Freud, Women, and Morality

FREUD, WOMEN, AND MORALITY

The Psychology of Good and Evil

ELI SAGAN

Basic Books, Inc., Publishers   New York

Library of Congress Cataloging-in-Publication Data

Sagan, Eli.
  Freud, women, and morality.

  Bibliography: p. 257.
  Includes index.
  1. Moral development. 2. Good and evil. 3. Mother
and child. 4. Father and child. 5. Freud, Sigmund,
1856–1939—Views on women. 6. Psychoanalysis.
I. Title.
BF723.M54S24 1988   150.19′52 87-47770
ISBN 0-465-02570-6

For Frimi

CONTENTS

vii

Contents

PART IV

TOWARD A RECONSTRUCTION OF THE
PSYCHOANALYTIC THEORY OF MORALITY

PART V

CONCLUSION: TIME PRESENT, TIME FUTURE

ACKNOWLEDGMENTS

I AM the fortunate beneficiary of the efforts of three superb readers: Robert Bellah, Burton Raffel, and Miriam Sagan. I am always amazed that, despite their exertions, mistakes in grammar and syntax, logical inconsistencies, and fanciful speculations manage to pass through their rigorous net.

From Karla Hackstaff and Jennifer Pierce—formerly my students, now my friends—I have learned a great deal. Their critical response to my teaching forced the clarification of my argument at many points.

To Jim Stockinger I owe much, especially the knowledge of Rousseau and his critique of reason.

From Kurt Thompson, also a former student, I have borrowed a superb insight into the relationship of Eros to warfare.

I am especially grateful to my children, Miriam, Rachel, Susannah, and Daniel, who have taught me much more about tyranny and equality than they possibly imagine.

Lloyd deMause has shared with me his vast knowledge of family and child-raising history.

Edmund Leites has taught me about Puritan culture and how to think about the history of the family and sexuality.

Neil Smelser helped me get back in touch with a critical insight at a point where I had lost contact with it.

Drs. Robert Gardner and Roy Schafer kindly met with me when my ideas were still in the embryonic stage, and encouraged me to go ahead. I cannot know how sympathetic they may be to the final result. Dr. Jacob Arlow graciously assisted me in clearing up a bibliographic reference to an idea of his.

John Calvin Batchelor, Nancy Chodorow, and Gordon Fellman read parts of this manuscript, and all made helpful suggestions for its improvement.

Acknowledgments

The librarians at the New York Psychoanalytic Institute could not have been more helpful to an inquiring scholar.

Joanne Nussbaum continues in her role as a superb typist.

I am in great debt to Steven Fraser, my editor, who urged me to widen and to deepen the scope of this work. The book is now substantially more ambitious than the original manuscript that came to his attention.

Persistent in her critique and yet unabashed in her encouragement and praise, Frimi Sagan is, for me, the closest thing to a Muse that the modern world allows.

PART I

CONSCIENCE
AND SUPEREGO

1

Freud's Dilemma and Freud's Solution

JULY 8, 1915, Sigmund Freud, fifty-nine years old, wrote a re-markable letter to J. J. Putnam in Boston. Putnam, a New England physician of some reputation, having become a convert to psychoanalysis in his late years and a correspondent of Freud's, urged the founder of psychoanalysis to speak out more on the relationship of morality to psychoanalytic principles.

Freud responded: "I think I ought to tell you that I have always been dissatisfied with my intellectual endowment and that I know precisely in what respects, but that I consider myself a very moral human being who can subscribe to Th. Vischer's excellent maxim: 'What is moral is self-evident.' I believe that when it comes to a sense of justice and consideration of others, to the dislike of making others suffer or taking advantage of them, I can measure myself with the best people I have known. I have never done anything mean or malicious, nor have I felt any temptation to do so, with the result that I am not in the least proud of it. I am taking the notion of morality in its social, not its sexual sense. . . .

"On one point, however, I see that I can agree with you. When I ask myself why I have always aspired to behave honorably, to spare others and to be kind wherever possible, and why I didn't cease doing so when I realized that in this way one comes to harm and becomes an anvil because other people are brutal and unreliable, then indeed I have no answer. Sensible this certainly was not. In my youth I didn't feel any special ethical aspirations, nor does the conclusion that I am better than others give me any recognizable satisfaction! You are perhaps the first person to whom I have boasted in this fashion. So one could cite just my case as a proof of your assertion that such an urge toward the ideal forms a considerable part of our inheritance. If only more of this precious inheritance could be found in other human beings! I secretly believe that if one had the means of studying the sublimation of instincts as thoroughly as their repression, one might find quite natural psychological explanations which would render your humanitarian assumption unnecessary. But as I have said before, I know nothing about this. Why I—and incidentally my six adult children as well—have to be thoroughly decent human beings is quite incomprehensible to me."[1]

What is so striking, in this circumstance, is that the man whose great historical role it was to reveal to us so much of the hidden shame of humankind—that, as children, we suffered from the wildest sexual longings; that our wishes included cannibalizing our enemies, eating our own feces, killing our fathers (or mothers), and sleeping with our mothers (or fathers)—that this same person, when faced with the human need for morality, found it "quite incomprehensible."

Such disclaimer of insight, however, was not destined to persist. Within eight years of the letter to Putnam, with the publication of *The Ego and the Id* in 1923, Freud announced to the world that the superego, which subsumed the moral function, was one of the three basic structures of the mind. In that work he proclaimed, with obvious pride, "If anyone were inclined to put forward the paradoxical proposition that the normal man is not only far more immoral than he believes but also far more moral than he knows, psychoanalysis, on whose findings the first half of the assertion rests, would have no objection to raise against the second half."[2]

It is of interest to observe that, by the time of the letter to Putnam, Freud was not as ignorant of the moral function as he claimed to be. He had already taken a first important step that would eventually lead to the discovery of the superego. "On Narcissism: An Introduction" was published in 1914. There Freud introduced the concept of the ego ideal, which was destined to become, within his theoretical structure, one of the component functions subsumed under the superego. The ego ideal resulted from a transformation of the belief in the possibility of perfection, a conviction that must be abandoned as the psyche matures: "[The child] is not willing to forego the narcissistic perfection of his childhood; and when, as he grows up, he is disturbed by the admonitions of others and by the awakening of his own critical judgment, so that he can no longer retain that perfection, he seeks to recover it in the new form of an ego ideal. What he projects before him as his ideal is the substitute for the lost narcissism of his childhood in which he was his own ideal."[3] Freud's letter to Putnam provides evidence that the ego ideal—the desire and capacity to live by certain perfect standards of behavior, the need to think well of oneself—can become intimately involved with moral action, at least with some individuals. Freud was consciously aware of boasting to Putnam about his own moral position.

That Freud chose not to reveal he had been working on the problem and confessed, instead, that he knew nothing about it is one small indication of Freud's ambivalence about morality, an ambivalence that profoundly affected his whole theoretical structure.

The Ego and the Id was a seminal work. It remains one of the basic foundation blocks of psychoanalytic theory, setting forth Freud's last global description of the psyche, the structural model. Three structures comprise the psyche and subsume all psychic action: ego, id, and superego. Because Freudian theory is always a theory of conflict, in this model all neuroses, ambivalence, and symptomatic behavior come from conflicts among, and within, these three structures. Within Freudian psychoanalysis today, though much controversy exists about the exact nature of ego, id, and superego, only a handful of theorists challenge the basic structural hypothesis.

Freud does not differentiate in *The Ego and the Id* between ego ideal and superego; he uses these terms interchangeably. Only later in his life did he consistently use the designation superego for the large psychical entity and assign to it three basic functions: self-observation, conscience, and maintaining the ego ideal, which demands greater and greater perfection.[4] A tendency on the part of some later theorists to

equate superego and conscience persists, and this failure to differentiate the two concepts seriously limits our perception of the way morality works within the psyche. The failure to discriminate sharply the
roles of superego and conscience, however, was already present in
Freud's work.

Of crucial importance for the nature of the superego is the fact that
it appears very late in the child's life—between the fourth and sixth
year. Unlike the ego and the id, which certainly exist as independent
psychic structures by the time the child is six months old, the superego
comes into existence only after the child has endured a long psychic
history. Whether or not the components of the superego, especially
conscience and the ego ideal, exist before the birth of the superego is
an enormously important question. If a three-year-old child already
has the beginnings of a conscience, which is destined to be preempted
and controlled by a superego that will appear roughly two years later,
then it is not impossible that certain basic conflicts may develop between conscience and the superego. Because a child lives a long psychic
life without any superego, it would not be unreasonable to hold that
the nature of the superego would be profoundly affected by the vicissitudes of psychic history that predate its appearance.

The late emergence of the superego is determined, Freud tells us, by
the fact that it comes into existence with the end of the Oedipus conflict. "The ego ideal [superego] had the task of repressing the Oedipus
complex; indeed, it is to that revolutionary event that it owes its existence." "The ego ideal [superego] is therefore the heir of the Oedipus
complex . . ."[5] This structure is established by incorporating the parents—and their moral imperatives—into the psyche. Moral commands, which have come from an external source, now speak with an
inner voice. That which in the past told us, for instance, always to
tell the truth now appears as an inner compulsion toward the same
behavior. All of these incorporated values, however, do not necessarily
have to be good for the psyche. Harmful imperatives are also internalized by means of the superego. The alien voice of parental authority
that had announced to the child "Don't masturbate" becomes transformed into an internal superego injunction: "Sex is bad!" External
authority becomes internalized.

It is crucial for the nature of the superego that it is born under both a blessing and a curse. The parents whose incorporation results in the creation of the superego have presented the child, in regard to moral values, with a double vision. They have been both nurturing and punishing, encouraging and defeating, loving and aggressive, sympathetic and castrating, estimable and frightful. The superego cannot select only the virtuous aspects of the parents. The parents are eaten whole; the superego becomes their agent inside the child's psyche. "But now that we have embarked upon the analysis of the ego we can give an answer to all those whose moral sense has been shocked and who have complained that there must surely be a higher nature in man: 'Very true,' we can say, 'and here we have that higher nature, in this ego ideal or superego, the representative of our relation to our parents. When we were little children we knew these higher natures, *we admired them and feared them*; and later we took them into ourselves.' "[6] And such is this "higher nature" in man that conscience, our most precious moral quality, is dependent for its efficacy on the fear of castration: "The superior being, which turned into the ego ideal [superego], once threatened castration, and this dread of castration is probably the nucleus round which the subsequent fear of conscience has gathered; it is this dread that persists as the fear of conscience."[7]

It is a grim picture. How paltry a figure Freud would have presented to Putnam (and himself) had he insisted that the reason he—and his six adult children—had to be "thoroughly decent human beings" was because they all feared castration if they ceased being so. This description of the functioning of morality should not be rejected, however, merely because it presents human beings as far from ideal creatures. Truth and what we wish for may be two very different things. The significant question is not how pessimistic but how accurate is Freud's account of the birth and the nature of morality.

Much evidence exists indicating that Freud himself did not quite believe his description of the relationship between conscience, Oedipus complex, and superego. Nothing in the whole of the psychoanalytic canon is as riddled with contradictions as Freud's narrative of the end of the Oedipus complex and the emergence of the superego. Freud himself displays a profound ambivalence about every aspect of this theoretical approach.

1. Though the superego incorporates both the nurturing, loving,

admiring parents and the punishing castrators, Freud, in theoretical works written after 1923, writes ten times as much about the harsh, punishing aspects of the superego as he does about its loving, benevolent attributes.

2. Civilization, which represents the unfolding of superego demands through history, is portrayed in some of Freud's works (but not in all) as the greatest contributor to neurosis in our time.

3. Women, to whom even sexist thinkers in the nineteenth century assigned the task of keeping alive the flame of moral values while their men sullied themselves in real-world achievement and corruption—women, Freud announces, are incapable of the same degree of superego development as men.

4. Though the superego subsumes conscience and the ego ideal, nonetheless at times Freud argues that one of the main purposes of psychoanalytic treatment is to free the ego from superego demands.

5. And when the end of the Oedipus complex is described in detail, Freud tells us that it is "smashed to pieces by the threat of castration."[8] As the superego is the heir of that catastrophe, one may wonder what kind of crippled, pathological moral imperative must result from such a birth trauma.

It would not be accurate to conclude from all this that Freud and psychoanalytic theory was antimorality, opposed to civilization, against nurturing and benevolence, and unredeemably sexist. Freud was proud of his own moral behavior; he could write about civilization and Eros with almost rapturous enthusiasm; he was keenly aware of how essential adequate nurturing is to psychic health; and he had a capacity to deal with and treat with women on a basis of equality that was rare in his time (the proportion of women to men who became analysts in Freud's day is remarkable). What is true is that Freud's psychoanalytic theory demonstrates the most profound ambivalence about everything that centrally or peripherally touches on questions of morality. And this ambivalence is all of a piece. That the superego (for men) is installed as a result of a tremendous fear of castration; that women are "castrated" before the Oedipus conflict and, therefore, never achieve a developed superego; that nurturing and love have, somehow, nothing to do with morality; that conscience and superego are confused with each other—all these inadequacies in psychoanalytic theory arise from a basic repression of the memory of the pre-oedipal mother and the love, identification, idealization—and hostility—the child (male and female) feels for her. Freud's world of Oedipus complex, castration, superego is a male world where women exist only as prizes awarded to conquerors.

It would be a mistake to look for the source of these confusions in some inadequacy of Freud's psyche or character. That could not explain why, with only slight modifications, four generations of analysts have held to these views. More important, such an approach would obscure the fact that the same ambivalence runs very deeply through the whole of Western culture. The splits between body and soul, between reason and feeling, which are intimately related to questions of nurturing and morality, are as old as Plato and St. Paul. In the twentieth century, ambivalence about morality, civilization, nurturing, and women define the moral agenda of our time. The observation that our culture has failed to resolve these ambivalences will provoke, I am sure, very little dissent. If certain aspects of Freudian theory have a strong antifeminine bias, it is important to comprehend that Freud lived in a pervasively sexist society and to accurately describe the precise nature of that sexism. If the psychoanalytic theory of morality is riddled with ambivalence, it is essential to understand the profound moral conflicts that characterized the social and political world of the nineteenth century. In part II of this book, we will explore the historical background of the superego in detail. Morality—and confusions about morality—can never be understood without regard for the historical situation in which it exists. Freud's superego, like everyone's, was profoundly determined by the society in which he lived.

The dependence of the superego on the *particular* society in which it exists underlines a fatal flaw in the theory of the superego as representing the *moral* function within the psyche. Far from carrying out the task of morality in the psyche, *the superego is essentially amoral and can be as easily immoral as moral. Within a slave society, the superego legitimates slavery. Within a racist or sexist society, the superego demands racism and sexism. And in a Nazi society, the superego commands one to live up to genocidal ideals.* A careful reading of the German catastrophe reveals that that whole Nazi enterprise would have been impossible without a strong and powerful superego passionately striving for its objectives.

The Superego and the Genocide of the Jews

In his book *The Nazi Doctors*, Robert Jay Lifton brilliantly documents the fact that the genocide of the Jews had its origins, first, in programs of sterilization and, second, in a project of euthanasia. The sterilization course was set in motion by the Nazis a few months after Hitler came to power in 1933. The original objects of these blood-purifying programs were not Jews but insane, mentally retarded, and habitually criminal *Germans*. These programs were embarked upon under the powerful superego injunction of purifying the race in the effort to create an ideal society, more perfect and more free of blemish than any that had ever existed. Konrad Lorenz, who attained international respectability and reputation for his work on animal behavior after this "grand" experiment proved a horrible failure, was just one of many who extolled the ideal nature of the program. He wrote in 1940:

> It must be the duty of racial hygiene to be attentive to a more severe elimination of morally inferior human beings than is the case today.... We should literally replace all factors responsible for selection in a natural and free life.... In prehistoric times of humanity, selection for endurance, heroism, social usefulness, etc. was made solely by *hostile* outside factors. This role must be assumed by a human organization; otherwise humanity will, for lack of selective factors, be annihilated by the degenerative phenomena that accompany domestication.[9]

Doctors played the central role in these programs because sterilization and euthanasia were doctors' business. As the emphasis changed in the late 1930s from sterilization to euthanasia, the superego was an essential element in bringing the doctors along. Rudolf Ramm was on the medical faculty of the University of Berlin and published an important manual that urged a doctor to become not only a caretaker of the sick but also a "cultivator of the genes," a "physician to the *Volk*," and a "biological soldier." Ramm made an easy transition from traditional moral values: "inner calling, high ethics, profound knowledge ... sacrifice and dedication," to "the idealistic *Weltanschauung* of National Socialism." And when this whole process ultimately led, after 1941, by inexorable logic, to the extermination of the Jews, the "moral" reasons for undertaking that "final solution" had already been clearly established.

> Pointing to the chimneys in the distance, [Dr. Ella Lingens-Reiner] asked a Nazi doctor, Fritz Klein, "How can you reconcile that with your [Hippocratic] oath as a doctor?" His answer was, "Of course I am a doctor and I want to preserve life. And out of respect for human life, I would remove a gangrenous appendix from a diseased body. The Jew is the gangrenous appendix in the body of mankind."[10]

One cannot read Lifton's book without being profoundly aware that we are not involved here with the psychological process of rationalization, wherein a person who wishes to perform sadistic acts and cannot admit to that desire invents a reasonable explanation for his actions. We are talking about profoundly corrupt but nevertheless dedicated and idealistic people. Without an ideology that they were performing a moral action—without the superego—the whole extermination process would have been impossible.

> These medical participants in mass murder were held to the regime behind the murder by the principles of what Dr. B. [an Auschwitz doctor] called 'coherent community' . . . and 'common effort' . . . in discussing his and others' sense of the Nazi movement's commitment to overcoming staggering national problems. . . . In all this, 'the bridge . . . is the ideology.' And that 'bridge' could connect the Nazi doctors to an immediate sense of community and communal purpose in their Auschwitz work.

Many of the Auschwitz doctors—whose job it was to make the "selections" on the entering ramp that determined how many were to be gassed immediately and how many sent to live in the camp—contended that their oath of loyalty to Hitler, which they took as SS officers, was much more important to them than the Hippocratic oath of their medical school days.[11] An oath—a superego mechanism—remarkably enough, remained essential.

This extraordinary mixture of idealism and sadism was noticed by many reflective people. Dr. Karl Brandt was one of the leaders of the euthanasia program directed against mental patients. One hero of the resistance to that genocidal design was the Reverend Fritz von Bodelschwingh, who protected his patients from the killers. Yet, after the war, it is reported that Bodelschwingh commented: "You must not picture Professor Brandt as a criminal, but rather as an idealist."[12] In one part of Brandt's mind, at least, the killing project was undertaken for idealistic, moral reasons. How the other parts of Brandt's mind judged these actions, to what intense conflicts he was subject, no one has yet been able to successfully elaborate.

Even the notorious Josef Mengele cannot be dismissed with a simplistic diagnosis—pathological, sadistic, near psychotic—because these words give no place to the "moral" fervor that propelled his work. Teresa W., an anthropologist prisoner at Auschwitz who was used by Mengele for his "research" on twins, commented that he was like "a religious man ... absolutely so committed that he will only consider the people going to church as the right people—or [those who] have the same face as he has." She was convinced that Mengele believed "that Hitler [was] doing something absolutely incredibly good."[13]

And this is not the first time in history we encounter this remarkable combination of sadism and idealistic behavior. The Inquisition burned many disbelievers to purify the world, and the Crusaders, when they finally took Jerusalem, slew every non-Christian being they found there—all for the greater glory of the superego.

What was so striking for Lifton in his research into this unbelievable human experience was the tremendous importance placed, over and over again, on doctors in the whole genocidal project. Doctors—the very symbol of healing, caring, and the value of life. There seems to be no question that it was a deliberate Nazi motive to bring all the force of the superego to bear on the killing enterprise. Lifton writes of "the powerful Nazi impulse, sometimes conscious and at other times inchoate, to bring the greatest degree of medical legitimation to the widest range of killing." The evidence of Auschwitz confirms this analysis:

> In terms of actual professional requirements there was absolutely no need for doctors to be the ones conducting selections: anyone could have sorted out weak and moribund prisoners. But if one views Auschwitz, as Nazi ideologues did, as a public health venture, doctors alone became eligible to select. In doing so, the doctor plunged into what can be called the healing-killing paradox.[14]

Freud's Dilemma and Freud's Solution

In summary, then, the Nazis used all the trappings of the superego to promote genocide: purifying, healing, curing; oath, community, the *Volk*, social usefulness, ideal society; sacrifice and dedication, ideology, idealism, and morality. The mechanism of the superego makes it possible to use almost any virtue in the most horrible of human projects. If the superego, man's "higher nature," is so susceptible to corruption, can it possibly be the moral instrument in the psyche?

Superego Pathology

It may be argued at this point that I have been describing not a healthy and robust superego but a diseased, pathological, or, at the least, corrupt one. The superego, the argument may run, can still be the moral instrument in the psyche even though it is prevented by pathology from doing its work. A diseased heart is a heart nevertheless. In my view, this analogy does not hold. First, we can observe that, throughout history, the corrupt superego—sanctioning slavery, racism, sexism—has been the *norm*, not the exception. Second, when we consider that most of the worst troubles that humankind has brought upon itself, including warfare, are impossible without the functioning of the superego, that is analogous to discovering an organ in the body whose function it is to bring disease. And last, it should be pointed out that the superego is Freud's discovery, and, at times, his description of it seems to assume its pathology: for instance, when he tells us that this moral instrument behaves like a "garrison in a conquered city"[15] and when he emphasizes its brutal and punishing aspects. If we accept the concept that the superego represents the moral function within the psyche, we are then faced with the frightening possibility that there is no moral capacity within the psyche at all.

When an organ in the body is diseased, its pathology usually results from having too much of something it does not need or too little of something it has essential need of. One may analyze the Nazi superego in this mode. Too much sadism and aggression; too much of the drives to dominate, degrade, and destroy other people. And too little of what?

CONSCIENCE AND SUPEREGO

The superego to be healthy needs a large component of love, what Freud liked to call "Eros." And a large component of *conscience*. It was precisely these qualities that were severely underrepresented in the Nazi superego.

When we call a sadistic superego "pathological" or "corrupt," by what standard are we judging it? Is there an instrument in the psyche that can differentiate between the moral and immoral attributes of the superego? It is the argument of this book that *conscience* is such an instrument; that conscience, unlike the superego, knows clearly which actions are moral and which immoral; that conscience, unlike the superego, is incapable of corruption and pathology. It may be silenced or paralyzed, but one can never accurately speak of a diseased conscience. Here we come upon a crucial distinction: *the superego always collaborates with its own corruption.* The relative health or pathology of the superego is dependent on how much or how little of conscience is operative in its functioning.

And conscience, unlike the superego, does not have to wait until the child's fourth or fifth year to make its presence felt. Conscience has its origins in the basic nurturing situation, and identification with the nurturer plays an essential role in its composition. Traditionally it is the mother, not the father, who presides over the birth of conscience, over the beginnings of morality. The Freudian theory of morality had to repress the memory of conscience in favor of the superego, because it was deeply involved in repressing the remembrance of the pre-oedipal mother and the overwhelming importance she has in the life of the child. In order to reconstruct the psychoanalytic theory of morality, it is necessary to lift that repression and to restore conscience and Eros to their rightful place at the very center of morality.

And conscience, not the superego, is the essential element in moral social progress. We may ask: What makes it possible for any child—grown to adulthood—to act more morally than his or her parents? What makes moral progress—the giving up of cannibalism, infanticide, slavery—realizable? The psychoanalytic theory of the superego, taken by itself, creates the necessity for answering these questions negatively: Nothing makes it possible. If the fear of castration by the parents is the foundation of morality, the overwhelming psychological imperative must be to incorporate the values of the parents (and society) in order to protect one's bodily and psychic integrity. This is an accurate description of much, if not most, psychosocial action, but it is not a description of *all* such behavior. People do triumph over inadequate nurturing. Society does change profoundly in regard to moral values. Conscience and Eros contribute a crucial portion to those forces that drive history.

2

Huckleberry's Dilemma: The Conflict Between Conscience and the Superego

HUCKLEBERRY FINN, fleeing the homicidal inclinations of his alcoholic, psychopathic father and liberating himself as well from the ministrations of those respectable members of the community who were determined to "sivilize" him, sets out on a raft to drift down the Mississippi River. Very soon after beginning his journey he encounters, and invites to join him, the black slave Jim, who is running away from his master, a Miss Watson, one of those dedicated to the salvation of Huckleberry's soul. Through a series of adventures, misadventures, and just drifting and looking at the sky, Jim and Huck become attached to each other. In a sublimated way, one could say they fall in love with each other, Jim being more conscious of this than Huck. Through this emotional tie Huck begins to perceive that a black man—and a slave—is a human being very much like himself. Love and identification reinforce each other.

With it all, Huck is ambivalent and resists the idea that a black slave could be his human equal. An amorphous feeling of guilt for having stolen away Miss Watson's "nigger" disturbs the preconscious part of his mind. Despite having learned the lesson of civilization only in part, he nevertheless feels that he is doing something profoundly wrong.

As the result of a complicated set of circumstances, at one point Huckleberry starts out to give Jim up to his pursuers. We are then witness to a dialogue within Huck wherein the superego, which demands the reenslavement of Jim, and humanitarian conscience, which pleads for Jim's freedom, struggle for Huckleberry's soul.

Huck begins by trying to convince himself that Jim would be better off back home. But that resolution won't work because Miss Watson would probably sell him down the river again, nothing would be accomplished, and Huck would be shamed in front of the whole town for having helped a "nigger" escape. And yet, returning him is seemingly the "right thing" to do.

> The more I studied about this the more my conscience went to grinding me, and the more wicked and low-down and ornery I got to feeling. And at last, when it hit me all of a sudden that here was the plain hand of Providence slapping me in the face and letting me know my wickedness was being watched all the time from up there in heaven, whilst I was stealing a poor old woman's nigger that hadn't done me no harm, and now was showing me there's One that's always on the lookout, and ain't a-going to allow no such miserable doings to go only just so fur and no further, I most dropped in my tracks I was so scared. Well, I tried the best I could to kinder soften it up somehow for myself by saying I was brung up wicked, and so I warn't so much to blame, but something inside of me kept saying, "There was the Sunday School, you could 'a' gone to it; and if you'd 'a' done it they'd 'a' learnt you there that people that acts as I'd been acting about the nigger goes to everlasting fire."

Resorting to prayer to assist him in his determination, Huck finds he cannot pray. "It was because my heart warn't right. . . . I was letting *on* to give up sin, but away inside of me I was holding on to the biggest one of all. I was trying to make my mouth *say* I would do the right thing . . . and go and write to that nigger's owner . . . but deep down in me I knowed it was a lie, and He knowed it. You can't pray a lie—I found that out."

Faced with the threat of castration from "Him," Huck has no choice but to write a letter to Miss Watson informing her where her slave is to be found.

> I felt good and all washed clean of sin for the first time I had ever felt so in my life, and I knowed I could pray now. But I didn't do it straight off, but laid the paper down and set there thinking . . . how near I come to being lost and going to hell. And went on thinking. . . . and I see Jim before me all the time . . . we a-floating along, talking and singing and laughing. But somehow I couldn't seem to strike no places to harden me against him. . . . I'd see him standing my watch on top of his'n, 'stead of calling me . . . and see how glad he was when I come back out of the fog . . . and would always call me honey and pet me . . . and how good he always was . . . and he . . . said I was the best friend old Jim ever had in the world . . . and then I happened to look around and see that paper.
>
> I was a-trembling, because I'd got to decide, forever, betwixt two things, and I knowed it. I studied a minute, sort of holding my breath, and then says to myself:
>
> "All right, then, I'll *go* to hell"—and tore it up.
>
> It was awful thoughts and awful words, but they were said. . . . I would take up wickedness again, which was in my line, being brung up to it. . . . I would go to work and steal Jim out of slavery again; and if I could think up anything worse, I would do that too; because as long as I was in, and in for good, I might as well go the whole hog.[1]

Twain's genius brings us a brilliant description of the way the superego operates. It is, indeed, the fear of the punishment of hell, the threat of castration from a father figure, that drives Huck to do "the moral" thing and return Jim to slavery. The difficulty, of course, is that the "moral" action is really immoral and the supposed immoral behavior is moral. Huck's response neatly demonstrates Freud's concept that when people do something at variance with what their superego dictates, they will feel guilt and expect to be punished. Huck does feel guilty about helping Jim escape. His actions can be accurately described as *feeling guilty about behaving morally*. This irony clearly demonstrates that something is radically wrong with a theory that equates morality and superego.

At this point, the objection may be raised that a work of fiction cannot be used as evidence for criticizing psychological theory. Huckleberry's dilemma, however, is one that many people face in their lives. Having been taught by the parents to hate Jews, despise Blacks, and cheat on one's income tax—all of which can be superego imperatives—a person may decide not to do any of these things, and will feel "guilty" and expect punishment for defying parental imperatives. Psychiatrist Robert Coles relates a very moving story of a young white man in the American South involved with the great conflicts over integrating the public schools. Like Huck's dialogue, it demonstrates how disorienting and exhilarating it can be to challenge superego commands in the interest of Eros:

> I didn't want any part of them here. They belong with their own, and we belong with our own—that's what we all said. Then those two kids came here, and they had a tough time. They were all by themselves. The school had to get police protection for them. We didn't want them and they knew it. But we told them so in case they were slow to get the message. I didn't hold back, no more than anyone else. I said, "Go, nigger, go," with all the others. I meant it. But after a few weeks, I began to see a kid, not a nigger—a guy who knew how to smile when it was rough going, and who walked straight and tall, and was polite. I told my parents, "It's a real shame that someone like him has to pay for the trouble caused by all those federal judges."
> Then it happened. I saw a few people cuss at him. "The dirty nigger," they kept on calling him, and soon they were pushing him in a corner, and it looked like trouble, bad trouble. I went over and broke it up. I said, "Hey, cut it out." They all looked at me as if I was crazy, my white buddies stopped and the nigger left. Before he left, though, I spoke to him. I didn't mean to, actually! It just came out of my mouth. I was surprised to hear the words myself: "I'm sorry." As soon as he was gone, my friends gave it to me: "What do you mean, 'I'm sorry!'" I didn't know what to say. I was as silent as the nigger they stopped. After a few minutes, we went to basketball practice. That was the strangest moment of my life.[2]

When the concept of the superego first made its appearance, Viennese psychoanalysts assumed it stood for the father who was commanding one to behave in a morally upright manner. Very quickly one critic of the concept inquired as to what happened to the superego if one's father was a criminal.* What is essential to understand is that the superego is not just the internal representative of the parents' moral values but of *all their values*, good and bad, moral and immoral. The same internalized voice that commands one to keep one's room clean,

---

* Otto Isakower, personal communication.

respect others, tell the truth, may also (and frequently does) give orders to hate Blacks, despise women, and repress sexual pleasure. Some part of the superego is always corrupt. Metaphorically speaking, everyone's father (and mother) is a criminal to some degree.

The psychoanalytic theory of the superego seems valid when it describes a revolutionary development at the end of the Oedipus complex wherein external commands are internalized, a process that results in the creation of many and varied internal imperatives. These imperatives are then modified and expanded as the child grows: its perception of its parents changes, teachers and other authority figures enter its life, and, as an adult, he or she becomes part of a community and a culture with a complex value system of its own. The theory of the superego does describe how and when a child internalizes moral commitments, but the theory can do nothing, by itself, to distinguish what is moral from what is immoral. It explains absolutely nothing about the child's capacity to judge the various—and many times contradictory—elements within this superego structure.

It is helpful to return to Huckleberry's dilemma. The humor, the pathos, the triumph all result from the fact that he is in a state of conflict, driven in two directions at the same time. We know what impels him in the direction of giving up Jim. The superego with its commitment to the current values of society, backed by its own particular psychic police power: guilt and the fear of punishment and castration. But what psychic power is it that gives Huck the capacity to say no to this corrupt aspect of the superego? What psychic function is it that gives any of us the ability to discriminate between moral and immoral aspects of the superego? "Conscience" is the word I use to describe this psychological function, though "morality" or "the moral capacity" can serve just as well. The advantage of all three expressions is that there is no ambiguity in their use, as there is with the concept superego. Huck's conscience or moral capacity would never command him to give Jim back. Conscience calls for the opposite behavior; for both Huck and for Coles's informant, conscience provides the power that defies superego imperatives.

Whereas Freud asserted that the superego, after its formation, subsumed the functions of the ego ideal, conscience, and self-observation,[3] it may be more accurate to say that only conscience, using the capacities of idealization and self-observation, has the capacity to judge the superego. Only conscience can tell us what is moral or immoral; only conscience can discriminate between the beneficial and the corrupt aspects of the superego. It is conscience, not the superego, that enables a person to behave more morally than his or her parents and provides the capacity for society to make moral progress. The superego, by itself, can only reproduce the exact same value system from generation to generation. Where there is no conflict between conscience and superego, society remains stagnant. All the great moral heroes of the world—including Freud—have championed the dictates of conscience against the inflexible commands of the corrupt superego.

It may be objected here that it is not conscience that keeps Huck from betraying Jim or Coles's informant from allowing the beating of the Black student. It is merely Eros, it may be argued, a not very sublimated sexual attachment between the men involved. Huck "loves" Jim; Coles's white student is attracted to the other's looks and demeanor. It is not morality, such an argument goes, it is nothing more than love.

Nothing more—and nothing less. There is no morality without love; "eternal Eros," Freud would say on occasion.[4] The mode of thought that separates morality from love is the same mode that brings us the harsh and punishing superego, that sees in the threat of castration the grounds of morality. The split between love and morality goes very deep within our culture and has brought us innumerable philosophical compromises, from utilitarian liberalism to the superego-as-morality. Freud, as we shall see, could argue passionately on both sides of this issue. Sometimes it is Eros, at most other times only a harsh demanding superego, that can save humankind from its own destructiveness.

I argue that conscience (morality, the moral function) has its genesis in the original nurturing situation between the child and its primary caretaker(s). Love and morality cannot be sundered. All morality is a sublimated and transformed manifestation of the Eros of nurturing. This proposition is a central tenet in the attempt, which occupies part IV of this work, to construct a different psychoanalytic theory of morality, an attempt that takes acute cognizance of the pre-oedipal life of the child.

A careful reading of Huckleberry's predicament reveals many important questions about morality and society, about morality and history. Slavery, and its imperatives against which Huck struggles, is an institution of society that legitimizes the ownership of one human being by another. The racism exposed within the story of Coles's informant cannot be considered an institution, since it has no legal foundation, but it is certainly institutionalized within the society (by the *de facto* existence of segregated schools). The permission to own slaves or practice racism is granted by the superego, which has incorporated the values of the parents and the society into the psyche. Twain, who created Huck's dilemma, despised "civilization" as much as did Huckleberry and liked to believe that only an individual living outside the boundaries of an unprincipled society could act morally. Society, and the superego that spoke for it, was, for Twain, almost totally corrupt. This is a romanticized view that ignores the fact that the very moral values Twain wishes to live by are themselves endorsed, even though in a hypocritical way, within the value system of the culture. The Sunday school from which Huck was truant did proclaim that one should love thy neighbor as thyself, and one of the great documents of the Republic announced that all men are created equal.

Twain would like to believe that from society he received only corruption and that moral insight came solely from himself. He would be all conscience and society all corrupt superego, but the truth is that the superego within society had institutionalized *conflicting* values, some moral, some immoral. Twain's insight into the malignant nature of slavery (and racism, since the book was written twenty years after slavery was abolished) was possible for him only because he lived in the nineteenth century when ambivalence about racism had grown to a degree of intensity unknown to the previous history of the world. If Twain had lived in ancient Greece, he probably would have written comedies, but they would not have been about the evils of slavery, because no one in that society was capable of this moral stance.

Conflicting values always exist within the superego. The essentially moral person, nonetheless, does not have to remain passive in this situation. Faced with conflicting and opposite superego imperatives (all men are created equal but it is proper to own slaves), conscience is the one autonomous instrument within the psyche that has the power to choose the moral alternative. To a certain but crucial degree, conscience is independent of society because it has its beginnings in the intimate infantile situation of child and nurturer. The autonomous nature of conscience makes moral progress possible.

The perception of the self-directing nature of conscience reveals a crucial theoretical truth about society and the individual's place within it: there is a moral system within the psyche *independent* of the value system of the culture; there is a moral insight within the psyche *independent* of the superego's conflicted system of values. One cannot, therefore, equate the moral system and the value system.

Slavery and its passing, racism and its longed-for passing—all these are facts of history. The moral destiny of human beings is revealed, ultimately, through historical process. Before we can proceed to examine and critique the psychoanalytic theory of morality and civilization, it is helpful to determine the theory's place in human history. Everyone's view of right and wrong is deeply imbedded in historical process. Conscience, though autonomous, is far from being totally free of society. No one enjoys full freedom from inherited values. Even Huckleberry on his raft, despite his every intention, had to deal ultimately with that fact. We turn to history to see what it may teach us about the possibilities, and limitations, of morality and conscience.

PART II

MORALITY
AND HISTORY

3

Tyranny and
Equality

I N REGARD to the critical question of whether moral values are universal for all people or merely relative to the particular society in which they are expressed, I will argue at great length, and attempt to demonstrate with psychological data, that the concept of a universal human morality is valid and that the exercise of any of the three fundamental forms of tyranny—over women, over children, over other men[1]—is always immoral, in any society, at any time in history, regardless of what the value system of the society may say in the attempt to rationalize it. Slavery, tyrannization of women, abuse of children are always immoral no matter what intellectual or psychological arguments may be raised in their defense. This universal human morality proceeds from a universal human psychology, which all people necessarily share. Great individual and social variety is not precluded by this concept of a universal psychology any more than human variety is abolished by a medicine, an anatomy, or a biology each of which is also true for all people.

I will argue that morality has its origins in the basic situation of nurturing between a child and its primary nurturer or nurturers (in most societies, until now, the mother). It is an absolute necessity of

27

our biological nature that human infants and children must be physically and psychologically nurtured. The unfed child will die; the unloved child will live on, at best, to endure a pathological existence.
Human nurturing, however, presents us with one profound problematic: it is ambivalent from the start. The human child receives not only
love, affection, and concern from the adults who care for it, but also
anger, animosity, and hostility. It is the ambivalent nature of human
nurturing that makes morality an absolute necessity of both our biological and our psychological existence. Moral action is essential for
psychic health because *all* critical human relationships are ambivalent:
Within them love and aggression struggle for hegemony, and it is one
of the fundamental functions of morality to resolve such conflicts on
the side of Eros.

It is a long road, both actually and theoretically, from the mother-
child dyad to a society that institutionalizes slavery, fascism, imperialism, or the domination of women. It is precisely that ground that this
book attempts to cover. I am interested herein primarily with social,
not personal, morality. The personal moral problems of cheating, ly-
ing, indulging oneself at others' expense are definitely related to but
are not the primary concerns of this work. Morality and immorality
within any particular society—and more especially the changes in
these manifestations as society develops—are.

On the question of whether it is appropriate to talk of moral truth,
or truths, that are valid for all societies, it is enlightening to look at
Aristotle's discussion of the moral rightness of slavery. Aristotle,
whose authority is by no means absolute, believed that a universal human morality did exist, defined by concepts that have been translated
into English by such terms as "natural," "by nature," "just." He begins
his discussion of slavery by distinguishing whether the institution exists by nature or merely by law or convention: "There are others . . .
who regard the control of slaves by a master as contrary to nature. In
their view the distinction of master and slave is due to law or convention; there is no natural difference between them: the relation of master
and slave is based on force, and being so based has no warrant in
justice."[2]

An institution grounded only in law or convention can, without vio-
lating justice, be changed or even abolished; an institution grounded

in nature or justice can be abolished only by a transgression upon what is natural, that is, universally moral. In the parlance of twentieth-century sociology, what Aristotle is delineating is a system of values or norms (what de Tocqueville calls the *mores* of society), on the one hand, and a system of universal moral imperatives, on the other—normative behavior, which varies from society to society, as opposed to moral behavior, which has a universal validity. In a slave-owning society, slavery is legitimized by the norms of the society; whether it is moral or not is another question.

When one reads Aristotle on the question of whether slavery conforms to an absolute standard of justice, one is almost compelled to bow down before the power of the human intellect and its capacity to distort the moral truth. Believing in the universality of justice, his defense of slavery must rest on universal principles. "We have to consider whether there are, or are not, persons who are by nature such as are here defined; whether, in other words, there are persons for whom slavery is the better and just condition, or whether the reverse is the case and all slavery is contrary to nature." After an involuted argument that cannot stand against a critique based on Aristotelian logic, the master concludes:

> The soul rules the body with the sort of authority of a master: mind rules the appetite with the sort of authority of a statesman or a monarch. In this sphere it is clearly natural and beneficial to the body that it should be ruled by the soul, and again it is natural and beneficial to the affective part of the soul that it should be ruled by the mind and the rational part; whereas the equality of the two elements, or their reverse relation, is always detrimental. . . . Again, the relation of male to female is naturally that of the superior to the inferior—of the ruling to the ruled. This general principle must similarly hold good of all human beings generally. . . . We may thus conclude that all men who differ from others as much as the body differs from the soul, or an animal from a man . . . all such are by nature slaves, and it is better for them, on the very same principle as in the other cases just mentioned, to be ruled by a master. A man is thus by nature a slave if he is capable of becoming . . . the property of another.[3]

For the moment, after making note that the superiority of men over women is a *first principle* for Aristotle, we pass on to explore what slavery in Greek society can teach us about the question of moral relativism or moral universalism. There was no significant ambivalence about slavery within Greek culture. No major figure spoke out against it; even the great Euripides, who almost alone was capable of challenging the fundamental Greek commitment to destructive warfare,[4] never questioned the validity of slavery. Who those "others" were who regarded slavery as immoral, against whom Aristotle is arguing, we have no way of knowing, since their works do not survive, and we cannot even be sure whether or not Aristotle was merely erecting straw men with straw arguments. The value system, the norms, the *mores* of Greek society were totally and unambivalently committed to the legitimation of the institution of slavery. What judgment may we make about this situation? Are we entitled to assert that slavery is immoral, unjust, unnatural in any society in any time in history because it violates a fundamental human moral position, namely, that the tyranny of one human being over another is a violation of justice?

The position of moral and cultural relativism argues that we cannot make such an assertion. We may not like slavery; it may even be considered immoral within *our* culture; but we cannot, such a position asserts, condemn slavery in *another* society because we are using, as the basis of that condemnation, only the value system of our society, which has no universal validity. If we had lived in Greek society, we would have considered slavery appropriate and just, as did everyone else. It is only an accident of history that we happen to consider slavery immoral. Essentially, the position of cultural and moral relativism asserts that there is no morality, there are only values. Or, more accurately, morals and norms are one.

We may not have the right to demand of any system of values that it be moral by "our" standards, but as the theory of moral relativism exists within *our* culture, and *our* culture demands a certain consistency for its norms, it would not be asking too much for the position of moral relativism to remain consistent, no matter into what area we extend it. What, then, shall we make of the severe physical and/or sexual abuse of children that we find as normative in certain societies at certain times? And what of the tyranny of men over women, which has been certified as natural and just in most societies throughout history? When we read that, in a few nonliterate cultures of South America, gang rape was an instrument of social control of men over women, does anyone really believe that it is *merely* the relative value system of our culture that makes us see this as a moral horror? And then we have the problem of Auschwitz and Bergen-Belsen. Are we to withhold judgment in that case also, recognizing the arbitrary and relative source of our revulsion? Even from the point of view of logic, there is a deep flaw within the concept of relativism: the view that *all* value systems are relative to the society in which they exist is in fact itself a universal statement. The pervasive persistence of cultural relativism, a morally and intellectually untenable position, is symptomatic of a deep moral ambivalence that suffuses our whole culture.

Interestingly enough, as an illustration of that ambivalence, the argument against moral universalism by proponents of relativism takes on a *moral* tone. Moral universalism, it is commonly asserted, is a throwback to the imperialism of Victorian times when it was used as a rationalization for white men who wished to dominate people of color all over the world. The white man's burden owed its existence to the "superior" morality of white culture. Moral universalism is seen, then, as an instrument of tyranny. What, however, is wrong with imperialism and white tyranny? Isn't it only by the *current* values of our culture that we are judging imperialism and tyranny to be an evil? Holding a consistent moral relative position, we are required to assert that we cannot stand in judgment on our nineteenth-century forebears; they were only doing what was *considered* moral in their society, and we (in condemning imperialism) are only doing what is *considered* moral in our society. We have no absolute standard of morality to judge between the two positions. It is merely an accident of history that we see imperialism and white domination of the world as an evil. Equally important, we really have no right to regard the change in values in society from a proimperialism to an antiimperialism (or at least an ambivalence about imperial domination) position as moral progress, because no such thing exists, for by what standard could we judge whether such a movement is progressive or not if there is no universal standard of morality? And if our society should move from its current ambivalence about imperialism to a reassertion of the nineteenth-century view of its absolute validity, we may not like it (for no one particularly likes a change in value system), but we cannot condemn such movement as morally reprehensible; we can merely lament that it goes against the values we were taught when young. The position of moral relativism makes it impossible to make a moral judgment on any change in the value system within society. We may wonder if that is not the reason for its existence. Relativism is not a theory of morality; it is a theory of no morality.

Tyranny, in all its manifold expressions, is the momentous social objective correlative of immoral behavior. The struggle for equality, and the erection of institutions that legitimize and manifest it, is the great social expression of morality. Equality between men and men; equality between men and women. As to children, there can be no true equality between them and adults; perhaps with children "mutuality" is a better word than "equality." Whatever word one uses, it seems clear that one of the major struggles of the last four hundred years has been to establish the equal validity of children's lives. These same four hundred years have seen a profound change in the amount of tyranny or equality within human society. We have yet to see a society that does not practice several forms of tyranny, but morality within society is always a matter of degree: more or less tyrannical, more or less equal. One cannot talk about morality within society without addressing oneself to history.

In this regard, there is still more to be learned from thinking about Aristotle and slavery. How is it that one of the most brilliant men of all times, a person passionately concerned with ethical problems, could not, would not, know that slavery was immoral? How comes it that, today, the average reader of the *New York Times* is capable of a moral insight that was impossible for the divine Aristotle? We know that slavery is unjust, unnatural, but he had to deny exactly that proposition. We have come to the great paradox* of social morality: morality, though universal and absolute, is only revealed and manifest through the development of society, through history. We know today (or, at least, some of us know) that slavery and sexism and racism and classism are immoral, not because we are more brilliant than Aristotle, nor even necessarily more moral on a personal day-to-day level, but because we are the heirs of the only history that really matters: that which has significantly lessened the degree of tyranny in human society and,

---

* *Paradox*: a seeming contradiction that is actually capable of being resolved.

proportionately, increased the degree of equality. I am not insensible to the fact that any conception of moral progress is subject to profound reservations. Every day the front page of our newspapers causes us to reflect, in some manner or other, on the great metaphors for the twentieth century: Auschwitz, Hiroshima, and the grinding tyranny of Stalinism. Rightfully acknowledging these catastrophes, the question remains: How is it that so many people today (although certainly not enough), people of average intelligence and without moral genius, are ready to abandon notions of racism and sexism to the same trash heap of history onto which slavery was consigned? With all the social tragedies of this century, it is still remarkable that you and I are capable of a moral vision more far-reaching than that of Plato, Aristotle, Rousseau, and Freud. Though we too are undoubtedly subject to certain moral blind spots, due to the still-limited nature of our society.

These historical considerations have a special significance in regard to the question of equality for women and men. The old saw about a dwarf standing on the shoulders of a giant being able to see farther is sometimes useful. But in regard to the moral question of equality for women, except for Freud, whose profound ambivalence will be analyzed at length, the just-mentioned great thinkers of the Western world were all dwarfs. They can teach us nothing about the moral and psychic cost of denying equality for women; they have, in respect to this question, no shoulders to stand on. They were great thinkers *for their time*, but the moral development of society has rendered many of their judgments inadequate. In the Western world, since about 1800, the question of equality between women and men has been a central item on the moral agenda of society, manifest by an erratic, but neverending, drive for equality, on the one hand, and an intense and sometimes brutal repression, on the other, and pervasively throughout, an acute ambivalence, a failure either to resolve the problem in a moral way or to cold-bloodedly repress it out of existence. Masculine anxiety about this demand for feminine equality has been so pervasive that it has influenced not only the specific question of feminism but it has also affected, unconsciously, every other moral dilemma in society: racism, classism, warfare. Masculine exercise of dominion over other men is by no means unrelated to deep unconscious struggles, rages, and anxieties concerning women.

33

This book is about Freud and psychoanalytic theory and the question of morality, but none of this can be discussed thoroughly without seeing certain problematics in their historical context. The moral agenda within society has changed enormously from the eighteenth to the nineteenth to the twentieth centuries. And, *pace* Marx, the rise of capitalism is not the only significant event to have occurred in that period. We cannot understand the twentieth century, its triumphs and its disasters, without comprehending the vastly complex moral agenda bequeathed us by the nineteenth century. And we cannot begin to understand that complexity without some sense of what the modern world has brought us besides industrialization. I am incapable of writing that history, but it can be of some value to take a look, no matter how briefly, at where we as a species have been and how far we have traveled in a mere four hundred years, a period of only sixteen generations.

1600 to 1800

In the year 1600 there was no democratic society anywhere on the face of the earth, except possibly in some small pockets of "primitive democracy" in the area destined to become Switzerland. Two great republics, the Venetian and the Dutch, managed to exist without a king, but neither of these was close to being a democracy; they remained aristocratic, oligarchic, plutocratic commercial states. Everything else, as far as the eye could see or the mind could travel, was in the hands of monarchs. Kingship was the fundamental form of social cohesion, that which held society together. Great emperors, grand monarchs, middling kings, and insignificant tyrants. Cruel despots and kindly rulers; warlike kings and peaceful lords; bureaucratically organized monarchs and adminstratively chaotic lords; great sensualists and intense ascetics; warriors and bankers; secular monarchs and princes of the church. All could agree on one fundamental social fact: politically speaking, there was no "people." Aristocrats and great bankers and merchants, who could obtain certain aspects of political power, yes, but "the people" did not exist.

In a similar fashion, and for similar reasons, there were no social movements that might in any way organize the disadvantaged into a social force. The great peasant revolts of the fourteenth century had been forgotten. The democratic communes of the Italian peninsula of the thirteenth and fourteenth centuries, wherein the *popolo* had obtained a voice, had all been transformed into various forms of monarchy *cum* aristocracy. There were no labor unions, no labor parties, no movements of peasants or workers that might crack the form of their invisibility. Nowhere did the ideal exist, and still less the reality, that the state had any obligation to care for its members. People were subjects, not citizens. No one, anywhere, had any "rights." Universal education for children was not even a mote in the vision of some wild-eyed reformer. A certain mild ambivalence about slavery existed, with periodic discussions and pronouncements concerning the validity of enslaving Europeans or Christians, but it was unimaginable that anyone would ever put an end to that institution.

Feminism, unlike democracy and peasant uprisings, did not even have a past. There had never been a call, of any kind, for equal rights for or treatment of women. Women had never acted together to attain any political or social advantage. Patriarchy, with all its cruel and gracious aspects, seemed unchallengeable. And children, it seems, were much more to be feared than loved. They were swaddled—wrapped in cloths that made the movement of arms and legs impossible—from the day they were born. They were regularly beaten either in the school or in the home, without any question as to the propriety of such discipline. Very few women of "quality" nursed their own children.

In such a society relations with one's children were not particularly close. Richer families put their infants out to wet-nurse [where the rate of infant mortality was two times greater than with children who were nursed at home], and when they returned, the advice of moralists, theologians and writers of domestic advice books, at least after the Reformation, was that the first duty of parents was ruthlessly to crush the wills of young children by physical force, as the only hope of containing Original Sin. Most children *of all classes* left home very early, between the ages of seven and fourteen, to work in other people's houses as servants or apprentices, to serve in a magnate's household, or to go to school.[5]

In summary, the world in 1600 had very little sense that the tyranny over men, women, and children should be ameliorated or abandoned. It was a world of autocracy, classism, sexism, slavery, and the psychological and physical abuse of children. A society wherein very few held any real power over their own lives.

Forty years into the seventeenth century, this oppressive world began to come apart, at least in England and in the new England of North America. Something momentous for the history of the world had been stirring within religious and private life since the last half of the sixteenth century, and in 1640 members of the middle and upper classes in England began the revolt against the king, eventually beheaded him, and proclaimed a Commonwealth. Equally significant for the future, the English Levellers became the first organized group in modern history to adopt a conscious ideology of equality for all men (but not for women). Despite the reluctance of even the Levellers to conceive of female equality, these revolutionary years witnessed the very beginnings of feminist political action:

> What is remarkable, however, is the way the breakdown of royal government in 1640, the prolonged political crisis between king and Parliament of 1640–42, the Civil Wars of 1642–45, and the emergence of many extremist independent sects and of a genuinely radical political party, stimulated the women of London and elsewhere to unprecedented political activity. On 31 January and 1 and 4 February 1642, women, operating without help from fathers, husbands or other males, took independent political action on the national level as women, for the first time in English history: they petitioned the House of Lords and Commons for a change of public policy. They numbered some four hundred or more, and were apparently composed of working women, artisans, shop-girls and labourers, who were suffering severe financial hardship as a result of the decay in trade.
>
> The next crisis came in April and May 1649 when very severe economic hardship coincided with a political showdown between the army and Parliament and the London-based lower-middle-class radical movement of the Levellers. Once again masses of women assembled at Westminster, complaining of the economic crisis and demanding the release of the Leveller leaders who had been imprisoned.[6]

The absolute sovereign power of the monarchy was permanently weakened by the revolution and was never to be reestablished. The cause of democracy, however, would have to wait two hundred years before the nineteenth century witnessed the establishment of the first stable democratic societies since the passing of Athenian democracy around 100 B.C. As for feminism, it would be three hundred years before it became a *permanent* issue for the whole of society.

No attempt will be made here even to touch lightly on the three hundred to four hundred years of struggle for political, economic, and gender equality, a struggle that still sharply defines, and threatens with extinction, the world we live in. Parallel to the public sphere of politics and economics, however, remarkable things were happening in the private realm of marriage, child rearing, and sexuality from 1600 to 1800. The great conflicts and ambivalences of the nineteenth century directly proceeded from these developments. If we are to understand the world as Freud found it (and as he left it, after the great Freudian revolution), it is essential to comprehend what changes had occurred since the beginning of the seventeenth century in the relationships between men and women, between adults and children, and among men, women, and children in relation to their own bodies. It is imperative to understand that we are talking about changes in the moral stance of society. The state of affairs between men and women, between adults and children, is always on an either/or continuum of tyranny and dominance, on the one hand, and equality and mutuality, on the other. The more there is of tyranny and dominance in such relations, the less there is of equality; the greater the degree of equality, the less of dominance and tyranny. Morality is of the essence in such a situation. When society moves in the direction of more equality between women and men, that is moral progress. When the movement is toward more dominance, that is moral regress.

The causes of such progressive or regressive movements are immensely complex—as are the causes of progress and regress on the large social scale of, let us say, racism and classism—and it is doubtful whether any two historians or theoreticians of such developments would agree as to the reasons for change. Two things, however, seem to be beyond argument. First, there have been prodigious changes in these areas in the last four hundred years, some progressive and some regressive. And second, in trying to understand these complex permutations, it is imperative that we deal with the moral implications, and possibly even the moral causes, of social developments.

The social historian Lawrence Stone has described the evolution of the family and marriage from about 1550 to 1800 as the rise of affective individualism; affective in the sense of warmth, full of emotion; individualism in the sense of the predominance of the nuclear family over larger kinship ties and the demarcation of a bounded private sphere of love and affectionate child rearing. "I believe this to have been perhaps the most important change in *mentalité* to have occurred in the Early Modern period, indeed possibly in the last thousand years of Western history."[7]

Prior to this development, real life seemed to be a direct imitation of Hobbes's description of it as nasty, brutish, and short. If life had continued in the preaffective mode, the anxiety-infused theory of Hobbes, rather than the optimistic liberalism of Locke, would have held dominion over the modern world. Indeed, the modern world might never have evolved:

> These four factors, the lack of a unique mother figure in the first two years of life [as a result of wet-nursing], the constant loss of close relatives, siblings, parents, nurses and friends through premature death, the physical imprisonment of the infant in tight swaddling-clothes in early months, and the deliberate breaking of the child's will all contributed to a "psychic numbing" which created many adults whose primary responses to others were at best a calculating indifference and at worst a mixture of suspicion and hostility, tyranny and submission, alienation and rage.
>
> ... it is remarkable how difficult it is to find in the correspondence and memoirs of that period that ease and warmth which is so apparent in the eighteenth century. So far as the surviving evidence goes, England between 1500 and 1660 was relatively cold, suspicious and violence-prone.[8]

After 1640, Stone asserts there evolved a veritable revolution in the value system of society as regards marriage and the family: the development of that which he calls the closed domesticated nuclear family, originating with the upper bourgeosie and squirarchy in the late seventeenth century and becoming the *predominate* mode of family existence in the eighteenth. There was, clearly, an intimate connection between this evolution and the profound changes that were occurring in political and religious life:

> It was a family organized around the principle of personal autonomy, and bound together by strong affective ties. Husbands and wives personally selected each other rather than obeying parental wishes, and their prime motives were now long-term affection rather than economic or status advantage for the lineage as a whole. More and more time, energy and money and love of both parents were devoted to the upbringing of the children whose wills it was no longer thought necessary to crush by force at an early age. Education loomed larger and larger in parents' minds, and among the wealthier members of society the new orientation towards children led to an active desire to limit their numbers in order to improve their life-chances. Patriarchal attitudes within the home markedly declined, and greater autonomy was granted not only to children but also to wives.[9]

The Puritans, and Puritanism, had a great deal to do with these remarkable transformations.[10] During the "sexual revolution" of the sixties and seventies of our own century, Puritan values became a symbol of everything against which people were rebelling. It was a historical confusion. There was a profound difference between the sexual repression that existed within Puritan ideology (no dancing, no bright colors, no religious pictures, no gay music; we may assume that sexual foreplay and variety in sexual congress were also severely inhibited) and the sexual repression of the nineteenth century, commonly designated Victorianism. Nineteenth-century sexual repression was aimed overwhelmingly at women and children; men were free, as long as a reasonable secrecy was maintained, to keep their mistresses, their seamstresses, and their whores. Puritan sexual repression, and the Puritan commitment to fidelity in marriage—the question of whether the latter comprises repression, or not, could fill a book in itself—applied with equal force to men and women. The Reverend Dimsdale was no less guilty than Hester Prynne. As far as I know, this was the first time in the history of Western culture when such an ideal of marriage held dominion over any large section of society. It was the slimy, patriarchal sexual repression of Victorian times that had to be overthrown in the twentieth century in order to establish sexual freedom—for women as well as men. If our current ideal—far from being realized—

includes both intense sexual pleasure and gender equality, we must not fail to understand that it is to Puritanism that we owe a significant beginning of equality.

Sexual equality in the marital circumstance went hand in hand with two other aspects of the Puritan ideal.[11]* Within marriage, both partners were supposed to achieve sexual satisfaction, even if that gratification may not have been of the order of intensity that we would find adequate today. And husbands and wives were supposed to be companions, helpmates to each other, an ideal that did not preclude, but rather included, the primacy of the male in the partnership. In its ideal form, Puritan marriage was friendly, emotionally gratifying, sexually satisfying, and of a degree of equality that was remarkable considering the history of the world up to the sixteenth century.

It is important to note, when trying to understand the course of moral development in all its complexities and ambiguities, that in regard to tyranny over children, the Puritan family ranks very poorly. It may even be reasonably suggested that the whole of the Protestant Reformation represents a regressive movement in regard to children, most especially in its definition of them as born with the tremendous burden of original sin that requires that their will—a manifestation of that sinful condition—must be broken as the primary condition of upbringing and socialization.[12] This dread of assertiveness on the part of the infant and child was bequeathed by the Puritans to the followers of evangelical religions in the eighteenth century. "With remarkable consistency and persistence, evangelicals through the centuries insisted that parents must control and break the emerging will of children in the first few years of life. The central issue . . . was this: the autonomous will and self-assertiveness of the child must be reduced to impotency, be utterly suppressed and contained, or the child ultimately would be damned for eternity. 'Break their wills,' urged John Wesley [the founder of Methodism], 'that you may save their souls.' "[13] It was not until the triumph of liberalism over autocracy and evangelicalism, in the eighteenth century, that children became, for most middle and upper-class parents (at least in England and North America), a source of joy and love rather than of dread.

* Edmund Leites, personal communication.

The moral advances that took place between 1600 and 1780 in England and America were extraordinary. Swaddling of infants was almost universal at the beginning of this period. Stone comments:

> The practice of tight swaddling in the first months or even year of life, resulting in what is virtually a prolongation of the inter-uterine condition of total immobility, is thought to isolate the infant from its surroundings. Thus there would be, and often was, a combination of sensory deprivation, motor deprivation and affect deprivation in the first critical months of life, the consequences of which upon the adult personality are now thought to be very serious and long lasting in reducing the capacity for warm social relationships.[14]

In the middle of the eighteenth century, the attack on swaddling was in full force, physicians began advocating its abandonment, and ultimately it ceased to exist.[15]

Wet-nursing was a practice whereby a newborn infant was taken from its home and deposited with a caretaker who nursed and provided for it for the first year or two of its life, whereupon it was returned to its "natural" mother. The traumatic impact of such shipment and the psychic confusion about who one's mother really was, and what truly constituted mothering, can be imagined. Throughout northwest Europe and North America this practice was under severe attack in the eighteenth century; mothers were urged, from all sides, to nurse their own children. Rousseau was one of the first persons, possibly even the first, to make the direct connection between children-rearing practices and the values of society on the whole: "Let mothers nurse their babies, and a general reform of morals will happen naturally."[16] This is the first insight that suggests democracy is impossible unless we have a democratic child rearing: that a stable, unfragmented psyche is a necessary condition for a stable, nonauthoritarian society.

The breaking of the child's will, as the primary condition for molding its nature, gave way, in most households, to a mode of care that proceeded from an optimistic assumption about human nature. The child's will was to be treasured and cultivated, along with other qualities. Around 1750 Henry Lord Holland gave instructions for raising his son, Charles James Fox: "Let nothing be done to break his spirit.

41

The world will do that business fast enough." Concomitant with this development, the beating of children at home and in school was coming under severe criticism. Locke had published in 1693 a widely accepted book that argued that boys in school should not be physically abused for academic failures. By the middle of the eighteenth century some of the most elite schools in England had forsaken this disciplinary device.[17] It is not suggested that such humane educational practice became universal—the beating of students remains legal in some parts of the United States today—but it is important to understand how indebted we are, in our highest ideals, to the moral advances of the 1700s.

As tyranny and domination diminish, equality, mutuality, and Eros flourish. To forsake swaddling, wet-nursing, and the breaking of the will is to release those emotions toward children that we regard as natural, but that are not nearly as natural as we might imagine. The loving of children in a full, open, joyous manner is a great triumph of the moral advance of culture, a position achieved with enormous effort against severe difficulties, a position capable of being abandoned at any time whenever acute social anxieties may demand it. To anticipate for the moment, in the nineteenth century a very powerful trend developed in society that reacted as if the humane and loving treatment of children had been a mistake in need of correction. A theory of moral social development, especially one based on a psychological foundation, has no problem with—actually needs for completeness—the possibilities and actualities of psychological and moral regression. The end of the eighteenth century, to return to our narrative, was one of the great periods in the history of the liberation of childhood.

The revolution in child-rearing practices was already noted at the beginning of the century. "As early as 1697 a French visitor could detect that a change was taking place, and that English children were being treated in an extraordinarily affectionate manner." Maternal breast-feeding was one factor that produced the situation wherein the mother was the dominant and ever-present figure in the child's life.[18] The kind of intense, optimistic, ever-praising mothering that many in our society take as a standard had its first full flowering among the comfortable and affluent classes in the eighteenth century.

Of keen interest for us today, when greater and greater emphasis is being placed—by some people—on the role of the father in infant and child care, is the fact that much of the data that we have about the affectionate nature of child rearing in the 1700s comes from fathers. "How delightful to see the childish amusements of our sweet boy," wrote Timothy Pickering of Salem, Massachusetts, in 1778, "to hear his fond prattle and view his wanton tricks? What joy and wonder to observe his growing mind? and what pleasure to communicate instruction?" And even more revolutionary, fathers were unashamed to wax eloquent about their infant daughters. Edward Chandler in the mid-1780s wrote to his American brother-in-law: "Hear is the Mother and daughter along side me and they make such a noise that it is impossible for me to proceed any farther at present—" "Wherefore must drop my pen and take my dear baby to play with." "Oh Samy, she is the loveliest Child that ever god Created. There is nothing in this world half so dear to me as my Child. And a beautiful babe she is—and every body is fond of her. I wish you was hear to see her."[19]

No attempt is being made to portray the end of the eighteenth century as a children's paradise. There was, undoubtedly, a great deal of child abuse, not-quite-conscious infanticide, and persistent attempts to break the child's will. It is impossible at this point to say exactly how many parents subscribed to the affectionate mode and how many still regarded the child as an object of dread. Two things seem clear, nonetheless. There were, in England and America, many, many parents like the Pickerings and the Chandlers. Two hundred years earlier, there had been hardly any.

This rise of an affectionate, caring, optimistic child rearing was impossible without a prior profound change in the relationships of men and women in marriage. Men and women who do not treasure each other cannot consistently cherish their children. An affectionate, liberating nurturing also enables boys, and then men, to resolve some basic ambivalences toward mothers and women, thereby making equality within marriage a greater possibility. A more moral marriage and a more moral parent-child relation are each the cause of the other. Where, within this system of double causality, change begins and new cultural forms arise is something we do not yet understand, in part because we cannot explain exactly what role the society as a whole plays in such transformations. It is beyond the boundaries of this book to attempt such explanations.

What we can see clearly is that, starting as early as the sixteenth century, a veritable revolution in the nature of marriage was realized in the societies we have been discussing. The traditional religious purposes of marriage had been to avoid fornication and to sire legitimate children. In his Prayer Book of 1549, Archbishop Cranmer added a third motive: "mutual society, help and comfort, that one ought to have of the other, both in prosperity and in adversity." So powerful was this radical conception that it grew and flourished to the point where, in the beginning of the eighteenth century, Benjamin Wadsworth in America could declare: "The indisputable authority, the plain command of the great God, required husbands and wives to have and manifest very great affection, love and kindness to one another." One essential change necessary for this particular great awakening was that the system of arranged marriages had to give way to marriage by choice. By the end of the 1600s "arranged marriage was coming under severe criticism from all quarters,"[20] and by the end of the eighteenth century, most parents retained, at most, a veto power over a proposed marriage that they imagined would prove to be disastrous. Romance, as each individual was free to conceive, or debase, it, became one of the fundamental grounds of marriage. In the fifty years before 1800, men and women loved each other—and liked each other—more gaily, more humanely, than possibly at any other time in the history of the world.

But the rose was sick. There was a canker within the bloom. Love, kindness, affection, companionship, mutuality are one order of human experience; sexuality, to our great sorrow, is another. The emphasis here is not on the soft, sweet, sensual, sublimated sexuality of love, but on the raw, primitive lust of anger and orgasm. Not of amiable Eros which brings all things together, but of obdurate libido, "the hectic in the blood,"[21] which can drive us apart at the precise moment when we need each other most. It is imperative to recognize the subtle but powerful distinction between making love and fucking. Even today, after one particular great advance in the process of sexual revolution, people still do not know how to accommodate fucking and loving in only one bed.

Tyranny and Equality

Two things have frightened men—not humankind, but *men*—more than the punishment of their master, more than the wrath of God, more than death. The first is their own sexuality. Why this should be so, we do not know; we have a deep sense of it, but no theoretical clarity. Freud could not tell us why; those who have come after have been correspondingly mute. The poets, dramatists, and novelists from whom Freud learned so much have known in their bones of this dread of libido. The history of sexuality, prostitution, pornography, rape, and child abuse confirm over and over again the existence of a profound anxiety where sex is concerned. And second, related to the first, but somehow autonomous in its own right, has been the masculine dread of female sexuality, especially female orgasm, most especially the notion that women are as capable of fucking as are men. This is the last, final equality that men refuse to grant women. There must be millions of men in the world today who are able, reluctantly but still persistently, to accept the idea that women share equality with men in the areas of love, affection, companionship, but who unconsciously maintain a prodigious anxiety that their own masculine identity will dissolve into nothingness should women, or at least their own particular woman, learn the secret of raw, uninhibited, primitive sexuality. Women have been denied, and are still denied, equality in the realm of enterprise not because female assertiveness is in itself so frightening but because such a wish to dominate in the real world symbolizes a more powerful desire (so the masculine mind imagines) to rule in that land of unsublimated concupiscence.

Freud says that in the unconscious there is no negative, that the id knows nothing of denial. The more one observes how difficult it has been for men to forsake the tyranny over women, the more it appears that in the deep recesses of primitive libido there exists no conception of equality, only a world of rule or be ruled.

Once the repression of sexuality begins to be lifted, these great problematics within the libido have to be dealt with and aspects of them severely defended against. It does not appear to be far from the mark to say that it is precisely the desire not to deal with the full threatening implications of female sexuality that constitutes one of the fundamental bases of sexual repression. Once the freedom of sexuality, for both men and women, starts to become a reality and the more tyrannical aspects of repression are lifted, men begin to deal with their sexual anxiety about women by a process of splitting: the goddess and the whore, the women one marries and the women one goes to bed with before marriage, the sexual things one does in the nuptial bed and those other things one does elsewhere. (I was told by a member of the generation before mine that going outside of marriage for oral sex was not cheating because "You don't get that at home.") Stone asserts that, by 1750, sexual repression had been substantially lifted, as indicated by the prodigious fact that sexual pleasure was no longer associated with sin and guilt. The resultant, however, was an ambiguous combination of both good and bad similar to that to which we have been witness in the last twenty years: sexual pleasure within marriage became more highly sought after and possible, and, at the same time, sexual chaos began to dominate the streets of large cities at night. "By legitimizing the sexual act within marriage for the purpose of mutual comfort and endearment, Protestant theology began the slow separation of sexual pleasure from procreation that ended in the late seventeenth-century spread of both *contraception* and *libertinism*."[22]

This defensive measure of splitting adopted by males in the attempt to cope with an almost unbearable anxiety concerning their own and female sexuality is analogous to a person who has to fight, singly, against two opponents. His only hope for survival is to separate them from each other and thereby combat each one severally. The whore or mistress who is allowed all the dangerous attributes of raw sexuality is isolated from affection, caring, loving; in every way but sex she is made into a thing. Because emotions are not engaged, one can deal more ably with the threat of being libidinally overwhelmed. Female sexuality becomes less dangerous. The case is similar and opposite within marriage; men are defended against being annihilated by a combination of affectionate and libidinal feelings by denying the marriage partner full sexual expression. The caring, nurturing aspects of love become, thereby, less full of dread. Sexism is built upon this rock.

And then, inevitably, one final thing occurs within society that frightens male tyrants almost beyond the reach of reason: women cease to be the passive objects of male "generosity" and begin to demand equality in their own right. Exactly that happened at the end of the eighteenth century, and no matter what the particular text of female demands—economic, social, legal, political—there always existed, and still exists, a powerful subtext of sexuality, full sexual rights to both feelings and actions, and both men and women unconsciously know that this subtext is, in many ways, the true text. The panic and the rage with which men react indicate that much more is involved than the question of who can eat in what club or, even more important, who can become a doctor. Were we not faced with the tremendous irrationalities of sexual equality, we might long ago have resolved many of the problems that still plague us.

Like almost all movements for reform, feminism began with both a liberal and a radical thrust. Feminist liberalism had antecedents in the actions of liberal men who began to abjure the worst forms of male tyranny. Already in the 1634 edition of Thomas Gouge's most popular marriage manual it was stated directly that a husband may not beat his wife, a sentiment that found official confirmation in the New World: "*The Liberties of the Massachusetts Colony*, adopted by the General Court in 1641 . . . placed strict limits on the use of judicial torture to extract information, and forbade husbands to beat their wives or maltreat their servants or apprentices."[23] When Daniel Ela told his wife, in 1682, that "shee was none of his wife, shee was but his Servant," that statement was reported to the authorities by the neighbors, and he was fined forty shillings by a Massachusetts court despite his wife's protest that she had "nothinge Agenst my husband to Charge him with." This new gift of freedom from the worst tyranny was, it must be emphasized, granted to women by men, a fact acknowledged by the sentiments of Samuel Willard who stated that a husband should so rule "as that his Wife may take delight in it, and not account it a Slavery, but a Liberty and Privilege."[24] Feminist liberalism accepted the rule of men but optimistically assumed that the despotism would prove benevolent:

> The association of boundless power with men was evident to Abigail Adams, who wrote in March 1776 asking her husband [John Adams] to "Remember the Ladies" in "the new Code of Laws" that he and his fellow legislators might make, and to "be more generous and favourable to them than your ancestors. Do not put such unlimited power into the hands of the Husbands." "Remember," she said, "all men would be tyrants if they could. . . . That your Sex are Naturally Tyrannical is a Truth so thoroughly

established as to admit of no dispute, but such of you as wish to be happy, willingly give up the harsh title of Master for the more tender and endearing one of Friend. Why then, not put it out of the power of the vicious and the Lawless to use us with Cruelty and indignity with impunity. Men of Sense in all Ages abhor those customs which treat us only as the vassals of your Sex."[25]

Had women stayed content to beseech, to mollify, to appease, the great masculine rage against women and the creation of severe sexual repression in the nineteenth century might never have reached such proportions whereby it came to dominate the culture. But once the repressive lid had been taken off love, affection, mutual care, and companionship, the full power of sexual energy was not to be easily denied. Radical feminism did not attempt to cajole men into granting a greater degree of equality. It demanded for women the same rights men were demanding for themselves; and full equality always means equal access to raw sexual power. Even in the early seventeenth century, Marjory, the wife of Viscount Fenton, had, after a particularly intense marital quarrel, torn the pages from the Bible which spoke of the subservience of women to men. And in 1673 the heroine of *The Careless Lover* declared for independence: "But Uncle, it is not now as it was in your young days. Women then were poor, sneaking, sheepish creatures. But in our age we know our own strength and have wit enough to make use of our talents." Directly after the turn of the eighteenth century, Mary Astell stated the radical position as clearly and as basically as it has ever been stated: "If absolute sovereignty be not necessary in a state, how comes it to be so in a family? Or if in a family, why not in a state? . . . Is it not then partial in men to the last degree to contend for and practice that arbitrary dominion in their families which they abhor and exclaim against in the state? . . . If all men are born free, how is it that all women are born slaves?"[26]

The feminist revolution, however, like the revolution in our economic relations, has been a long time coming, and most of the eighteenth century was to pass before a new wave of radical feminism, influenced directly by the American and French revolutions, developed at the end of the century. These feminists were "far more radical in their demands, their personal behavior and their religious attitudes than their predecessors had been a century earlier." Mary Wollstonecraft was remarkably modern, even post-Freudian, in her insistence that children be enlightened about the facts of pregnancy and birth; in her biting analysis and criticism of the system of upper-class French marriage, wherein each partner engaged in adulterous affairs with the tacit consent of the other, as an expression of "sentimental lust"[27]; and in her call for sexual equality.

The reaction against this feminism that stood for sexual parity and radical politics (the French Revolution) was immediate and intense. Exactly as today, liberal feminists felt threatened by this demand for full equality, and the periodical *The Lady's Monthly Museum* attacked Wollstonecraft, declaring that "the champions of female equality . . . are no longer regarded as sincere and politic friends, but base and insidious enemies." But it was the men who tried to defend against an almost uncontrollable anxiety with the expression of savage aggression. Wollstonecraft was, in the famous epigram of Horace Walpole, "that hyena in petticoats."[28] Knowing much more today about the nature of unconscious conflict, we can read a deeper meaning into that metaphor: she has a hyena under her petticoats. Her genital organ is incarnadine, salivied, and betoothed. Such was the male vision of a woman with full libidinal impulses.

The panic flight from this terrible image of freedom would become intense in the century that was to follow. The bold eighteenth-century attempt to build "Jerusalem in England's green and pleasant Land"[29] was to be smothered by the sickly smog of industrial capitalism. And the affectionate, caring, companionate nuptial bed was, for many if not most, to be transformed into a place where men and women would misunderstand and mistreat each other; sex, even within marriage, was to become as much feared as enjoyed. Aggression against children increased conspicuously. The larger social world, remarkable to tell, would witness some of the most extraordinary moral advances ever: stable, permanent democracies would be established; slavery would finally be completely destroyed; social movements would bring the first *permanent* conditions of power to those who had been powerless since the beginning of time. The great Age of Ambivalence was upon us.

4

The Great Refusal

ANY ATTEMPT to understand the moral promise and the moral chaos of the last two hundred years is doomed to failure as long as it concentrates only on the large public world of economics and politics and neglects the private world of men and women, parents and children. We will never be able to comprehend fascism, for instance, if we look only at economic and political history and fail to observe the manner in which children were being raised, and the vast changes that were occurring in that crucial area, from 1800 onward. No attempt is being made here to reduce all sociology to psychology. But in our striving to understand the last two centuries can we ignore the facts that Germany was one of the last countries in Western Europe to give up swaddling and that in the Soviet Union today even the most sophisticated people still swaddle, "but only for the first three months"?*

Similarly, if we are to understand "what happened?" in the nineteenth century—what caused the great moral advances of the previous 250 years to start to come apart, what transformed a great promise into a great refusal—we must look not only to capitalism, the rise of nationalism, and democracy, but also to the prodigious conflicts

---

* Intourist guide, Moscow. Personal communication, July 1985.

within marriage, sexuality, and child rearing. When we truly begin to comprehend the dialectic between the public and the private worlds, our theoretical capacity will have increased immensely. This book makes no claim of being able to do more than underline certain crucial sociological questions. But it does take as its premise the concept that an enlightened, nonreductionist psychology has a vast amount to contribute to the theory of society.

The great public world of economics, religion, and politics was relegated to a background phenomenon in the previous chapter in the attempt to concentrate on the tale of women, men, and children. These two worlds of public and private, though each demonstrates a definite autonomy, are nevertheless acutely dependent one on the other. As one example, feminism in both its liberal and radical manifestations is unimaginable in a world where there is no masculine challenge to the tyranny of men over men. "The issue had already been debated on the stage in 1697, when in Vanbrugh's play *The Provoked Wife* Lady Brute applies Locke's breakable contract theory of the state to her own situation: 'The argument's good between the King and the people, why not between the husband and the wife?' "[1] Similarly, but moving in the opposite causal direction, men's deep psychological panic over the demand for female sexual equality, and the defensive resort to increased repression, cannot fail to have affected the views and actions such men took in regard to slaves, workers, and the nonwhite peoples of the earth.

No one-to-one correlation between the lifting of tyranny in one world and the equivalent phenomenon in the other world is postulated here. Our theoretical task would be easy if the historical record demonstrated that, for instance, more equality in the realm of politics always produces more equality in the relations of men to women. Sometimes that seems to have been so; at other times, however, exactly the opposite was the case. A certain insidious trade-off appears to occur in the complex world of tyranny and dominance: when tyranny is ameliorated in one area of social life, many times it seeks greater satisfaction in another, as if to compensate itself for loss. There is much evidence that indicates that the position of women in ancient Athens grew worse in the fifth century B.C. than it had been in the previous two centuries. And it was precisely in that fifth century that Athenian democracy achieved its greatest degree of equality. It is almost as if men, no longer able to oppress other men with the same degree of harshness, were compelled to heighten the tyranny over women.[2] A bare recitation of the moral triumphs and immoral catastrophes of the nineteenth century can make one wonder whether something similar but even more complex was occurring at that time.

Even the world of masculine dominance over other men demonstrates no moral developmental consistency. An unexpected relationship appears to exist between democracy and imperialism. In Athens, again, the fifth century was the great age of Athenian imperialism; the Athenian empire ruled unchallenged in the Aegean Sea, an empire with no inclination to soften the harshness of its hegemony. Pericles, the great spokesman for democracy, was also the supreme imperialist. Striking is the comparison with Europe in the nineteenth century. Democracy and imperialism, the Reform Act and the Empire, were the great political innovations. It may be wondered whether men, no longer able to tyrannize to the same degree over other men at home, did not seek some foreign "other" on whom to satisfy their *libido dominandi*. An analogous twentieth-century situation comes to mind if one recalls the pathetic figure of the solitary Lyndon Johnson, having been raised in a violently racist society and having become the champion of civil rights at home, slowly driving himself almost mad over the war against the "yellow gooks."

The problematic within all moral and psychological advance is that such advance requires the giving up of psychological defenses. All expressions of aggression, all forms of tyranny and dominance, are defenses against anxiety. People are racist and sexist in good part because such reduction of other people to objects helps contain anxiety and the tendency to panic. The only manner in which moral and psychological progress is possible is by the creation of new, less primitive, more sublimated mechanisms of defense, all of which allow the traditional modes of defense to be abandoned. When a society prematurely progresses morally and psychologically—that is, when it begins to disparage the more primitive modes of defense without having yet created new, effective mechanisms—that society becomes psychologically overextended. Great conflicts arise. Remarkable moral advances occur simultaneously with the worst moral catastrophes. What nation, for instance, shall ultimately speak for the culture of the twentieth century? A nonimperialist democracy or Nazi Germany?

The nineteenth century in Europe was such a time of moral and psychological tension. And twentieth-century society throughout the whole world remains trapped in the same moral bind from which it cannot liberate itself. Old forms of tyranny and dominance—racism, classism, sexism—are under attack everywhere, but nowhere are they truly given up, and to the despair of humankind, new forms of tyranny are created to contain the almost unbearable anxiety of the modern world: fascism, Stalinism, genocide, religious fundamentalism, and even the national suicide of Cambodia.

In the eighteenth century, the moral advances in both the public and private worlds seemed to be in harmony with each other. The amelioration of tyranny and the advance of equality in regard to women and children were at one with the moral advances in political life. Historians debate at great length "the true causes" of the American and French revolutions. Regardless of these intellectual controversies, it seems clear that both prerevolutionary societies had accomplished something that made revolution possible, or even inevitable. Within the value system of each society, an ideal of constitutional government, of citizenship (that is, the amelioration of tyranny), and of equality had evolved. Such an accomplishment is not possible within only one generation. These revolutions, whatever their immediate and individual causes, were at least eighty to one hundred years in the making. In England a similar moral advance was taking place in the eighteenth century: a stable constitutional monarchy, a proto-democracy. Liberalism and the Enlightenment were the social equivalents of the growth of equality within the family. Each was the cause of the other.

This momentous partnership, this "inevitable" progress of human reason and the human spirit, exploded in the nineteenth century. No longer can we observe one predominant progressive trend of companionate marriage, mother nurturing, *liberté, égalité*. The English massacre of six hundred peacefully demonstrating, lower-class men, women, and children at Peterloo in 1819 gave notice that there was a dark, horrific strain in the human spirit; a force that would not be easily tamed and civilized; a view that found the concept of equality maddening, as if those demanding it were so many reptiles or insects who had to be exterminated in order to make the world orderly. And it was not long before women within marriage and children within the family were to feel the effects of this calculating attempt at counterrevolution:

> The only conclusion to be reached is that, despite internal dissension within the medical profession, for the first time in Western history there was a strong body of opinion which actually denied the existence of the sexual drive in the majority of women, and regarded the minority who experienced it to any marked degree as morally, mentally or physically diseased. A marriage manual of 1839 stated as a fact that sterility was caused by any female who displayed "excessive ardour of desire," and advised that "tranquility, silence, and secrecy are necessary for a prolific coition."[3]

Certain specific acts of maltreatment of children—the beatings and the psychological abuse (those scenes in Dickens that one never forgets)—were probably no more severe or prevalent than in the eighteenth century; we have no means of weighing accurately this kind of historical data. But a definite trend away from freedom was observable in the early part of the century. Around 1800 one of the most popular books on child rearing was Maria Edgeworth's *Practical Education*, which delighted in the child's being. When once asked how she had learned so much about children, Edgeworth replied: "Why, I don't know, I lie down and let them crawl all over me." By 1820, however, the advice of Hannah More had become more popular than the humane Edgeworth. More expounded: "Is it not a fundamental error to consider children as innocent beings, whose little weaknesses may, perhaps, want some correction, rather than as beings who bring into the world a corrupt nature and evil dispositions, which it should be the great end of education to rectify?"[4]

This latter view was, of course, merely rehashed evangelical Original Sin. But in the area of infantile sexuality, the nineteenth century was to invent, as the century progressed, its own, unique mode of abusing children. Childhood masturbation became an obsession of parents and their medical and nonmedical advisers. Predictions abounded that it would cause insanity and a host of lesser psychological disabilities. Instruments to prevent its indulgence, some of them almost out of the catalogue of a medieval torturer, were invented, sold, and put into operation. And long before Freud had invented the term castration anxiety, that dread became the primary means of repressing masturbatory activity:

> As one American child psychologist put it, when a child of two rubs his nose and can't be still for a moment, only circumcision works. Another doctor, whose book was the bible of many an American nineteenth-century home, recommended that little boys be closely watched for signs of masturbation, and brought in to him for circumcision without anaesthetic, which invariably cured them. Spitz's graphs on different advice given for masturbation, based on 559 volumes surveyed, show a peak in surgical intervention in 1850–1879, and in restraint devices in 1880–1904. By 1925, these methods had almost completely died out.[5]

The culture was fundamentally ambivalent, however, and for every piece of data entered in the child-abuse column, one can find counterindication that children were deeply thought about, cared about, and treasured. English novelist Elizabeth Gaskell and journalist William Cobbett (who was jailed for protesting the flogging of soldiers) raised their children in a manner that was a full anticipation of Dr. Spock. French historian François Guizot, "who studied examples of conjugal love throughout history, claimed that never before had parents lived on such affectionate terms with their children."[6] Such positive attitudes toward nurturing eventually led to the discovery of one of the most important means of dealing with the dark conflicts within the human psyche. Jacob Abbott, in 1871, wrote perceptively about the need to differentiate between repression and sublimation, without knowing either term:

> In a word, we must favor and promote, by every means in our power, the activity of children, not censure and repress it. We may endeavor to turn it aside from wrong channels—that is, to prevent it manifesting itself in ways injurious to them or annoying to others. We must not, however, attempt to divert it from these channels by damming it up, but by opening other channels that will draw it away in a better direction.[7]

What we can perceive is a society in an acute state of ambivalent conflict, unable to move decisively in either a primarily moral or fundamentally reactionary direction. Or—more accurately, but presenting us with a logical contradiction—intensely doing both things at the same time. These ambivalent phenomena are also observable recently and are currently present in our society. Consider the days when the public view on the war in Vietnam was running 60–40, or 55–45, or 50–50; or consider today, when the question of abortion fractures our culture. This intense moral divide in many crucial areas began in the nineteenth century: we are the heirs of that incomplete moral agenda. From 1867 to 1869 the correspondence columns of the *Englishwoman's Domestic Magazine* were the focus of an intense debate concerning the appropriateness of corporal punishment of girls at home. Half of those who wrote in found the whole idea appalling; many had a mixed reaction; and a goodly number were fierce advocates of the practice.[8]

So pervasive was this moral ambivalence, in both the private family world and in the large world of politics, that it characterized the culture as a whole. We search in vain for any one distinguishing moral trend, such as can be found in the eighteenth century. No claim is being made here that the eighteenth century was a moral paradise, or even close to it. Like any century, it demonstrated in a multitude of ways the human capacities for domination and destruction. It did, however, exhibit in northwest Europe and America a consistent trend of moral improvement without any compensating, symptomatic, fierce regressions. To even begin to comprehend the nineteenth century, we need first to understand that moral triumphs and moral catastrophes followed each other in rapid succession. As with us today, it seemed almost impossible to decide where society was heading.

The list of moral catastrophes must begin with the brutality of early capitalism, with small children laboring twelve to fourteen hours a day, with wages close to the starvation level, and with the beatings and killings of workers who had the temerity to protest. White imperialism, starting with England and quickly spreading to almost every country in Europe, dominated the political agenda by the end of the century. At its worst, massacre became an instrument of public policy. At home, opposition to the growing democracy was fierce. As each new group demanded participation in the polity, the countertactics of humiliation, beating, and jailing took their human toll; political martyrs came to be canonized in the way that religious sufferers once had been. We take our democracy today so for granted that we forget how recent an invention it is, how difficult was the struggle to secure it, and how many currently democratic societies almost did not succeed. We may find it unsettling to learn, for instance, that all through the nineteenth century the Catholic Church in France was fiercely opposed to full democratic institutions.

And in the private world of the family, we have already touched upon the new assault—from some quarters—on women and children. "Patriarchy" as a word to describe the tyranny of men over women has become greatly overused. Its use in a vague general way keeps us from differentiating the crucially distinct forms of patriarchy. Certainly, the patriarchy of the Roman *paterfamilias*, and the patriarchy of the sixteenth century, and the patriarchy of the 1800s were very different phenomena. Critical for the purposes of this book is the understanding of the particular brand of patriarchy produced in Victorian times. Based on the intense sexual repression of "respectable" women and the acute concern with and anxiety about infant sexuality, Victorian patriarchy created a father who was armor-plated with psychological defenses; a full-bodied authoritarian, who took his particular morality very seriously and threatened and/or delivered extreme punishment for "moral" waywardness. Freud was born into a world of such fathers and such an authoritarian conception of morality. Every patriarch was an imitation Jehovah in the household: distant, demanding, castrating. It is no wonder that Freud's concept of the superego—for him the moral instrument in the psyche—should take exactly this form.

Simultaneous with these moral retrogressions, in certain areas of concern nineteenth-century society was making magnificent progress. Slavery, after more than ten thousand years of existence, was for all practical purposes eliminated from the earth. The drive toward full democracy was inexorable, despite all the opposition. The moral revulsion against the Peterloo massacre helped fuel the movement that culminated in the Reform Act of 1832 in England. By the end of the century complete male suffrage was an important ideal in every country of Europe: either a reality or a political battleground. Concomitant with this impulse was the drive for universal public education; our unambivalent belief in its appropriateness is an inheritance from the last century. Of fateful consequence for the present was the fact that, building on the ideal of equal political rights, a call was raised for full economic equality, a demand that was to become a *permanent* aspect of the world's moral agenda. When in the fourteenth century John Ball had declared that "the matter goeth not well to pass in England, nor shall not do so till everything be in common,"[9] his call for action had no lasting significance. But the identical nineteenth-century appeal has become the essence of twentieth-century history. In the last century child-labor laws, trade unionism, working-class and radical political parties all challenged the propensity of industrial capitalism to do its worst.

Continuing with our outline of moral advance, note has already been taken of the uninterrupted humane and delightful treatment of children, at least by some people. And "Victorian" marriage, it is becoming more and more apparent, was not as disastrous for all couples as we once imagined. There were many relationships that reflected and built upon the companionate marriage of the eighteenth century, combining both emotional delight and sexual intensity.[10]

The historical and sociological problem becomes one of numbers. We can quote one or two personal diaries to prove practically anything we want about the nature of nineteenth-century sexuality and marriage. The question remains: How many people are represented by any particular point of view? We face the identical lack of certitude in trying to understand contemporary society. We are probably able to describe eight or ten or twelve characteristic lifestyles of present-day married life. But how many people are living each of those styles? How can we say exactly what late twentieth-century marriage "is"? We lack this mathematical accuracy. But even if we had it, our theoretical problems would not be solved. What is necessary is constantly to relate one aspect of moral relations within society to others, in order ultimately to shed light on each of them. We know, for instance, that despite the efforts to repress women, female sexuality, and children; despite the enthronement of authoritarian, intrusive patriarchy; despite all forms of legal and psychological harassment—the feminist movement would not go away. And that speaks to the notion that something very positive was still going on within marriage and child rearing—again, at least within some households. One cannot produce the likes of Elizabeth Cady Stanton, Susan B. Anthony, and Mrs. Pankhurst—and hundreds of thousands of their followers—in a family situation where women are taught by their mothers and fathers that they have no worth. The feminist movement grew in an atmosphere of *political* and *familial* enlightenment; it could not be otherwise. If the nineteenth century was the beginning of the Age of Ambivalence, it was ambivalent in a manner that made enormous moral progress possible. That kind of ambiguity is impossible to understand by all forms of simplistic social theory. A culture may be racing in two opposite moral directions simultaneously.

The growing feminist movement in the nineteenth century concentrated most of its energy on the question of suffrage. The political reaction against the French Revolution and against the growing demands for universal male suffrage produced a quiescent effect on the women's movement in the first thirty or forty years of the century. But starting around 1840, in both England and America, the drive for women's suffrage became inexorable. It took eighty years and thousands of demonstrations and arrests, however, before the male masters of society relented and renounced that particular form of domination.

What was so frightening to the masculine mind of the idea that women should vote? What was it that men imagined they would lose? There is no question that men reacted like people deeply threatened. The masculine response was totally irrational; there was no conceivable threat to society or to capitalism in giving women the vote. In the attempt to understand a deeply irrational problem we should not offer a thoroughly rational explanation. "Capitalism" alone will not explain the deep irrationalities and ambivalences of the nineteenth century. Even capitalism itself is simply one system of male domination over other men; it cannot be taken as a given; it also has to be understood psychologically, as do all systems of domination. The call by women for full political, social, and sexual equality is one of the most frightening demands men have ever had to face, equal in its capacity to engender panic as the insistence that masters give up their slaves, or that economic lords renounce total power over their workers, or that the aristocratic-plutocratic rulers of society share their sovereignty with "common" people. Economic and political rulers, however, are never more than a handful of people, whereas every man in a sexist society is a potential tyrant. Feminism threatens every level of society. The masculine negative response to feminist demands is so powerful that it has the capacity to shape society's whole moral direction.

On the question of whether or not the rise of capitalism explains the moral retrogressions of the nineteenth century, it is of interest to note that the retreat from the advances of the eighteenth century were already visible by 1770, many years before industrial capitalism and its bourgeoisie became the rulers of society. Lawrence Stone remarks: "The next stage in the evolution of the family was marked by a strong revival of moral reform, paternal authority and sexual repression, which was gathering strength among the middle classes from about 1770."[11] A similar insight had been expressed earlier by historian Gordon Taylor, who commented: "Everything points to the fact that the period of decisive moral change was not at the time of Victoria's accession, or even the nineteenth century at all, but that it took place during the decade 1790–1800."[12] We cannot rely only on the capitalist explanation to guide us through the ambiguities of the nineteenth century. There is a logic even within the world of irrationality: a psychologic. If all moral progress necessitates the abandonment of reasonably effective mechanisms of defense (on the part of those exercising domination), such renunciation—even partially—of old defenses greatly increases anxiety. Therefore, no one gives up such mechanisms without a struggle. For these reasons, the chances of violent moral regression are always present.

This is the true cause of the possibilities of malignancy that constantly threaten human civilization—possibilities that became only too real in this century. One cannot comprehend the causes of psychological and moral regression within the family in the nineteenth century—sexual repression of children and women, the reconstruction of authoritarian patriarchy—without understanding the acute panic that men felt as women advanced toward equality. Nor can one comprehend those causes without being aware of how powerful the exercise of domination is as a defense against anxiety. Men are capable of any degree of tyranny or destruction in the attempt to overcome inner terror. The twentieth century has surely taught us that.

The great thinkers of the middle and latter part of the nineteenth century lived in a far different world than the Enlightenment and the

Age of Reason. The limits of rationality were what Dostoevski, Marx, Freud, and Nietzsche attempted to understand. *Irrationality*—that which lies below the reasonable, ordered surface of life—was their subject. Each of them insisted that, in order to understand individual and social life, we must seek what cannot be seen directly. Dostoevski insisted that there was a child rapist and axe murderer in each of us, no matter what surface of civility. Marx asserted that, if we would understand the structure of society, we must look not to religion or philosophy or common morality but to the hidden and disguised system of domination that truly holds it together. Nietzsche's whole philosophy is an intense critique of the rational and an ambivalent glorification of the illogic, chaos, and power of irrationality. All of them, along with Freud, insisted that if freedom is possible, it can only become a reality by first understanding the cage in which we are imprisoned.

Though ultimately committed to freedom, each of these thinkers maintained a profound ambivalence toward one or several of the concerns on the great nineteenth-century moral agenda: political freedom, economic equality, the renunciation of prejudice, feminism, sexual freedom, and the nonauthoritarian treatment of children. Freud, born in 1856, and not the others, is the subject of our book; what he would and would not see. Despite his moral and intellectual genius, he was a child of the nineteenth century—in many ways, an extraordinarily characteristic child. Ultimately adding more to the store of human freedom than most of the world's great men have even dreamed of doing, he himself was, in certain areas, far from free. That human ambiguity is the true subject of this work.

Freud and Ambivalence

It is a comparatively easy task to demonstrate the strong antifeminine bias in Freud's work. That women are less capable than men in the area of morality; that most women over thirty are already beginning to show definite signs of being exhausted by life; that the child's first protector against fate is the *father*—all this is readily available in the Freudian texts; no great detective work is necessary. We will traverse this ground in the chapters that follow. If that were the primary thrust of this work, however, it would be a very slim book, with no real reason for existence, because this ground has already been expertly covered by feminist critics of Freud. This book is written for a larger purpose: to demonstrate that Freud's anxiety about women produced not only antifeminist theory on matters directly concerning women but also crucially important theoretical distortions in areas that, on the surface, do not bear directly on the question of male-female equality. It will be argued that as the result of a hidden antifeminine bias the psychoanalytic theory of morality is inadequate. Similar distortions of the truth enter into Freud's thought on the great questions of civilization and the instincts and the role of science within human culture. On both of these issues, as on the question of morality, Freud displays a pervasive ambivalence that is the direct product of his ambivalence about, and anxiety concerning, women.

The superego, for Freud, is the crucially important psychic instrument of morality. In Freud's description of that function, the superego partakes almost totally of masculine attributes. Born of the oedipal struggle between a boy and his father, harsh and punishing in its stance toward misconduct, making use of the threat of castration as its principal mode of police power—this superego, along with its discoverer, has almost completely repressed the memory of the pre-oedipal mother who nurtured the child (male and female alike) for the first four or five years of its life. Because the true origins of morality, I argue, lie precisely in that mother-child dyad, any theory of morality that pays no attention to that time in the child's development must necessarily be seriously lacking in accuracy.

That this harsh, punishing, castrating superego is a perfect symbolic representation of the nineteenth-century reconstructed version of the patriarch seems clear. The theory of the superego, as elaborated in Freud's work, is the product of an authoritarian child rearing wherein the father assumes a crucial role—at a certain point in the child's life— the role being as different from a loving, nurturing mother as is imaginable. It is only the breakdown of that Jehovah-like patriarchy and the movement of culture toward a more liberating child rearing that has enabled us to perceive the inadequacies in such a view of the origins of morality. That the superego cannot represent the moral function within the psyche will be discussed at length in the critique that follows. We will pay close attention to the facts that in a slave society, *it is the superego that legitimizes slavery*; that in a sexist culture, it is the superego that encourages sexism; and that in a fascist society, it is the superego that condones fascism. The superego function within the psyche exists—the opposite will not be argued here. But if we are to understand human morality, we will have to comprehend much more.

Freud's desire to construct a masculine world uncontaminated by feminine reengulfment anxieties similarly committed him to a view of science and reason as two indomitable, erect, penislike instruments that men would use to forge the future of humankind. Reason and science, for Freud, were the great replacements for religion in the continuing progress of culture. That these two, uncontrolled by the authority of morality, can bring us untold misery, Freud must have known. But in the theoretical works he was incapable of abandoning his reliance on a masculine, magical road to salvation.

On the question of civilization, Freud was probably more ambivalent than on any other topic he addressed. For him civilization is both loving, nurturing, and moral—the representative of eternal Eros; and also, simultaneously, harshly repressive of the sexual instincts. It is, therefore, both feminine and masculine; and Freud, though he talked much about the inherent bisexuality in everyone, was incapable of dealing unambivalently with the feminine elements within himself, except within the therapeutic situation. In his theory, masculinity and femininity are at war with each other, and the theory of civilization was one great casualty of that war.

With Freud it was not a question that oedipal matters, being the more recent and therefore more available to an adult, would become the center of the theory in the beginning, and that the earlier pre-oedipal relationships would be discovered later. To a certain degree, this was so. However, as will be demonstrated at length in the chapters that follow, Freud was consistently engaged in the repression of the memory of the pre-oedipal time, a time when women rule and little boys suffer from great conflicts of gender identity. No adequate theory of morality, of civilization, of science and reason can be constructed so long as it is erected upon a primarily oedipal foundation and ignores and represses the first four years of a child's life. Freud attempted exactly that feat and the attempt ended in failure.

I have provided a lengthy historical introduction in order that we can understand the ambivalences within Freudian theory against the background of nineteenth-century conflicts over women, sexuality, and authoritarian child rearing. To conceive of the problematics within psychoanalytic theory as a question merely for Freud, and not as characteristic of Western culture, is to miss an opportunity for deep insight into the workings of the value system within society. Freud's antifeminine bias can be understood alongside Aristotle's views on slavery, but even here there is a difference. Whatever ambivalence Aristotle felt about the justice of the institution—and he must have felt some because he was impelled to argue against the "others" who condemned it—the precise nature of that ambivalence is very difficult to establish. With Freud the theoretical conflicts are pervasive and easily apparent, in good part because he accomplished two enormously important, positive things in the area of female equality: he welcomed women into the analytic profession without prejudice; and he did more to liberate sexuality from repression than any person who ever lived. True, he had his doubts at times whether women's sexual feelings could ever be as strong as men's, but he never once denied the importance of female sexuality, nor ever implied that women should be denied sexual pleasure. The current stage of the feminist revolution—the most progressive and permanent stage yet—owes much to Freud and to the profound changes in child rearing that have resulted from the Freudian revolution. Ambivalence is the key. Ambivalence is what we must understand.

The plan of this book is to present in part III a thorough critique of the theory of the superego. After two chapters devoted to that task, the origin of this theoretical distortion in antifeminine defenses is examined. Part III closes with a chapter each on the theory of civilization and of reason/science, underlining in each case how the conflicts concerning masculinity and femininity have significantly misshaped the theory.

The object of this work is not only critical, however. Part IV represents a serious attempt to reconstruct a psychoanalytic theory of morality based on conscience as the primary moral mechanism in the psyche. Conscience, which grows directly out of the relationship of the infant and child to its primary caretaker(s)—that is, in most cultures until today, the mother. After a discussion of the origins of conscience and morality, a chapter is devoted to the crucial psychic mechanism of idealization, a mechanism without which morality could neither develop nor prosper. The last chapter in this part undertakes the task of traversing the path from mother-child dyad to a full adult living in a complex society. Social values within the culture and the personal psychic state of adolescence both take on fundamental significance in the endeavor to understand this intricate developmental process.

Because moral values within the social environment have been the fundamental concern of this work, it becomes appropriate to close the book with a discussion of current moral problems. Here, once again, the concept of ambivalence becomes of crucial importance. Part V elaborates, first, on the concept of the overwhelming importance of the value system for society, and examines the question of how likely it is that we may see a fundamental change in the system of values. The book closes, appropriately enough, with an attempt to describe what a society that decides to resolve some of the great ambivalences of the twentieth century on the side of Eros would *feel* like—because no one but visionaries can know what it will look like. We have already been lamentable witnesses to several actual attempts to resolve those ambivalences on the side of destruction. A work about morality or conscience is always about the choosing of death or life.

PART III

THE PSYCHOANALYTIC THEORY OF MORALITY— A CRITIQUE

5

The End of the Oedipus
Complex and the Formation
of the Superego

FREUD'S DESCRIPTION of the end of the male child's Oedipus complex reads like a nightmare. Panic-stricken by the notion that his desires to murder his father and sexually possess his mother will lead to severe retaliation by the father—that his father will cut off his penis—the boy renounces the most assertive (in Freud's terms, the most masculine) impulses he has ever experienced; renounces, that is, any real hope of ever becoming a man himself, in the narcissistic interest of preserving his anatomy. All possibilities of heroism are over; any prospect of rivaling the father is abandoned; childhood—and neurosis—are destined to last forever. At best, the boy identifies with the aggressor (his father) and participates wholeheartedly in repressing these oedipal wishes. At worst, the boy renounces all hopes of being a man, identifies with the mother, and presents himself to the father as a sexual object. It is a world in which there is only *one* father—*the* father—and no little boy can ever aspire to attain such an awesome office. It is the very essence of a pathogenic situation. Freud would have us believe that there is no escape from this catastrophic outcome. Within his own work, however, he demonstrates that this nightmarish description is only a part, and by no means the whole, of the oedipal saga.

It is not my intention to challenge the basic psychoanalytic position on the nature and importance of the Oedipus complex and the fact that, at its conclusion, the superego makes its appearance as the heir to that conflict.* I take these theoretical positions as given. What remains to be discussed is whether Freud's description of the manner in which, and the reasons why, the Oedipus complex dissolves, and the way in which the superego takes up its inheritance describe a pathological or a normal psychological progression. For every stage of psychological development there are characteristic pathological nonsolutions as well as normal, healthy resolutions. One may describe the early oral stage, for example, and state that all children, at some point and at some times in that stage, experience almost uncontrollable cannibalistic rages. If one were to conclude from this, however, that *all* adults will be subject to uncontrollable rages that will make it impossible for them to grant reality to the existence of other people, making love unattainable—if such were one's conclusion, it would be important to argue against that kind of deduction. Such rages in an adult would represent only one pathological possibility inherent in the early oral stage. This kind of analysis gives no weight to the healthy modes of overcoming such distress. There will, however, still be a great deal of insight and truth contained within the description of the pathological outcome, though it will not be the whole truth. It will be argued here, similarly, that Freud's description of the dissolution of the Oedipus complex, brought about by the fear of castration and the subsequent

---

* Whether that which is designated "superego" is an actual structure or department of the mind, or merely a series of discrete but related psychic impulses that we characterize as a structure because we cannot think about them in any other way, is a very important theoretical issue but not germaine to this discussion. My own position is that there are no such structures or departments as ego, superego, id, and that when Freud talks about these various psychic impulses as if they behaved like the Department of the Interior (which has an office—a place where you can go; which has its own interests that are opposed to interests of other departments; and so on), this is a mythical anthropomorphization similar to that which makes the north wind into a person blowing air.

institutionalization of a harsh and punishing superego, is a portrayal of a pathological outcome of an important crisis. We can learn much from such a narrative, but it may also hide from us the fact that there exists a much healthier way to resolve oedipal conflicts, a way that, in fact, most people take to some degree or other.

It is of interest to observe that in regard to this question, as with so many other theoretical problems discussed in this work, Freud himself—at some point—clearly perceived both sides of the issue. In *New Introductory Lectures*, published in 1933, which represent a summary of his work after World War I, Freud succinctly states the discipline-and-punish canon: "Under the impression of the danger of losing his penis, the Oedipus complex is abandoned, repressed and, in the most normal cases, entirely destroyed, and a *severe superego is set up as its heir*."[1] Seven years before this, however, in an essay *The Question of Lay Analysis* (1926), Freud stated the exact position that will be argued here—that the severe superego is a pathological formation: "Estrangements between the ego and the superego are of great significance in mental life. You will already have guessed that the superego is the vehicle of the phenomenon that we call conscience. Mental health very much depends on the superego's being normally developed—that is, on its having become sufficiently impersonal. And that is precisely what it is not *in neurotics, whose Oedipus complex has not passed through the correct process of transformation*. Their superego still confronts their ego as a strict father confronts a child; and their morality operates in a primitive fashion in that the ego gets itself punished by their superego."[2]

No statistical study is necessary to determine which was the official Freudian position and which the aberration. This last quote is the only one I find of this nature. The castration–severe superego postulate is reiterated over and over again. In regard to present-day status, a reading of current psychoanalytic journals unequivocally demonstrates the perpetuation of the official Freudian stance, although a few analysts have argued against it.[3]

Whether the harsh and punishing superego represents a normal or a pathological outcome of the oedipal crises obviously has vast significance for the nature of morality. To equate morality with the superego and then to equate the superego with discipline and punishment is clearly to make a cripple of the moral function, to consign it to a diseased existence. It may be that for many, if not most, people their morality partakes precisely of this pathological formation, but we are not, therefore, obliged to call it health.

Let us look in detail at Freud's narrative of the dissolution of the Oedipus complex. In *The Ego and the Id*, he was already arguing that not only is the superego the heir to that complex, but also that the repression of the complex cannot be accomplished without the formation of the superego, whose first job is to put an end to oedipal wishes. The dissolution of the Oedipus complex and the formation of the superego are simultaneous; they are each the cause of each other:

> The ego ideal [superego] had the task of repressing the Oedipus complex; indeed, it is to that revolutionary event that it owes its existence. Clearly the repression of the Oedipus complex was no easy task. The child's parents, and especially his father, were perceived as the obstacle to a realization of his Oedipus wishes; so his infantile ego fortified itself for the carrying out of the repression by erecting this same obstacle within itself. It borrowed strength to do this, so to speak, from the father, and this loan was an extraordinarily momentous act. The superego retains the character of the father [in his most prohibiting, punishing aspects], while the more powerful the Oedipus complex was and the more rapidly it succumbed to repression (under the influence of authority, religious teaching, schooling and reading), the stricter will be the domination of the superego over the ego later on.[4]

In colloquial language, we may say that repressing the Oedipus complex is the job the superego is born to do. The very first words out of its mouth are: "Thou shalt not!" Do not desire thy mother or father, compete with thy father or mother, pretend to an adequate genital organ, overstep the limits of thy childhood. It understands authoritarianism at birth; we wonder how—if ever—it learns of democratic process.

In an essay published a year later, "The Dissolution of the Oedipus Complex" (1924), Freud discusses this problem at length. He begins by inquiring what causes the Oedipus complex to dissolve and give way to the latency period. Simply by asking that question Freud was doing something unusual; part of the answer is implied in the fact that the question is asked. Freud had never asked why, or for what reason, the oral stage is dissolved and gives way to the anal stage, or the anal to the genital. These questions did not seem worth asking because the assumption was that the developmental progression, oral-anal-genital, is a biopsychological given of everyone's psyche. The oral stage gives way to the anal stage because that is the way we are; our psyches are programmed at birth to undertake such a journey. With the oedipal stage, however, Freud finds such reasoning inadequate and, strangely enough, discovers the causes for the dissolution of the Oedipus complex in *actions taken by the parents*, not in the course of an inevitable biopsychological development. He begins the argument by stating and then rejecting the developmental concept. "Another view is that the Oedipus complex must collapse because the time has come for its disintegration, just as the milk-teeth fall out when the permanent ones begin to grow. Although the majority of human beings go through the Oedipus complex as an individual experience, it is nevertheless a phenomenon which is determined and laid down by heredity and which is bound to pass away according to programme when the next pre-ordained phase of development sets in. This being so, it is of no great importance what the occasions are which allow this to happen, or, indeed, whether such occasions can be discovered at all."[5]

This eminently reasonable argument, however, is rejected by Freud and, after a long discussion about the threat of castration, he declares with dogmatic certitude: "These connections justify the statement that the destruction of the Oedipus complex is brought about by the threat of castration."[6] A year later, in an essay concerned with the anatomical distinctions between the sexes, there has been an acceleration of the amount of violence needed to keep those oedipal wishes under control and Freud announces: "The Oedipus complex . . . in boys . . . is not simply repressed, it is literally smashed to pieces by the shock of threatened castration."[7] We may imagine that the severity of the superego, whose function it is to carry out this suppression, is increased accordingly. The more intense the oedipal strivings, the more energy is necessary to keep them under control, the harsher and more punishing the superego must become.

It is important to understand that, for Freud, the threat of castration is not simply an inward psychic anxiety that the child projects onto the parents. He believes that the intimidation is ever-present in the real world. Parents always, according to Freud, threaten that someone will remove the child's genital organ. In the world in which Freud lived, this was more than likely the case. In the case study of "Little Hans," Freud sets the background by describing Hans' parents, who were followers of Freud, people of progressive inclination who were attempting to raise their child in the most intelligent, humane way possible. On the very next page, Freud recounts that when Hans attempted to masturbate, his mother announced that she would call the doctor who would forcibly remove the child's penis.[8] We can imagine how, in that society, the less progressive, less humane parents behaved toward their children. For Freud, this openly stated threat to remove the child's penis is *the* precipitating cause of the dissolution of the Oedipus complex:

> When the (male) child's interest turns to his genitals he betrays the fact by manipulating them frequently; and he then finds the adults do not approve of this behavior. More or less plainly, more or less brutally, a threat is pronounced that this part of him which he values so highly will be taken away from him. Usually it is from *women* that the threat emanates; very often they seek to strengthen their authority by a reference to the father or the doctor, who, so they say, will carry out the punishment. In a number of cases the women will themselves mitigate the threat in a symbolic manner by telling the child that what is to be removed is not his genital, which actually plays a passive part, but his hand, which is the active culprit . . .
>
> Now it is my view that what brings about the destruction of the child's phallic genital organization is this threat of castration. Not immediately, it is true, and not without other influences being brought to bear as well. For to begin with the boy does not believe in the threat or obey it in the least. . . . It is not until a *fresh* experience comes his way that the child begins to reckon with the possibility of being castrated, and then only hesitatingly and unwillingly, and not without making efforts to depreciate the significance of something he has himself observed.
>
> The observation which finally breaks down his unbelief is the sight of the female genitals . . . . with this, the loss of his own penis becomes imaginable, and the threat of castration takes its deferred effect.
>
> . . . If the satisfaction of love in the field of the Oedipus complex is to cost the child his penis, a conflict is bound to arise between his narcissistic interest in that part of his body and the libidinal cathexis of his parental objects. In this conflict the first of these forces normally triumphs: the child's ego turns away from the Oedipus complex.
>
> . . . The object-cathexes are given up and replaced by identifications. The

authority of the father or the parents is introjected into the ego, and there it forms the nucleus of the superego, which takes over the severity of the father and perpetuates his prohibition against incest, and so secures the ego from the return of the libidinal object-cathexis. . . . The whole process has, on the one hand, preserved the genital organ—has averted the danger of its loss—and, on the other, *has paralyzed it—has removed its function*. This process ushers in the latency period, which now interrupts the child's sexual development.[9]

Thus is our morality, mankind's "higher nature," born in the environment of the penitentiary. Freud does not tell us what happens to the Oedipus complex in households where the parents never threaten castration. Such a situation is, clearly, unimaginable for him.

We may gain insight into the sources of this kind of distortion from observing the process of Freud's thought. After writing the text just cited, he is impelled to address the problem of the differences between men and women, boys and girls. He immediately recognizes that his description of the birth of the superego has gotten him into trouble when attempting to relate the developmental process in girls. It seems to me a more than reasonable conjecture that Freud's own infantile perception of the anatomical distinctions between the sexes was profoundly disturbing for him, that it did raise intense anxiety about the permanence of his own genital, and that he never quite recovered from this shock of nonrecognition. Confirmation of this hypothesis may be provided by the fact that nearly everything Freud has to say on the subjects of castration threat, the anatomical *and psychological* differences between boys and girls, and the relationship of the superego to these psychic events is touched with an air of fantasy, projection, and defensive theorizing. Directly after writing the long passage just quoted, Freud asks: "How does the corresponding development take place in little girls?" He goes on to wrestle with the question:

At this point our material—for some incomprehensible reason—becomes more obscure and full of gaps. The female sex, too, develops an Oedipus complex, a superego and a latency period. May we also attribute a phallic organization and a castration complex to it? The answer is in the affirmative; but these things cannot be the same as they are in boys. Here the feminist demand for equal rights for the sexes does not take us far, for the morphological distinction is bound to find expression in differences of psychical development. "Anatomy is Destiny," to vary a saying of Napoleon's.

It is no mere coincidence that Freud's most famous putdown of women occurs right after a discussion of castration anxiety as midwife to the superego. Degrading women is one very significant masculine defense against castration anxiety. Freud goes on:

> The little girl's clitoris behaves just like the penis to begin with; but, when she makes a comparison with a play fellow of the other sex, she perceives that she has "come off badly" and she feels this as a wrong done to her and as a ground for inferiority.... The essential difference thus comes about that the girl accepts castration as an accomplished fact, whereas the boy fears the possibility of its occurrence.

Because in this world the threat of castration is essential for the establishment of the moral quality in the psyche, it follows that little girls will have very little motivation to develop a conscience because they cannot have anxiety about what has already happened:

> The fear of castration being thus excluded in the little girl, a powerful motive also drops out for the setting-up of a superego and for the breaking-off of the infantile organization.... The girl's Oedipus complex is much simpler than that of the small bearer of the penis; in my experience, it seldom goes beyond taking of her mother's place and the adopting of a feminine attitude towards the father.

The "beyond" in the last sentence, of course, refers to the erection of a strong, powerful, harsh and punishing superego. Toward the end of this discussion, Freud offers a caveat that does nothing except to underline his own ambivalence about these questions: "It must be admitted, however, that in general our insight into these developmental processes in girls is unsatisfactory, incomplete and vague."[10]

That lack of certitude did not prevent Freud, however, from making an even stronger statement, only one year later, about feminine failure to develop mankind's highest quality:

> In girls the motive for the demolition of the Oedipus complex is lacking. Castration has already had its effect, which was to force the child into the situation of the Oedipus complex. Thus the Oedipus complex escapes the

fate which it meets with in boys: it may be slowly abandoned or dealt with by repression, or its effects may persist far into women's normal mental life. I cannot evade the notion (though I hesitate to give it expression) that for women the level of what is ethically normal is different from what it is in men. Their superego is never so inexorable, so impersonal, so independent of its emotional origins as we require it to be in men. Character-traits which critics of every epoch have brought up against women—that they show less sense of justice than men, that they are less ready to submit to the great exigencies of life, that they are more often influenced in their judgments by feelings of affection or hostility—all this would be amply accounted for by the modification in the formation of their superego which we have inferred above. We must not allow ourselves to be deflected from such conclusions by the denials of the feminists, who are anxious to force us to regard the two sexes as completely equal in position and worth.

And then comes what we, in this age of female demand for equality, have come to expect from men who both see and will not see the justice in the claim; we get the half apology: I-did-not-really-mean-to-set-myself-up-above-all-women:

but we shall, of course, willingly agree that the majority of men are also far behind the masculine ideal and that all human individuals, as a result of their bisexual disposition and of cross-inheritance, combine in themselves both masculine and feminine characteristics, so that pure masculinity and femininity remain theoretical constructions of uncertain content.[11]

It is of great importance for us to try to understand why the foremost thinker of the twentieth century was capable of, and insisted upon, this kind of simplistic debasement of women. A full discussion of this belongs to a later chapter. But it is imperative to emphasize that a pathological anxiety about castration casts its dark shadow over the whole discussion. And this castration anxiety for the young boy comes not only—as Freud himself tells us—from the father as part of the oedipal struggle, but also significantly from the mother. She often is the parent who gives voice to actual castration threats; the sight of her genitals with the missing penis finally convinces the boy that there is a real danger that he will lose his own genital organ. She also, as Freud relates and as we shall discuss more fully later, wants a penis, wants a penis to replace the one she has "lost." What sensitive, intelligent little boy, intensely interested in such matters, would not conclude that the penisless mother wants nothing less than *his* own genital?

I am not arguing that Freud is telling us outlandish untruths. Little boys undoubtedly do suffer castration anxiety when their mothers threaten to have their penises cut off; that anxiety can, understandably, be heightened by the perception of the "organless" female genital; and all boys in the oedipal stage certainly assume that their fathers will counterattack and not allow the fulfillment of oedipal impulses. To conclude from all this, however, that in all circumstances—diseased as well as within normal range—the Oedipus complex is "literally smashed to pieces by the threat of castration" is to make a serious error. This last is a description of pathology. If the first experience the boy has with genital sexuality ends in such a traumatic way, everything we know about the compulsion to repeat and the formation of neurosis would indicate that when such a child—grown to adolescence—again faces the problems of genitality, heterosexuality, love, and adult sexual behavior, he will miserably fail to achieve a satisfactory resolution of these conflict situations. Adolescence, as we know, is a time of revisiting and redoing the oedipal situation. What adolescent male can have the courage to revisit, or the health to reexperience and transform, an Oedipus complex that ended so disastrously the first time round? Many, if not most, adolescents and young men find themselves in this exact state of neurosis: it is the job of a successful psychotherapeutic situation to lessen significantly castration anxiety that causes sexual dysfunction and makes loving impossible.

Freud, we may grant, has given us an accurate and penetrating description of the pathological ending of the Oedipus complex. Is there an alternative narrative, one wherein health triumphs, one that makes adult sexuality and love possible? Not quite surprisingly, such a description can be found within the body of Freud's own work. It is never openly stated that such a nonpathological resolution of the Oedipus complex is either desirable or possible; what we have are certain strong, unconscious indications in this direction—something more than a hint but less than a theory. The data that Freud gives us, however, speak for themselves.

At the end of *Totem and Taboo* (1912–13), Freud tells us an etiological myth about the brothers of the primal horde and their father that purports to explain the origins of religion, civilization, moral order, and democracy. In this horde, mankind's original social situation, the father was an authoritarian monster who kept all the women to himself, leaving the younger men (his sons) with no possibility of heterosexual fulfillment. One day the sons united among themselves, overthrew, murdered, and ate the father, and took the women for their own uses. Determined that no one should ever again assume such absolute authority, they lived in a state of equality with each other. The totem feast, wherein a godlike figure is eaten, was subsequently introduced to commemorate this awesome revolutionary experience and this, Freud comments, "was the beginning of many things—of social organization, of moral restrictions and of religion."[12]

It has never been established with any certainty whether Freud actually believed such an event had happened—once or a thousand times—in history, or whether he was merely trying to reconstruct the psychodynamics behind certain social and religious forms. What is certain is that Freud had absolutely no evidence of such an event or events, and therefore, no matter what he imagined it was, it was definitely a made-up story. Having been made up, Freud could have constructed it any way he wanted. He does *not* tell us that the brothers, intent on rebellion and parricide, got together and then became paralyzed by the threat of castration by the father, abandoned their oedipal goals in the interest of preserving their anatomy, and settled down to be obedient, latency children. Civilization, religion, social and moral order were not produced, as Freud tells it, by a renunciation of oedipal aims, but *by their fulfillment*. Only when the brothers succeeded in doing what every little oedipal boy imagines doing—killing the father and possessing his women—did a higher level of human existence become possible. Success in the pursuit of oedipal goals, not failure, makes adult life achievable.

What Freud gives us in *Totem and Taboo* is a parable for what really goes on in the successful, nonpathological resolution of the Oedipus complex. The healthy Oedipus complex dissolves for reasons exactly opposite to what Freud offers in his theoretical discussion. The male child imagines—in a way that is not quite clear—that he has accomplished its goals; he has obtained the mother and eliminated the father; he has taken his father's place. The father has been successfully dispatched and ingested, as in the story of the brothers. And it is this act of orally incorporating the father that produces the superego. The person who used to command "Do this! Don't do that!" is now inside the psyche's stomach, now barking orders that seem to be internal, not external—much as the duck in *Peter and the Wolf* continues to quack even when inside his devourer. It is a primitive process based on the original incorporation of the oral mother, but a process absolutely necessary for psychic health. Freud himself, in one of his last theoretical works, made the connection between cannibalism and the formation of the superego. "The basis of the process is what is called an 'identification'—that is to say, the assimilation of one ego to another one, as a result of which the first ego behaves like the second in certain respects, imitates it and in a sense takes it up into itself. Identification has been not unsuitably compared with the oral, cannibalistic incorporation of another person."[13] It seems clear from everything we know about the superego—the irrationality with which it can act, its inability to distinguish between positive and negative traits taken over from the parents, its commitment to harshness and brutality as well as benevolence— that its formation is truly an act of primitive incorporation.

It is not strange that the Oedipus complex should end with an incorporation, since every previous stage of libidinal development had been overcome and surpassed by a similar incorporative mechanism. The child moves from the oral to the anal stage only by incorporating the oral mother into itself, and the child who cannot accomplish such incorporation remains at least partially fixated in the oral stage. Having succeeded in introjecting the oral mother into itself, the child is free to expend its libidinal energies in another direction. The anal stage, similarly, is not left behind until anal cathexes to people or things have been incorporated into the psyche. This method of cathexis, incorporation, movement to another stage, is a fundamental given of psychic development. Why, then, should the oedipal stage be an exception? Why should the oedipal stage be the only psychic stage to end on a note of renunciation? The psyche is free to move on from the oedipal situation only when it has succeeded in incorporating its sexual and emotional cathexes.

The oedipal differs from previous stages of libidinal development in that it has a complex unconscious narrative underlying it: the killing of the same-sex parent and the possession of the parent of the opposite sex. Even for a child of five, to accomplish such acts in reality must appear bizarre and (as Freud has said) frightening. And yet, psychic health and development demand that the child have the courage to imagine it. Failure to accomplish these acts imaginatively means failure to incorporate the cathexes of the Oedipus complex, and fixation in that stage. Hans Loewald has underlined this strange irony in human development: "Insofar as human beings strive for emancipation and individuation as well as for object love, parricide—on the plane of psychic action—is a developmental necessity." "On the plane of psychic action" refers clearly to what I am calling imaginative acts. The child does not have to do the acts; he or she is required to have the courage to imagine doing them. Loewald elaborates: "Without the guilty deed of parricide there is no autonomous self. And further, from the viewpoint of received morality, individuality and its maturity—I am not speaking of an unbridled individualism—is a virtue, . . . at any rate in modern Western civilizations. To live among these paradoxes appears to be our fate for the time being."[14]

Seen from this point of view, the threat of castration becomes not the essential situation for the establishment of a healthy superego but the greatest hindrance to accomplishing that result. The greater the actual or imagined threat of castration, the less the child will be inclined to risk—imaginatively—the accomplishment of oedipal goals, the more the child will retreat from the Oedipus complex, the less the superego will be internalized and the more it will speak in an external, authoritarian voice. The less the actual or imagined threat of castration, the more the child will be willing to risk the accomplishment of oedipal inclinations, the more the superego will be incorporated and speak with an internal voice. These two descriptions relate to each other as do sickness and health.

Everyone to some degree, even a rather neurotic person, imaginatively accomplishes the oedipal task. The revisiting and reworking of the Oedipus complex in adolescence is a crucial preparation for adult life. This recollecting of that experience works because the original oedipal adventure ended, to some degree, on a note of triumph. It is the job of adolescence to recall that triumph and expand upon it, enabling the young person to become independent of the sexual and emotional ties of childhood. Should a heightened threat of castration persist, along with the accompanying harsh and punishing superego, the chances of success are proportionally diminished.

When the natural process of liberation from infantile and childhood attachments fails, psychotherapy may provide an answer. And it is in one of Freud's case studies—that of "Little Hans"—that we find corroboration of each of the points being made here concerning the threat of castration and a healthy resolution of the Oedipus complex. Hans was the young son of a Viennese couple who were believers in Freud's theories and method. At the very beginnings of the oedipal phase Hans developed strong phobic reactions to going out into the street and expressed a particular acute anxiety about horses. The parents consulted with Freud, and it was decided that the father should become Hans' therapist with Freud as the supervising doctor. On the basis of the original evidence and the material that Hans brought up in the treatment, it was agreed by all the adults concerned that Hans was suffering from intense castration anxiety, not necessarily brought about, but certainly intensified, by his emerging Oedipus complex. After many months of therapy, Hans overcame his phobias and made a remarkable recovery from his illness.

Near the end of the treatment Hans had two significant dreams. The first was of a thinly disguised situation where he had managed to marry his mother and have many children with her. The second brought Hans a penis as large as his father's. Concerning the second dream, Freud relates the father's communication to him:

'On May 2nd Hans came to me in the morning. "I say," he said, "I thought something today." At first he had forgotten it; but later on he related what follows, though with signs of considerable resistance: "*The plumber came; and first he took away my behind with a pair of pincers, and then gave me another, and then the same with my widdler* [penis]. He said: 'Let me see your behind!' and I had to turn round, and he took it away; and then he said: 'Let me see your widdler!' " '

Hans' father grasped the nature of this wishful phantasy, and did not hesitate a moment as to the only interpretation it could bear.

'*I*: "He gave you a *bigger* widdler and a *bigger* behind."
'*Hans*: "Yes."
'*I*: "Like Daddy's because you'd like to be Daddy."

'*Hans*: "Yes, and I'd like to have a moustach like yours, and hairs like yours." (He pointed to the hairs on my chest.)'

So successful was this imaginative fulfillment of oedipal strivings that it immediately produced remarkable changes. "In the course of the next few days," Freud writes, "Hans' mother wrote to me more than once to express her joy at the little boy's recovery."[15]

In summary, Freud writes unequivocally of the importance of these fantasy accomplishments for psychic health.

> We have already considered Hans' two concluding phantasies, with which his recovery was rounded off. One of them, that of the plumber giving him a new and . . . a bigger widdler, was not merely a repetition of the earlier phantasy concerning the plumber and the bath [an expression of castration anxiety]. This new one was *a triumphant, wishful phantasy, and with it he overcame his fear of castration.* His other phantasy, which confessed to the wish to be married to his mother and to have many children by her, did not merely exhaust the content of the unconscious complexes which had been stirred up by the sight of the falling horse and which had generated his anxiety. It also corrected that portion of those thoughts which was entirely unacceptable; for, instead of killing his father, it made him innocuous by promoting him to a marriage with Hans' grandmother. *With this phantasy both the illness and the analysis came to an appropriate end.*[16]

And Anna Freud, in her first major work, deals with this case at length, reemphasizing the importance of imaginative working through. "The analyst (who was Hans' father) had no difficulty in recognizing in these fantasies the fulfillment of the two wishes which had never been fulfilled in reality. Hans now had—*at least in imagination*—a genital organ like that of his father and also children with whom he could do what his mother did with his little sister."[17]

It seems almost unnecessary, at this point, to emphasize that we are not told that Hans achieved psychic health by reconciling himself to the fact that his Oedipus complex was smashed to pieces by the threat of castration. The intensity of that threat, in fact, was the cause of Hans' illness. He did not overcome the intense anxiety manifested in his phobic reactions by withdrawing from oedipal impulses. Exactly the contrary. Health came when he had the courage—in his particular case, with his father's permission and reassurance—to play the role of

Oedipus with all his imaginative power. The picture that Freud drew, in the later part of his life, of the dissolution of the Oedipus complex and the establishment of a harsh and punishing superego cannot endure as anything except a description of a situation fraught with the probability of pathology. Consummation, not renunciation, is the way to psychic health.

Why did Freud reject, in his conscious theoretical works, a truth that had been clearly perceived unconsciously with Hans and the etiological myth of the brothers? Inadequacy of intellect cannot be the answer. We must look to the area of psychic conflict for explanation. Almost all of our evidence points to the fact that Freud was fixated on the problem of castration anxiety, a fixation that made it impossible for him to think clearly about the dissolution of the Oedipus complex and the beginnings of the superego. Castration anxiety for Freud is not limited to the male child's concern that the father will eradicate his penis. An earlier stage of castration anxiety also exists, one that centers on the prohibition of masturbation, and here the primary emasculator is the mother. She threatens castration as the punishment for masturbation; her penisless genital provides the final proof that the permanent removal of the penis is a real possibility.

When Freud, therefore, began to discuss the dissolution of the Oedipus complex and its relation to castration anxiety, these two stages of anxiety and the two executioners (female and male) became conflated one with the other. The father's projected threat to retaliate on the small boy for the latter's oedipal desires could not be thought of independently of the more ancient anxiety centered on the mother. The dread of the mother and the rage engendered by her prohibition of sexual pleasure, therefore, cast their shadows on the whole discussion of the termination of the Oedipus conflict and the origin of the superego. Freud revenged himself on all women-mothers by constructing a theory that established their genital and moral equipment as vastly inferior. The theory of morality was a casualty of that unnecessary vengeance. The superego took on a harsh and brutal configuration, not only because it incorporated the father in his most merciless aspects, but also because it internalized the disciplining and punishing mother who had her own singular reasons for separating the boy from his penis. The denial of full equality for women makes it impossible to think clearly about a theory of morality. The first step in constructing an adequate psychoanalytic moral theory is to disavow the need to take retribution from women and mothers. Freud was incapable of that renunciation; the moral theory of the harsh and punishing super-ego was the consequence.

6

The Harsh and
Punishing Superego

FREUD BELIEVED that the catastrophic circumstances inherent in the origin of the superego determined its nature throughout its existence. Born in "the valley of the shadow of death," it became permanently characterized by harsh and punishing attributes. A brutal and disciplining superego was as inevitable for Freud as the Oedipus complex itself.

Freud gave very little indication that he understood that the superego is historically determined, that it changes profoundly as society changes. His overriding tendency was to regard the superego as immutable, like the drives, biologically not socially determined. "For this superego is as much a representative of the id as of the external world. It came into being through the introjection into the ego of the first objects of the id's libidinal impulses—namely, the two parents . . . Only in this way was it possible for the Oedipus complex to be surmounted. This superego retained essential features of the introjected persons—their strength, their severity, their inclination to supervise and to punish.[1] He never distinguished between the biopsychological inevitability of the superego and the *particular form* (harsh or loving; authoritarian or liberating; racist, sexist, or egalitarian) it takes. Freud had as much trouble imagining a loving and benevolent superego as he had envisioning a nonbrutal end to the Oedipus complex.

In the usual circumstance, the superego does not take on its more or less permanent attributes until late adolescence or very early adulthood. Social and cultural circumstances play a crucial role in determining its final form. No matter what may have been the particular narrative of the oedipal—castration—enthronement-of-the-superego time in the life of an individual psyche, the superego of a conforming person (and most people fit this description) in a Nazi society will differ profoundly from that of a conforming person in a liberal, democratic society. As one further proof that the superego, as such, may not be equated with morality, it is of interest to observe that one cannot argue that a conforming Nazi will have *less* superego than a conforming liberal democrat. It is easy to imagine a young Nazi berating himself and feeling guilty or ashamed about his failure to live up to Nazi ideals; his superego would certainly punish him for his sins against the Nazi faith. A Nazi superego would differ in quality from a liberal, democratic superego, but it would not be any less of a superego. We who live in a liberal, democratic, racist, sexist society should not be shocked to discover strong evidence of liberalism, democracy, racism, and sexism in our superegos. Every superego is more or less corrupt, more or less immoral. A Nazi-society superego is merely the exaggerated form of the moral contradiction existent within any superego.

One very important reason that Freud writes so often of the superego as enemy is the fact that he lived his life in a culture that was repressive of healthy sexual expression and activity. And that repression was impossible without the power of the punishing superego. Freud's picture of a superego intent on repressing instinctual drives and an ego trying to mediate between an authoritarian conscience and legitimate drives desiring fulfillment results from living within a culture intent on degrading the sexual function. As methods of child rearing since Freud have become less authoritarian, as the repression of legitimate (healthy) sexual desires has lessened, there is no question that the typical superego in our society has become less harsh and punishing, less in conflict with the demands of the sexual drives. In regard to sexuality, at least, our superego has become less corrupt.

Once we grant that the particular attributes of the superego are subject to change under social influence, we have opened the door to a much more complex view of moral control than that given in Freud's id-derived (biologically determined) approach. Even if we grant that the superego is always, *to some degree*, harsh and punishing, we may observe that a good part of the history of the world derives from the changes and permutations in *that degree*. The malleability of the superego, its capacity to integrate more and more of the dictates of conscience, is what makes moral progress within society possible.

Since Freud, there has been a rather faint chorus of demurral from psychoanalytic theorists on the question of the inevitable brutality of the superego. Both Heinz Hartmann and Roy Schafer have recognized that the crucial consideration in regard to superego formation is that it is constructed with what is given, not with what is necessarily moral. "I mention the well-known fact," writes Hartmann, "that pleasure premia are in store for the child who conforms to the demands of reality and of socialization; but they are equally available if this conforming means the acceptance by the child of erroneous and biased views which the parents hold of reality."[2] And Schafer tells us: "Exhibitionistic tendencies transmitted from parent to child will carry with them implied or explicit ideals for maximally satisfying display. Some show-offs may succeed more than another. The same for parental passion, greed, cruelty, sensuality, etc."[3] Neither Hartmann nor Schafer used this fundamental insight in an attempt to reconstruct the theory of the superego. The theorist who most perceptively understood the unacceptable rigidity in Freud's concept of the superego was the psychoanalytically influenced sociologist Talcott Parsons, who made use of insights about the nature of the superego to construct a global theory of society. It is of value to quote him at length:

> Freud's insight was profoundly correct when he focused on the element of moral standards. This is, indeed, central and crucial, but it does seem that Freud's view was too narrow. The inescapable conclusion is that not only moral standards, but *all the components of the common culture* are internalized as part of the personality structure. Moral standards, indeed, cannot in this respect be dissociated from the content of the orientation patterns which they regulate. . . . the content of both cathetic-attitudes and cognitive-status definitions have cultural, hence normative significance. This content is cultural and learned. Neither what the human object *is*, in

the most significant respects, nor what it *means* emotionally, can be understood as given independently of the nature of the interactive process itself; and the significance of moral norms themselves very largely relates to this fact.

... the cognitive definition of the object world does not seem to have been problematical to Freud. He subsumed it all under "external reality," in relation to which "ego-functions" constitute a process of adaption. He failed to take explicitly into account the fact that the frame of reference in terms of which objects are cognized, and therefore adapted to, is cultural and thus cannot be taken for granted as given, but must be internalized as a condition of the development of mature ego-functioning. In this respect it seems to be correct to say that Freud introduced an unreal separation between the superego and the ego—the lines between them are in fact difficult to define in theory.... the distinction which Freud makes between the superego and the ego—that the former is internalized, by identification, and that the latter seems to consist of responses to external reality rather than of internalized culture—is not tenable.... internalization is a very special kind of learning which Freud seemed to confine to the superego.

... The essential point seems to be that Freud's view seems to imply that the object, as cognitively significant, is given independently of the actor's internalized culture, and that superego standards are then applied to it. This fails to take account of the extent to which the constitution of the object and its moral appraisal are part and parcel of the *same* fundamental cultural patterns; it gives the superego an appearance of arbitrariness and dissociation from the rest of the personality—particularly from the ego—which is not wholly in accord with the facts.[4]

The superego is as much conditioned by reality as is the ego. It has many fewer "eternal" attributes than were given to it by Freud.

Is the harsh and punishing superego a pathological configuration? In places, Freud argued that it was. "We can either accept it as a fact that in obsessional neurosis a superego of this severe kind emerges, or we can take the regression of the libido as the fundamental characteristic of the affection and attempt to relate the severity of the superego to it. And indeed the superego, originating as it does from the id, cannot dissociate itself from the regression and defusion of instinct which have taken place there. We cannot be surprised if it becomes harsher, unkinder and more tormenting than where development has been normal."[5] And in another essay Freud discusses the formation of symptoms—a pathological event—as the result of repression of an instinctual impulse, and says of such a symptom:

The ego finds its unity threatened and impaired by this intruder, and it continues to struggle against the symptom just as it fended off the original instinctual impulse. All this produces the picture of a neurosis. It is no contradiction to this that, in undertaking the repression, the ego is at bottom following the commands of its superego—commands which, in their turn, originate from influences in the external world that have found representation in the superego. The fact remains that the ego *has* taken sides with those powers, that in it their demands have more strength than the instinctual demands of the id, and that the ego is the power which sets the repression in motion against the portion of the id concerned and which fortifies the repression by means of the anticathexis of resistance. The ego has come into conflict with the id in the service of the superego and of reality.[6]

Severe superego repression and neurotic symptom formation, we are being told, are two aspects of the same process.

It is interesting to observe in this last quotation from Freud a demonstration of the unreal split between ego, superego, and id that Parsons argues against. Freud says that the ego, in order to serve the interests of the superego and of reality (that is, the parents and society) represses an instinctual impulse of the id. Ego interests and id interests clash. But if we ask ourselves *why* the ego would want to serve the interests of the parents and the community, is it not clear that it does so because it wants love and approval from them? Is the desire for love and approval not an id impulse? The conflict is not between the ego and an id impulse. The conflict arises from the ego's attempt to satisfy two opposing id impulses: one that would fulfill the drive and the other that wants to be loved by parents who, for whatever reason, oppose the drive. Parents and society dead set against adolescent sexual fulfillment is a perfect representation of such a symptom-forming situation. That the superego would tend to grow in severity and harshness in such a situation seems obvious.

When Freud comments that the task of psychoanalysis is to free the ego from the demands of the superego, he does so because he has only the punishing, pathological aspects of its form in mind. Roy Schafer is one of the few analytic theorists who has clearly perceived these relationships. He observes: "In other words, severity of superego function testifies to the inadequacy of superego formation. It is therefore no great jump to recognize that disturbances in the parental superego play a double role in disturbing the child's superego development: it exaggerates the oedipal conflict and provides a faulty model for dealing with it. In this way, superego pathology is perpetuated." And health involves leaving the comforting and encouraging aspects of the superego in place: "The ego values, depends on, and loves this inner, paternal source of strength and organization. As with the id, the ego's relations with the superego are not simply antagonistic and the therapeutic task with regard to the superego is not simply to establish the ego's independence from it."[7] One may wonder how an ego free from all superego incentives, such as encouragement and approval, could function at all.

It may seem strange that there was need within the psychoanalytic community to make the argument that the superego was, in addition to its punishing-disciplining activities, also involved with imperatives about honesty, love, loyalty, concern with other people. It was Freud's overwhelming involvement with the pathological aspects of superego formation that made it necessary for Hartmann to state: "Not only the prohibitions of the parents, but also their love survives in the relation of the superego to the ego." He goes on to argue: "The much discussed questions of whether morals are, because of their origins, of necessity 'authoritarian' is, it seems to me, not always put in the right way. Every moral system has its origins in the relations of the child to adults who are not only loved and hated but also persons in authority. However, the value systems evolving from these origins may have an authoritarian, a nonauthoritarian, or an antiauthoritarian character."[8] The implication in this, though Hartmann does not spell it out, is that the relative authoritarian or nonauthoritarian nature of the moral system is intimately dependent on the relative harshness or benevolence of the superego. It was Schafer in his important article "The Loving and Beloved Superego in Freud's Structural Theory" who finally elaborated the importance of the nonpunishing aspects of superego functioning:

> There is a loving and beloved aspect of the superego. It represents the loved and admired oedipal and preoedipal parents who provide love, protection, comfort, and guidance, who embody and transmit certain ideals and moral structures more or less representative of their society, and who, even in their punishing activities, provide needed expressions of parental care, con-

tact, and love. The maturing child will identify himself with these parental aspects. . . . By means of this identification the child ultimately attains the position of being able to love, protect, comfort, and guide himself and his children after him, and of doing so according to relatively ego-syntonic, culture-syntonic and impersonal sets of ideals and moral standards.[9]

It is another testimony of Freud's ambivalence about moral questions that he also knew all this to be true. The transference is an essential instrument in any successful therapy, and the superego, Freud argues in one of the last things he wrote, is essential for the operation of transference: "If the patient puts the analyst in the place of his father (or mother), he is also giving him the power which his superego exercises over his ego, since his parents were, as we know, the origin of his superego. The new superego now has an opportunity for a sort of *after-education* of the neurotic; it can correct mistakes for which his parents were responsible in educating him."[10] Clearly the task of psychoanalysis is not to free the ego from the superego but to use the benevolent, encouraging aspects of the superego for therapeutic effect. This becomes possible because, regardless of the actual parents' adequacy or inadequacy, the superego has the capacity for idealization. The superego carries within itself an image of ideal parents, ideal nurturing, ideal psychic functioning. These ideal images are manifest in the positive therapeutic transference. Any individual whose aptitude for such idealization is severely crippled will be incapable of an adequate positive transference and, therefore, incapable of being helped by psychoanalytic therapy. The possibilities of idealization make the after-education and the correction of mistakes that Freud discusses a reasonable aim of the therapeutic situation. The harsh, punishing, pathological aspects of the superego are a hindrance to such a positive resolution, and have to be overcome if therapy is to be successful.

It is a reasonable assumption, I believe, that this whole discussion, both here and within the psychoanalytic community, would have been unnecessary had not Freud argued so vehemently the position that the superego is, essentially, corrupt. In *The Ego and the Id*, where it first makes its appearance, we are immediately told that the superego is erected around the dread of castration and that "even ordinary normal morality has a harshly restraining, cruelly prohibiting quality. It is from this, indeed, that the conception arises of a higher being who deals out punishment inexorably."[11] This Old Testament morality continues when Freud argues, a year later: "It is easily conceivable that, thanks to the defusion of instinct which occurs along with this introduction into the ego, the severity was increased. The superego—the conscience at work in the ego—may then become harsh, cruel and inexorable against the ego which is in its charge."[12] And, finally, in *New Introductory Lectures* (1933), where Freud summarizes his position on many issues, we are told that we cannot escape a corrupt superego even if the parents have been kind and loving. A harsh and punishing conscience is humankind's fate: "The superego seems to have made a one-sided choice and to have picked out only the parents' strictness and severity, their prohibiting and punitive function, whereas the loving care seems not to have been taken over and maintained. If the parents have really enforced their authority with severity we can easily understand the child's in turn developing a severe superego. But, contrary to our expectations, experience shows that the superego can acquire the same characteristic of relentless severity even if the upbringing had been mild and kindly and had so far as possible avoided threats and punishments."[13] Since neither Freud—nor anyone else as far as I can discover—has presented us with case material wherein a kind and loving upbringing has resulted in a relentlessly severe superego (and, certainly, Hans' parents with their threats of actual castration will not do), there seems to be no support for this most inconsistent argument.

Putting aside Freud's exaggerated vocabulary in regard to morality, there seems to be nonetheless a tendency of superego judgments toward harshness and severity. I am reminded of an occasion that occurred when one of my daughters was quite young. I was reading her Bible stories and had arrived at the narrative of David and Absalom. Why did that happen? she inquired. I, making use of my own interpretation and version of the story, explained that God was punishing David for taking away another man's wife. She stopped to meditate for a full forty seconds and then commented: "The punishment was too great." Anyone with a sensitive relationship to his or her own moral imperatives recognizes that superego punishments are inclined to be much more severe than the trespass would indicate. This tendency toward severity, if established as a truth, does not necessarily present a picture of psychic health. In itself it may be one important contribution to the fragility of the human psyche, one significant and inevitable distortion of reality that a healthy psyche must deal with and overcome.

Freud and others have given many reasons for the harshness of the superego. First, there does seem to be a very primitive form of expectation of punishment as a result of trespass. The trespass may be of a purely ritualistic, magical nature with absolutely no moral content and the expected punishment equally primitive. The concept of taboo, which we have observed in nonliterate cultures, represents this archaic trespass-punishment configuration. It seems probable that all children in our culture go through a stage, in infancy or early childhood, where they believe in the inexorable workings of taboo as much as did the ancient Hawaiians. The Orthodox Jew in our culture, whose every meal is surrounded by taboos, demonstrates the staying power of such primitive notions. This sense of taboo, this primitive conception of trespass-punishment, is somehow related to the more developed concepts of morality and guilt, and the superego incorporates these more ancient attitudes into its own structure. The Orthodox Jew, for instance, undoubtedly feels moral about the observation of dietary laws and a keen sense of guilt should he break them. Freud, of course, observed this when writing *Totem and Taboo*: "If I am not mistaken, the explanation of taboo also throws light on the nature and origin of *conscience*. It is possible, without any stretching of the sense of the terms, to speak of a taboo conscience or, after a taboo has been violated, of a taboo sense of guilt. Taboo conscience is probably the earliest form in which the phenomenon of conscience is met with."[14]

Taboo morality, taboo conscience, taboo guilt, taboo anxiety are all primitive conceptions; they are included in the superego and contribute to its severity. In the healthy, mature psyche they play a small, not a major, role in determining morality. In some preliterate cultures the food of the chief is taboo to anyone else; should someone eat it, even unknowingly, he or she is subject to death. In our society many people cannot go against the wishes of the president simply because he *is* the president. Both these circumstances represent a morality—of sorts. A superego overly dependent on taboo mechanisms for its functioning is a superego a mature person learns to live without.

A second factor that contributes to the severity of the superego is actual harsh treatment by the parents. As we shall see, Freud's ambivalence about analyzing this situation was complete; a harsh superego can result *both* from cruel treatment *and* from a loving and mild upbringing. "If the father was hard, violent and cruel," writes Freud in *Dostoevsky and Parricide* (1928)—and no one can read *The Brothers Karamazov* without comprehending the relationship of cruelty and the harsh superego—"the superego takes over those attributes from him and, in the relations between the ego and it, the passivity which was supposed to have been repressed is reestablished. The superego has become sadistic, and the ego becomes masochistic. . . . A great need for punishment develops in the ego, which in part offers itself as a victim to Fate, and in part finds satisfaction in ill-treatment by the superego (that is, the sense of guilt). For every punishment is ultimately castration and, as such, a fulfillment of the old passive attitude towards the father."[15]

In *Civilization and Its Discontents*, however, Freud argued the opposite and the same view in one paragraph: "Experience shows, however, that the severity of the superego which a child develops in no way corresponds to the severity of treatment which he has himself met with. . . . A child who has been very leniently brought up can acquire a very strict conscience. But it would also be wrong to exaggerate this independence; it is not difficult to convince oneself that severity of upbringing does also exert a strong influence on the formation of the child's superego. What it amounts to is that in the formation of the superego and the emergence of a conscience innate constitutional factors and influences from the real environment act in combination."[16] It is a most reasonable argument, I believe, that constitutional factors do affect the harshness or mildness of the superego; some people are born with an inclination toward an inflexible, harsh moral control system. To say this, however, is a long way from saying that a child can develop a "very strict conscience" even if gently brought up or, as Freud said in the quote from *New Introductory Lectures* cited earlier, that a relentless, severe superego may result even from "mild and kindly" upbringing. One wonders what, or whom, Freud had in mind. He never gives us any actual data that would indicate such a denouement.

It is possible that Freud was thinking of the situation of "spoiling" the child. We can imagine that when parents place almost no limits on a child's behavior, indulge it to the utmost in its inclinations, seemingly give the opposite of a harsh and cruel upbringing—and the child responds negatively to such parental aggression—that in such a case a child may develop a severe superego. Spoiling is not a case of kindly nurturing, but its opposite. Parents spoil a child either out of aggression toward it or because of a fear within themselves of showing any aggression toward the child. Such spoiled children end up furious with their parents; in certain circumstances where the parents demonstrated an intense ambivalence about the spoiling behavior, it may happen that the child, out of anger toward them and the perception of their aggression and ambivalence toward him, develops an inflexible, harsh superego in an attempt to resolve these conflicts. Spoiling is not love. A child brought up unambivalently lovingly will evolve a severe superego—because of innate constitutional factors—only in rare circumstances, circumstances so rare that a theory of the superego cannot be built upon them. Constitutional factors are significant, but in regard to punishing or loving aspects of the superego, they cannot compare with the importance of the quality of nurturing the child receives.

A third factor contributing to the severity of the superego is what Freud describes as "the defusion of instinct," which happens at the end of the Oedipus complex and the first formative moments of the superego.[17] What precisely this means is anyone's speculation. It represents Freud at his most metapsychological; the phrase was never explained by him or anyone else. He must have dimly perceived some process going on, but he was not able to tell us about it in conscious argument.

A fourth mechanism that increases the severity of the superego is that whereby aggression that cannot be expressed outward is turned inward toward the psyche itself. We are now most familiar with this psychic procedure. People who have difficulty in expressing normal amounts of aggression, people who deny themselves a reasonable amount of aggressive satisfaction and sublimation, may become masochistic or depressed—or both—as the repressed aggression turns back onto the self. Because the superego, in Freud's view, begins with the refusal to live through oedipal aggressive inclinations, the aggression that was originally aimed at the father or mother—being incapable of even imaginative satisfaction—allies itself with the newborn superego and tyrannizes over the ego.

> His aggressiveness is introjected, internalized; it is, in point of fact, sent back to where it came from—that is, it is directed towards his own ego. There it is taken over by a portion of the ego, which sets itself over against the rest of the ego as superego, and which now, in the form of 'conscience', is ready to put into action against the ego the same harsh aggressiveness that the ego would like to satisfy upon other, extraneous individuals. The tension between the harsh superego and the ego that is subjected to it, is called by us the sense of guilt; it expresses itself as a need for punishment. Civilization, therefore, obtains mastery over the individual desire for aggression by weakening and disarming it and by setting up an agency within him to watch over it, like a garrison in a conquered city.[18]

That grisly metaphor should alert us that there may be something which Freud is not expressing. Does it make any difference, at that crucial moment of the genesis of the superego, how the parents behave? Even with garrisons in conquered cities there is a vast degree of difference in the amount of rape, pillage, and just plain tyranny exhibited by, for instance, the Huns and the British. As conquest is inevitable, all of us, I assume, would rather be garrisoned by General Braddock than by Attila. Does the parents' behavior help determine whether the domination of the superego is more or less tyrannical? No question that it does. A father or mother who actually threatens castration; or merely expresses great anger at the child's ordinary misbehavior; or communicates to the child, in the way that parents know so well, that the child must be a most sinful and despicable person to even imagine doing such terrible things to its parents—such instruction cannot help but affect the degree of repression of aggressive feelings that the child imagines is necessary. As the severity of the superego is dependent on the child's repressing its own anger at the parents, if repression admits of degree, so must the severity of the superego. The relative harshness with which the child is treated during the oedipal stage cannot help but influence the kind of superego that results.

A fifth contribution to superego severity *is* independent of the parents' behavior. All children, but particularly those with a strong aggressive component in their temperament, will try to deal with their own inclinations toward aggression by projecting these onto the parents. The child denies its own anger by pretending the anger originates in the caretakers, saying, in effect: "It is not I who am furious with them, but they who feel hateful toward me." Anger projected onto the parents will easily settle in the superego, one of whose jobs it is to contain aggressive inclinations, and the superego will take on the intensity of the original anger toward the parents. "The authority now turns into his superego and enters into possession of all the aggressiveness which a child would have liked to exercise against it."[19] This process will unfold itself regardless of whether the parents are essentially loving or hostile toward the child, but here again the parents' stance cannot help but influence the manner in which this conflict is ultimately resolved.

The last circumstance I shall consider that is purported to intensify superego severity—the situation wherein the child is prevented from expressing legitimate aggressive feelings—is related to other phenomena that have already been discussed. Herman Nunberg observes:

> One might therefore assume that the intensity of the sense of guilt is dependent on the severity of the person who rears the child. This is, however, not always valid, since an excessive feeling of guilt may develop in boys, for instance, whose fathers were indulgent and weak, or in a boy whose father was absent altogether while he grew up surrounded by women who spoiled him. The more love a child receives and the more indulgent his parents are, the more his aggression may be inhibited and changed into feelings of guilt. Thus children grow up who are exceedingly good and who suffer enormously from the excessive burden of their feeling of guilt. The aggression prevented from reaching the outside world is bound to turn against the ego and to perform its work of destruction inside [within the superego].[20]

Nunberg is confusing the situation of spoiling and the circumstance where the child is prohibited from expressing his or her aggressive feelings. To say that the more a child is indulged, the more his aggression is inhibited is a contradiction in terms. To be indulged means to be permitted an excess of instinctual satisfaction; it means an emphasis on drive impulses over the reality principle. The truly spoiled child is permitted too much aggression toward the parents. But let us take the case wherein the child is told over and over again how much the parents love it, in return for which the child must express only affection toward his or her nurturers. There comes a time in every child's life when it feels the need to express toward the parents, with great intensity, "I hate you." In any reasonably nonauthoritarian household, the child will at some point risk open expression of such words. If the parents express dismay or horror—or extreme anger—that the child could entertain such devilish feelings, then there is no question that the repression and turning inward of these hostile emotions may, especially in households where superego prerogatives are held in high esteem, result in severe superego formation. In such circumstance, the child's distress is augmented because the parents maintain a very problematic relationship to their own aggression.

It is of importance to observe that every one of these circumstances which contribute to the harshness of the superego—whether the initial conflict begins with the parents, the child, or the "diffusion of instinct"—reveals, as an initiating cause, the failure to deal adequately with aggression. In each situation of conflict, if aggression is handled in a more productive manner, the superego maintains itself at a lesser degree of severity. Since Freud we have become increasingly aware of how important aggression is in the etiology of neurosis; it is certainly as important as, if not more important than, sexual dysfunction. If the failure to adequately sublimate, repress, and diffuse aggressive energy produces a pathological psyche, it would not be unreasonable to assert that the harsh and punishing superego, which evolves from the same inadequate psychic transactions, deserves the attribution "pathological."

The emphasis upon the severity of superego imperatives within psychoanalytic thought has exaggerated the importance of guilt and the desire for punishment as guides to moral action. There has been a tendency to regard as the same mechanism that which produces remorse and the need for punishment in Raskolnikov and that which keeps us from axing an old lady in the first place. As Freud correctly pointed out many times, people feel guilty about aggressive desires that they never really intend to carry out, and this is especially important for children in the oedipal phase who feel strong aggressive inclinations toward the parents. If we ask, however, what it is that keeps a reasonably healthy adult from acting out his or her hostile inclinations (some of which have a primitive intensity), guilt and the fear of punishment are too simplistic as answers. The Raskolnikov syndrome of acting out followed by intense guilt is itself a pathological configuration. "Let us recall the type of patients," writes Edith Jacobson, "who constantly act out impulsively and then pay for their sins with depressive conditions and the destructive results of their actions; persons whose superego is punitive but, in spite of this, never serves either as a moral preventative or as a moral incentive. Fundamentally their moral conflict appears to survive and to remain unchanged from one depression and one impulsive action to the next."[21] The problem with the harsh and punishing superego is that it is not, in itself, capable of forestalling such acting out in the first place; the difficulty with guilt as the regulator of moral action is that, many times, it exhibits no preventive power.

Unlike Raskolnikov, the average reasonably healthy human being is prevented from acting out primitive aggressive inclinations by the fact that he or she is not that primitive. Ordinary human beings refrain from killing old ladies because they are not that ill, and a crucial indicator of their health is a system of moral control—as deeply indebted to conscience as to superego—that operates *before* the act. Conscience is never pathological. The same cannot be said of the harsh, punishing, severe superego, riddled with guilt and a masochistic need for punishment.

A fundamental concern, if not *the* fundamental concern, in evaluating the relative health or pathology of the superego is the determination of whether it speaks with an internal or an external voice. When one hears the clear voice of the moral imperative, is it "them" talking or "me" talking? Psychoanalyst Otto Isakower has said that the "trick" in raising a child is to get the superego inside its head.* We are discussing relative internality or externality. No one presents such a picture of psychic integration that he or she completely perceives moral injunctions as coming only from the self; and conversely, even the most pathological person has some internal recognition of behavioral dictates. The more external the superego is perceived to be, the more pathological its formation, the less capable it is of curbing acting out in a preventive way and the less useful it becomes for integrating the whole psyche. The significant internalization of the superego is a pro-

---

* Personal communication, 1956.

found moment in the history of an individual psyche and in the history of culture. The transcendent scene in the First Book of Kings, where the prophet Elijah ascends to the top of the mountain to communicate with God and finds that the Lord is not in the "great and strong wind" or the earthquake or the fire but in a "still small voice"[22] is a profound symbolic narrative of the internalization of the superego, its reunion with the conscience.

For Freud, however, except at rare moments, God is always in the fire and the earthquake. "The institution of conscience was at bottom an embodiment, first of parental criticism, and subsequently of that of society—a process which is repeated in what takes place when a tendency towards repression develops out of a prohibition or obstacle that came in the first instance from without. The voices, as well as the undefined multitude, are brought into the foreground again by the disease, and so the evolution of conscience is reproduced regressively. . . . His conscience then confronts him in a regressive form as a hostile influence from without."[23] And no more profound metaphor for the externality of the superego can be imagined than Freud's image, given earlier, of a garrison in a conquered city. In Freud's narrative of the birth of the superego, keeping it primarily external is a requirement of health. Who could completely internalize an intense threat of castration without suffering severe pathology? An unremediable split between ego and superego is a necessary postulate in the Freudian canon. Such a split requires, and results from, the externality of the superego.

What enables us to separate ourselves from the theoretical bind that enclosed Freud's thought on this issue is not the fact that he suffered from a defect of personality, of which we are free. The basic disagreement with Freud on this issue arises out of a profound change in culture to which he, in great part, contributed. We view the superego differently because we disagree profoundly with the culture in which Freud lived on the question of how children should be raised, particularly in regard to how much authoritarianism (force, threat of punishment, preservation of the harsh aspects of hierarchy between parents and children) is necessary to the process. We endeavor to get the superego inside the child's psyche as much as is possible. Freud's culture could not even understand that as a goal: an external conscience, it was felt, was a necessity for adequate worldly functioning. In regard to parents and children the question is how hierarchical and tyrannical, as against how mutual and equal, the nurturing process should be. Full equality between parents and children is not possible, but that does not imply that the necessary hierarchical (and tyrannical) stance does not admit to degree. The harsh, punishing, severe, and *external* super-ego is the inevitable precipitate of an authoritarian child-rearing pattern. The loving, comforting, encouraging, *internal* superego proceeds from a concept of child care that insists that "maternal" nurturing need not disappear when the father enters the child's life.

Jean Piaget wrote about a post-Freudian generation, struggling to free itself from the cultural pattern of authoritarian child rearing:

> Such a form of education leads to that perpetual state of tension which is the appanage of so many families, and which the parents responsible for it attribute, needless to say, to the inborn wickedness of the child and to original sin. But frequent and legitimate in many respects as is the child's revolt against such methods, he is nevertheless inwardly defeated in the majority of cases. Unable to distinguish what is good in his parents and what is open to criticism [in the terms of the discussion here, because the superego by itself cannot make such a distinction], incapable, owing to the "ambivalence" of his feelings towards them, of criticizing his parents objectively, the child ends in moments of attachment by inwardly admitting their right to authority they wield over him [the severe superego being a perfect instrument to accomplish such a process]. Even when grown up, he will be unable, except in very rare cases, to break loose from the affective schemes acquired in this way, and will be as stupid with his own children as his parents were with him.[24]

In essence, what Piaget is saying is that as long as the authoritarian superego reigns supreme, no one can really grow up. This emphasizes how important it is, if a culture wishes to produce real adults, that the Oedipus complex end on a note of triumph, not disaster. Only then can the superego lodge primarily inside the child's head.

The existence of a primarily external superego becomes probable in a psyche habituated to the process of psychic splitting. The mechanism of splitting between the good mother and the bad mother, between the positive, loving aspects of nurturing and the negative, aggressive efflorescences of the process, has been emphasized in the writings of Melanie Klein. Health, Klein tells us, depends on the healing of that inevitable split, and pathology results from the failure to achieve reconciliation. It is my view that an emphasis on the severe, punishing aspects of the superego emanates from the need to perpetuate that original divide, from an uncurable ambivalence toward the primary nurturer. Klein writes cogently and simply about what is necessary to achieve reconciliation.

> For I assume the ego develops largely round this good object, and the identification with the good object shows externally in the young child's copying the mother's activities and attitudes; this can be seen in his play and often also in his behavior towards younger children. A strong identification with the good mother makes it easier for the child to identify also with a good father and later with other friendly figures. As a result, his inner world comes to contain predominantly good objects and feelings, and these good objects are felt to respond to the infant's love. All this contributes to a stable personality and makes it possible to extend sympathy and friendly feelings to other people. It is clear that a good relation of the parents to each other and to the child . . . play a vital role in the success of this process.[25]

It is more than probable that Freud would have found such an analysis—unencumbered with any reference to the drives and their diffusion and vicissitudes—inadequate, if not sentimental in the extreme. It would be profitable to attempt to discover the ambivalence Freud demonstrates toward the great, omnipotent, engulfing, pre-oedipal mother: the primary nurturer. We may discover that the harsh and punishing superego not only owes its nativity to the threatened loss of the penis, but also that it is brought into being partially to substitute for the hard, indomitable, overpowering penis itself—that penis, one of whose main functions is to make impassable the road that runs backward to the powerlessness of infancy. One of the primary functions of the harsh and punishing superego—and the belief in its inevitable formation—is to forbid regressive tendencies that may lead to reengulfment by the mother. Only when we overcome intense anxiety on this latter account, only then will we be free enough to abandon the commitment to a pathological system of moral control.

7

Freud's Ambivalent Stance toward Women and the Pre-Oedipal Mother

APART FROM the direct interests of psychoanalytic theory and therapy, and the cause of sexual liberation, Freud was no radical. He had little sympathy and no love for the deprived classes in society; found the ideal of equality anathema; was a good democrat but no socialist at a time when many intellectuals, especially Jewish intellectuals, felt the capitalist system to be inadequate. His lifestyle and his ambition placed him solidly in the center of the bourgeois world; he had practically no interest or sympathy with avant-garde art, music, or architecture at a time when Viennese culture was remarkable in its modernism. Outside of psychoanalysis, he was a good, solid bourgeois liberal—nothing less and nothing more.

In this two-hundred-year-old Age of Ambivalence, liberalism, though it remains our principal bulwark against reaction, is incapable of resolving the fundamental moral conflicts of our era. Only a radical change in the value system, most especially in the system of morals within that value system, can progressively and significantly alter the course of history. Without such a revolutionary change in morals, even the best of current societies is condemned to eternal cyclical swings between the finest and worst aspects of liberal society, without ever resolving fundamental problems. The demands of feminism play a crucial role in the attempt to radically alter values. In the twentieth century, sexism takes its ground on the repression of the memory of the pre-oedipal mother. And it is precisely the moral values we learn from her—pity, compassion, conscience—that are essential to the moral revolution. To repress women necessitates the repression of those values and the perpetuation of liberal ambivalence into infinity. Freud, it is easy to demonstrate, played his part in this continuing failure of nerve.

In the latter part of the twentieth century, it is possible to be a liberal and something of a feminist. In the latter part of the nineteenth century, this was almost impossible. Freud was no exception; not being a radical, he could not become a feminist. Feminism, however, is something—unlike avant-garde art—that it is impossible to be neutral about. Any intellectual, thinking person who is not a feminist must spend much psychic energy keeping the feminine drive for equality repressed, and, as we shall see, Freud did his share of that. Not everyone in Freud's immediate circle shared his views. Alfred Adler, for instance, in the first decade of this century was as close to Freud as anyone, and he was both a socialist and a feminist.

Freud stated his own position succinctly in the summing-up volume, *New Introductory Lectures*: "Psychoanalytic education will be taking an uninvited responsibility on itself if it proposes to mould its pupils into rebels. It will have played its part if it sends them away as healthy and efficient as possible. It itself contains enough revolutionary factors to ensure that no one educated by it will in later life take the side of reaction and suppression."[1] Though the commitment to democratic values and the refusal to assume a reactionary position were, and are, admirable things, they were by no means revolutionary in the year 1933. Holding such views placed one at the center of liberal thought. A classical liberal, Freud shared a belief in utilitarian mores to the point where he could discuss love of mankind in terms of the utilitarian value it brought to the lover. To Romain Rolland he wrote: "I revered you as an artist and apostle of love of mankind many years before I saw you. I myself have always advocated the love for mankind not out of sentimentality or idealism but for sober, economic reasons: because in the face of our instinctual drives and the world as it is I was compelled to consider this love as indispensable for the preservation of the human species as, say, technology."[2] It is more than ironic to observe the person who most taught us how inadequate reason is in regard to the instincts and the drives explaining how humankind is to overcome its destructive urges by reasoning out the *utility* of loving others. Obviously, something rather complex—and hidden—is going on here.

The problem with liberals and liberalism is that, while often representing the best in current mainstream society, they cannot mount a radical critique of current social values even when such criticism is essential to preserve a consistent moral stance. World War I and the American war in Vietnam were two critical times for liberalism. At the very beginning of World War I, Freud's incapacity to take a radical political stance forced him to rally to the support of the Austro-Hungarian Empire. Reading the letter that Freud sent to Karl Abraham on July 26, 1914, is an almost eerie demonstration of the power of culture:

> It is of course impossible to foresee whether conditions will now permit us to hold the congress. If the war remains localized in the Balkans, it will be all right. But the Russians are unpredictable.
>
> However, for the first time in thirty years I feel myself to be an Austrian and feel like giving this not very hopeful Empire another chance. Morale everywhere is excellent. Also the liberating effect of courageous action and the secure prop of Germany contribute a great deal to this. The most genuine symptomatic actions are to be seen in everyone.[3]

It is true that Freud very quickly grew disillusioned with the war. But it is still remarkable that this fiercely independent mind was capable of being illusioned in the first place, especially if we note that the "courageous action" which comes in for praise inevitably involved killing other people or assisting others who were so engaged.

It is not my intention to "indict" Freud for his failure to become a political radical, but if we are to comprehend his views toward the feminist demand for equality, we must see that his opposition in this regard was all of a piece with other fundamental social views. For instance, the masses, Freud tells us in 1927, "are lazy and unintelligent;

they have no love for instinctual renunciation, and they are not to be convinced by argument of its inevitability; and the individuals composing them support one another in giving free rein to their indiscipline."[4] The lower classes, we may say, are all id, and can never be put in a relationship of equality with those who have the capacity for ego and superego modes of behavior: "Anyone who has tasted the miseries of poverty in his youth and has experienced the indifference and arrogance of the well-to-do, should be safe from the suspicion of having no understanding or good will towards endeavours to fight against the inequality of wealth among men and all that it leads to. To be sure, if an attempt is made to base this fight upon an abstract demand, in the name of justice, for equality for all men, there is a very obvious objection to be made—that nature, by endowing individuals with extremely unequal physical attributes and mental capacities, has introduced injustices against which there is no remedy."[5] Freud was not the first individual—nor the last—who, having risen from penury into the middle class, felt threatened by the continued existence of deprived peoples and needed some wall—theoretical and political—between himself and those who had failed to make the same journey upward.

In this situation of discrepant life comforts, the only thing that can unite those who have "made it" with those who have not is identification: pity, compassion, love. Freud recognized that this was so but argued that the Christian injunction to "love thy neighbor as thyself" was a utopian impossibility: "But if he is a stranger to me and if he cannot attract me by any worth of his own or any significance that he may already have acquired for my emotional life, it will be hard for me to love him. . . . But if I am to love him (with this universal love) merely because he, too, is an inhabitant of this earth, like an insect, an earth-worm or a grass-snake, then I fear that only a small modicum of my love will fall to his share—not by any possibility as much as, by judgment of my reason, I am entitled to retain for myself."[6] A radical moral view would argue that it is not necessary to love one's poor neighbor as much as oneself. What is essential to a moral stance is to exercise that love to some degree and to hold to a generalized sense of what it means to be human, based on a broad identification with humanity as such and a deep commitment to the notion that there are no insects or grass snakes among human beings.

The moral problematic within nonradical liberalism is that it so easily splits off those whom one is supposed to love or care about from others who are outside the pale of identification. One is concerned with Blacks but not women; or women and not Blacks; or American boys uselessly dying but not Asian boys; or respectable people but not "lazy riff-raff." The words omitted from the last quote of Freud's demonstrate his facile capacity to do this, when he gives a very strange argument for not loving someone who is unknown, or unattractive to him. "Indeed, I should be wrong to [love such a one], for my love is valued by all my own people as a sign of my preferring them, and it is an injustice to them if I put a stranger on a par with them."[7] The phrase "all my own people" immediately lets us know that, as wide as was Freud's genius, he was a person of almost ordinary morals. This capacity for splitting was revealed in a letter Freud wrote to his future wife almost fifty years before *Civilization and Its Discontents*, and there the problem of feminism is addressed directly. Arguing with J. S. Mill, who was a radical in such matters, Freud writes: "For example he finds an analogy for the oppression of women in that of the Negro. Any girl, even without a vote and legal rights, whose hand is kissed by a man willing to risk his all for her love, could have put him right on this."[8] In 1883 this was the most that good, solid, decent liberalism could achieve.

That Freud gave voice to numerous hostile remarks about women has been documented by many people. A full demonstration here is not necessary, though it may be of value "to catalogue the ways" and quote briefly, in order to give the full flavor to Freud's need to maintain a position of inequality between men and women:

1. In the letter to his fiancée where he discusses Mill, he also asserts that "legislation and custom have to grant to women many rights kept from them, but the position of woman cannot be other than what it is: to be an adored sweetheart in youth, and a beloved wife in maturity."[9]

2. The *Studies on Hysteria* discusses the case of Frau Emmy von N. and praises her for the "moral seriousness with which she viewed her duties, her intelligence and energy, which were no less than a man's."[10]

3. The *Three Essays on Sexuality* states that all libido is masculine whether it is active in a man or a woman.[11]

4. In remarks to the Vienna Psychoanalytic Society in 1908, Freud

stated that Mill was wrong in his analysis of women's economic oppression because no woman could both earn her living and raise a family: "Women as a group profit nothing from the modern feminist
movement; at best a few individuals profit."[12]

5.   Women have a small capacity to sublimate their instincts, and
this results in the intellectual inferiority of so many of them.[13]

6.   Unlike men, "it is extremely questionable whether the erotic life
of women is dominated by sudden mysterious impulses."[14]

7.   "Indeed, we had to reckon with the possibility that a number of
women remain arrested in their original attachment to their mother
and never achieve a true change-over towards men. This being so, the
pre-Oedipus phase in women gains an importance which we have not
attributed to it hitherto."[15] The corresponding fact—that many men
never overcome their pre-oedipal attachment to their mothers—was
never discussed by Freud.

8.   Much is made of the built-in biological impediment to full, adult
orgasm for women, resulting from the two-stage (clitoris and vagina)
structure of female sexual development. Whether this concept has any
validity at all—and a vast literature today is devoted to arguing this
question—it is of interest that Freud never once discusses the fact that
men have a similar problem: many men are physiologically potent but
yet lack a certain psychological potency because their orgasm has a
infantile, pregenital quality to it, resembling an agitated urination as
much as full, adult orgasm. The quality of orgasm may change radically for the better for many men, who previously had no physiological
problems with orgasm, as a result of therapy or analysis. One wonders
whether the theory of clitoral (infantile) and vaginal (adult) orgasm is
not a projection onto women of a masculine problem.

9.   I have already touched upon the concept that the superego in
women is never as fully developed as in men. This is said in various
ways at various times by Freud, one of the most pungent being "I cannot evade the notion (though I hesitate to give it expression) that for
women the level of what is ethically normal is different from what it
is in men."[16]

10.   "A man of about thirty strikes us as a youthful, somewhat un-
formed individual, whom we expect to make powerful use of the possibilities of development opened up to him by analysis. A woman of the

same age, however, often frightens us by her psychical rigidity and unchangeability. Her libido has taken up final positions and seems incapable of exchanging them for others. There are no paths open to further development; it is as though the whole process had already run its course and remains thenceforward insusceptible to influence—as though, indeed, the difficult development to femininity had exhausted the possibilities of the person concerned."[17] It is true that Freud does not say—or even imply—that women are to blame for being anatomically, psychologically, and morally handicapped. His refusal, however, to pay any attention to the facts of social oppression leaves him with the understanding that there is almost nothing that we can do about the situation. Had he lived in ancient Rome, Freud might have observed that the thirty-year-old slave was—for some reason—less capable of intellectual development than a freeman of the same age.

11. And finally, when challenged (even if only inside his own head) by a sexually passionate, intellectually capable, morally active female, Freud was prepared with the kind of answer that critics of psychoanalysis despair of—an Alice-in-Wonderland argument where the words mean precisely what I say they mean, and nothing else. "For the ladies, whenever some comparison seemed to turn out unfavourable to their sex, were able to utter a suspicion that we, the male analysts, had been unable to overcome certain deeply-rooted prejudices against what was feminine, and that was being paid for in the partiality of our researches. We, on the other hand, standing on the ground of bisexuality, had no difficulty in avoiding impoliteness. We had only to say: 'This doesn't apply to *you*. You're the exception; on this point you're more masculine than feminine.' "[18] In days gone by, it was the custom among certain gentiles who had a few Jewish friends to explain to them that they were the exception to the otherwise valid derogatory generalizations that could be made about the people of the Book. In such symptomatic behavior did ambivalence express itself.

Whether all this—a rather complete catalogue of opinions, if not of individual expressions, garnered from nearly thirty volumes of published works, letters, and meeting reports—adds up to the fact that Freud deserves the appellation "misogynist" may not be the most important question to be derived from this material. Anyone who lives in a misogynist and sexist society, and who does not subject the values of that society to a radical critique, will incorporate misogynist and sexist values into his or her own psyche—*the superego will see to that*. As Freud and society were at one in their refusal to allow feminist demands for equality, understanding either Freud or society will also help us understand the other. What additional psychological phenomena can we find that would seem to be intimately related to a persistent sexist stance?

It is worthy of note that Freud perceived very clearly certain aspects of pre-oedipal life, but not others. Early in his psychoanalytic work he distinguished the oral and anal stages of libidinal development. He had no problem with this insight; it was a question of energy, instincts, drives. But the mythological, personal, anthropological aspects of pre-oedipal life were extraordinarily problematic. Who reigned over life in the oral and anal stage? What omnipotent divinity ordered the child's world during that time? Were these oral and anal energy charges directed toward any particular person? With whom did the child identify at this primitive stage of development? Though obvious to us now, the answers to these questions were shrouded in the mists of prehistory for Freud. History began with the Oedipus complex because in the land of Oedipus, men ruled—the father was the god and the tyrant. To his enormous credit, late in his life Freud attempted to see into that beclouded past. Amazed by what he perceived, he felt like the discoverer of a new era of history: "Our insight into this early, pre-Oedipus, phase in girls comes to us as a surprise, like the discovery . . . of the Minoan-Mycenean civilization behind the civilization of Greece." We know why Schliemann's task was so difficult and his achievement so remarkable: Mycenae was buried under tons of rubble. It would be of enormous value to know what it is that forces most men to encase the Mycenaean part of the mind in conscious obscurity. "Everything connected with this first mother-attachment," Freud writes, "has in analysis seemed to me so elusive, lost in a past so dim and shadowy, so hard to resuscitate, that it seemed as if it had undergone some specially inexorable repression."[19] Freud never satisfactorily explained the causes of that repression, and could not, because he was too much a part of it. In this very quote, for instance, he is talking only of women.

Almost all of Freud's discussion of the importance of pre-oedipal life has to do solely with women. Having mentioned that many women (but not men) never go beyond their attachment to their mothers, and that this fact points toward the importance of pre-oedipal life, Freud proceeds with some fancy logistic maneuvers in the attempt to "save the phenomenon" of the Oedipus complex. What is most important for us here is that this intricate discussion was never extended to little boys:

> Since this phase allows room for all the fixations and repressions from which we trace the origin of the neuroses, it would seem as though we must retract the universality of the thesis that the Oedipus complex is the nucleus of the neuroses. But if anyone feels reluctant about making this correction, there is no need for him to do so. On the one hand, we can extend the content of the Oedipus complex to include all the child's relations to both parents; or, on the other, we can take due account of our new findings by saying that the female only reaches the normal positive Oedipus situation after she has surmounted a period before it that is governed by the negative complex.[20]

And directly after this paragraph comes the Mycenaean metaphor—a civilization, possibly, where only women dwell.

Symptomatic of this repression of the attachment to the pre-oedipal mother is Freud's insistence that a child's first relationship of dependency-support and first identification involve the *father*. At the very beginning of *Civilization and Its Discontents*, he addresses the "oceanic" feeling (mystical sensation of oneness) and its relationship to religion. Correctly perceiving that it arises out of the infant's situation of helplessness and dependency, he then proceeds to a remarkable statement: "The derivation of religious needs from the infant's helplessness and longing for the father aroused by it seems to me incontrovertible, especially since the feeling is not simply prolonged from childhood days, but is permanently sustained by fear of the superior power of fate. I cannot think of any need in childhood as strong as the need for a father's protection."[21]

On a par with this is the repression of the memory of early identifications with the mother. "This leads us back to the origin of the ego ideal; for behind it there lies hidden an individual's first and most important identification with the father in his own personal prehistory." Ambivalence now requires a footnote to this sentence, "Perhaps it would be safer to say 'with the parents . . . ,' " a disclaimer that is followed by a discussion of the importance of the penis in distinguishing father and mother. Even girls, we are told, may arrive at the age of four or five without having identified with their mothers: "In a precisely analogous way, the outcome of the Oedipus attitude in a little girl may be an intensification of her identification with her mother (or the setting up of such an identification for the first time)."[22]

Massive denial is going on here. The father of six children, who had a deep professional and personal interest in observing the behavior of infants and children, who was no stranger to the nursery, who could then write about an infant's first seeking protection from Fate with the father protector—such a parent is refusing to see what is clearly in front of him. If the task of observing the true relationship between the child and its primary caretaker (its mother) was so difficult for Freud— a man living at the turn of the twentieth century who spent his whole life revealing what goes on within the repressed and the defended-against parts of the psyche—we get some notion of why it has taken human culture a million years before even raising the question of male-female equality with any sense of urgency. Though morally indefensible, the motives that caused male culture to oppress women for so long have had—and still have—enormous power.

The memory of the pre-oedipal mother, the recollection of the time when women were omnipotent and little boys helpless, the reliving of the era when a boy was profoundly uncertain about his maleness and the permanent possession of his penis, the evocation of an age when the fear of reengulfment by the symbiotic mother was a fundamental and overpowering anxiety—all this is profoundly disturbing for an adult male, the cause, if not of panic, of intense concern that one's identity as a person and as a male is exceedingly fragile. Freud has clearly taught us what we do with such anxieties: repress their content and defend against the return of the repressed. The various modes of degrading women or, as in Freud's case, the putting-down of women, is a masculine defense erected against the return of the memory of the pre-oedipal mother and the various fears and anxieties associated with her. For adult males the pre-oedipal mother becomes a contaminated person who must be quarantined and isolated and forgotten as much as is possible.

The exaggerated importance that Freud gives to the concept of penis envy is a mechanism of defense erected against conflicts with and anxieties about the pre-oedipal mother. I do not wish to argue, as some feminist critics of psychoanalysis have argued, that there is no such thing as penis envy, that it is a worthless notion. There is too much clinical evidence confirming the fact that certain women have a strong, pathological inclination to possess a penis—with complex symptomatic behavior built upon this wish. It is, also, undoubtedly true that—to some degree—all women have a wish to have a penis, just as it is equally true that all men—to some degree—have a longing to bear children. The important theoretical questions in both instances are: to what degree of intensity are these wishes entertained, and are they intense enough to indicate pathology? Freud, however, went much further. He made the feminine wish for a penis a basic building block in the theory of psychic development.

Freud uses penis envy, for instance, to answer the fundamental theoretical question of what begins the little girl's Oedipus complex. Once he began thinking about pre-oedipal development in girls, Freud quickly identified a crucial theoretical problem that has not been satisfactorily answered even today. In the oral stage, the mother is the primary object of oral libido for both girls and boys; the same is true for the anal stage. Even in the early genital stage the mother is the object of this first genital libido. In the oedipal stage, however, the little girl, unlike the little boy, has to change her object from the mother to the father; genital sexuality has to make a transition from homosexuality to heterosexuality. What causes this great metamorphosis? Although no one today seems to have a satisfactory answer, Freud inclined to think about envy and loss of the penis whenever he wrestled with pre-oedipal problems, and therefore comes up with the answer: penis desire and disappointment in its capacity to be fulfilled force the girl to turn from her mother to her father and begin her Oedipus phase: "at the end of this first phase of attachment to the mother, there emerges, as the girl's *strongest motive* for turning away from her, the reproach that her mother did not give her a proper penis—that is to say, brought her into the world as a female."[23] One could argue, with equal illogic, that the girl, furious at not possessing a penis and jealous of those who do, *cannot* turn to the father and decides to spend her sexual life with those who are penisless. Both these arguments are equally illogical, among other reasons because they attempt to explain with logic a situation that has little to do with logic. That Freud felt that penis envy could account for such a fundamental step in psychic development indicates how much weight he gave to this particular phenomenon.

Although it is highly questionable exactly how much we can learn about little girls from Freud's discussion of penis envy, there is no question that we can learn a great deal about little boys, especially what it is that they fear, what threats they feel for their anatomy. Whether all little girls passionately desire a penis at some stage of development or not, one thing does seem clear: a little boy's fear of castration centers as much, if not more, on his mother as on his father. I have already touched upon Freud's insistence that real-world threats of castration are essential for the dissolution of the Oedipus complex. The role of the mother in these admonitions is elaborated by Freud:

When the (male) child's interest turns to his genitals he betrays the fact by manipulating them frequently; and he then finds that the adults do not approve of this behavior. More or less plainly, more or less brutally, a threat is pronounced that this part of him which he values so highly will be taken away from him. Usually it is from women that the threat emanates; very often they seek to strengthen their authority by a reference to the father or the doctor, who, so they say, will carry out the punishment. In a number of cases the women will themselves mitigate the threat in a symbolic manner by telling the child that what is to be removed is not his genitals, which actually plays a passive part, but his hand, which is the actual culprit.[24]

In the primitive part of the little boy's psyche, it appears reasonable to presume, there is a very good reason why women want to cut off the penises of little boys—the genital regions of women are lacking a penis. What is more natural than that they want to acquire one to fill up that void? What is most disturbing to the male is that girls and women want not *a* penis but *my* penis.

For to begin with the boy does not believe in the threat of castration or obey it in the least. Psychoanalysis has recently attached importance to two experiences which all children go through and which, it is suggested, prepare them for the loss of highly valued parts of the body. These experiences are the withdrawal of the mother's breast . . . and the daily demand on them to give up the contents of the bowel. [In both circumstances the pre-oedipal mother is the cause of the separation.] But there is no evidence to show that, when the threat of castration takes place, these experiences have any effect. It is not until a *fresh* experience comes his way that the child begins to reckon with the possibility of being castrated, and then only hesitatingly and unwillingly, and not without making efforts to depreciate the significance of something he has himself observed. The observation which finally breaks down his unbelief is the sight of the female genitals. . . . With this, the loss of his own penis becomes imaginable, and the threat of castration takes its deferred effect.[25]

This perception of the penisless female genital, Freud tells us, is so frightening that it may permanently distort the male's relationship to women. "This . . . leads to two reactions, which may become fixed and will in that case, whether separately or together or in conjunction with other factors, permanently determine the boy's relations to women: horror of the mutilated creature or triumphant contempt for her."[26] What we are being told is that contempt for women is a *defense mechanism* erected by males to protect the fragile existence of the penis and, we may add, to preserve a brittle male identity. On a scale of intensity that runs from horror to contempt to putting-down to denying equality, we may assume that the exact same mode of defense is in operation, always for the same reason.

One seeming solution for this situation of intense anxiety is to buy the women off by giving them a penis of their own, so they will no longer seek to separate the male from his. Here, however, there is a balance-of-power problem: if women have as large and as effective a penis as a man, male dominance is over. The *realpolitik* solution is to give the women a little penis—not large enough to be threatening to men, but something to be content with. And Freudian theory does exactly that. As is well known, the clitoris, for Freud, is not a clitoris; it is a small penis and behaves just like a penis. "Anatomy has recognized the clitoris within the female pudenda as being an organ that is homologous to the penis; and the physiology of the sexual process has been able to add that this small penis which does not grow any bigger behaves in fact during childhood like a real and genuine penis."[27]

Not only are girls endowed with a little penis, Freud argues that their first experience with genital sexuality is a *masculine* one. In the oral and anal stages of libidinal development, there is no differentiation in response along the lines of male and female; the stages are sexually undifferentiated. The same is true for the first genital stage; boys and girls react alike. But in this particular case Freud is not content to leave the description as undifferentiated. Here, he insists, boys and girls are both masculine. "At the following stage of infantile genital organization, which we now know about, *maleness* exists, but not femaleness. The antithesis here is between having a *male* genital and being *castrated*. It is not until development has reached its completion at puberty that the sexual polarity coincides with *male* and *female*."[28] Freud calls the first genital stage of development, in both boys and girls, the "phallic" stage.[29]

The defensive maneuver in regard to the horror of the mutilated female genital is now complete. Women have been endowed with a little penis that responds with phallic capacities to sexual excitement. If a boy of four can be spoken of as "a little man," a girl of the same age can now be regarded as "a little, little man." This defensive action is related to the psychic mechanism involved in ritual sacrifice—the powers in the cosmos demanding one's life can somehow be bought off with a finger or a foreskin. In a similar manner, it is hoped that the threatening female divinities may be pacified with a gift of a miniature penis and the entitlement to phallic experience.

Within Freudian theory, this defensive-projective distortion of reality, known under the rubric "penis envy," has significance far beyond the theory of sexual development and of gender identity. It leads directly into the theory of morality and the superego and co-opts a philosophy of moral behavior as an ally in a not-too-subtle war against women. It makes it impossible to have an adequate view of conscience, morality, and the superego until the desires to dominate and degrade women have been abandoned. Lest this appear as an exaggeration of the Freudian position, it may be of value here to quote at length a passage from Freud, pieces of which have been used previously in this discourse:

> In girls the motive for the demolition of the Oedipus complex is lacking. Castration has already had its effect, which was to force the child into the situation of the Oedipus complex. Thus the Oedipus complex escapes the

fate which it meets with in boys: it may be slowly abandoned or dealt with by repression, or its effects may persist far into women's normal mental life. I cannot evade the notion (though I hesitate to give it expression) that for women the level of what is ethically normal is different from what it is in men. Their superego is never so inexorable, so impersonal, so independent of its emotional origins as we require it to be in men. Character-traits which critics of every epoch have brought us against women—that they show less sense of justice than men, that they are less ready to submit to the great experience of life, that they are more often influenced in their judgments by feelings of affection or hostility—all this would be amply accounted for by the modification in the formation of their superego which we have inferred above. We must not allow ourselves to be deflected from such conclusions by the denial of the feminists, who are anxious to force us to regard the two sexes as completely equal in position and worth; but we shall, of course, willingly agree that the majority of men are also far behind the masculine ideal and that all human individuals, as a result of their bisexual disposition and of cross-inheritance, combine in themselves both masculine and feminine characteristics, so that pure masculinity and femininity remain theoretical constructions of uncertain content.[30]

The fateful consequences of denying the equality of men and women, the inevitable result of defending so thoroughly against the memory of the pre-oedipal mother, the irremedial distortion of theory resulting from seeing women primarily in the role of menacing one's masculinity—the final precipitate of all this is the necessity to downgrade the moral virtues we all learn from that same pre-oedipal mother: nurturance, pity, compassion, love, conscience. No repression of women is possible without the repression of these great virtues as well. The enthronement of the superego as the primary instrument of moral control, and the overwhelming emphasis on its harsh and punishing aspects, are part of a subtle, unconscious conspiracy to maintain the tyranny of men over women.

8

Ambivalence about Civilization

WHEN A CIVILIZATION sets itself a new moral agenda that it refuses to carry out; when such a culture dances on the cliff edge of ambivalence, not knowing whether to take the leap for freedom or retreat in panic—as Western civilization has done for the last 150 years—one significant result of this profoundly vacillating behavior, and the emotional exhaustion that it produces, is that many sensitive people of traditional good morals begin to question the legitimacy of society, culture, and civilization themselves. Society becomes thoroughly indecisive about cultural progress because it has no way of knowing whether it will ever take the steps necessary for moral resolution. And in the thought of those reflecting, sensitive people civilization itself becomes the villain in the piece; it is identified as the primary cause of our distress. The truth is, however, that we are the creators of our malaise. Our failure to live up to our own best ideals creates the theoretical necessity of constituting civilization as scapegoat. We project onto it our incapacity to unravel moral conflicts and rebuke it for our own irresolution.

Freud's thoroughgoing ambivalence about civilization was commensurate with this analysis. We may define "civilization," especially

119

as he used the term, as a progressive ordering and control of primitive impulses. Such regulation makes possible the erection of all the great cultural institutions and symbolic forms: art, literature, music, law, philosophy, science, humanistic learning, great universities, democratic politics. It should become immediately clear that civilization, so understood, has an intimate relationship to the concept of the superego. If any philosophical exhortation announces "Civilization demands that . . ." "superego" can easily be substituted for "civilization." Both the superego and civilization demand the containment, the repression, the sublimation of the more primitive manifestations of the drives.

On the question of civilization and its relationship to the biopsychological instincts of libido and aggression, Freud at one time or other argued every conceivable position. Civilization is erected on the repression of both the aggressive and the sexual instincts; civilization is erected *primarily* on the repression of the sexual instincts; civilization is erected *primarily* on the repression of the aggressive instincts. The progress of civilization and the increasing repression of sex may lead to the extinction of human life; but also, the advance of civilization may lead to a better (more fulfilled) life than we currently know. Civilization, by repressing and sublimating aggression, frees Eros and makes communal life and the progressive love of mankind possible; on the other hand, the advance of civilization produces an excess of guilt, neurosis, and the debasement of sexuality. Civilization is both the repressor and the liberator of human existence.

Admittedly, the relationship of civilization to the instincts or drives is not an easy thing to think about; it is a large and difficult question. Freud, however, managed to solve—or at least illuminate—many more difficult problems in his lifetime. With regard to no other theoretical issue did he display such diverse positions over the years.

Freud's first extensive discussion of the impact of civilization occurred in a paper, " '*Civilized*' Sexual Morality and Modern Nervous Illness," published in 1908.[1] Here there is already a lack of clarity in distinguishing the roles played by the repression of sexuality and the suppression of aggression in the formation of civilization. He begins with a discussion of repressed sexuality: "If we disregard the vaguer ways of being 'nervous' and consider the specific forms of nervous illness, we shall find that the injurious influence of civilization reduces itself in the main to the harmful suppression of the sexual life of civilized peoples (or classes) through the 'civilized' sexual morality prevalent in them." The grounds of the argument, however, quickly change: "Generally speaking, our civilization is built up on the suppression of instincts. Each individual has surrendered some part of his possessions—some part of the sense of omnipotence or of the *aggressive* or *vindictive* inclinations in his personality." The following paragraph returns again to the question of the suppression of sexuality: "The sexual instinct ... places extraordinarily large amounts of force at the disposal of civilized activity, and it does this in virtue of its especially marked characteristic of being able to displace its aim without materially diminishing in intensity. The capacity to exchange its originally sexual aim for another one, which is no longer sexual but which is psychologically related to the first aim, is called the capacity for *sublimation*."[2] No discussion of the sublimation of aggressive drives is attempted. Theoretically, we are left with a vague fusing of the instincts of sex and aggression, as if we are being told that civilization is built on the repression of the aggressive sexual drives, or of the sexual aggressive drives.

Four years later (in 1912), in an article significantly titled "On the Universal Tendency to Debasement in the Sphere of Love," Freud speculates that the sexual drives may not be capable of satisfaction, in part because it is impossible, even as an adult, to separate out sadistic from erotic needs. These reflections quickly lead into ruminations about civilization itself. "It is my belief," the argument begins, "that, however strange it may sound, we must reckon with the possibility that something in the nature of the sexual instinct itself is unfavourable to the realization of complete satisfaction." First, since the original objects of sexual excitement are unattainable because of the prohibitions on incest, all adult sexual partners will never serve as adequate substitutes for the real thing. Second, the original sexual drive is composed of several discrete components, some of which are incompatible with adult sexuality—those having to do with feces, for instance. Freud goes on, "The same is true of a large portion of the sadistic urges which are a part of erotic life. But all such developmental processes affect only the upper layers of the complex structure. The fundamental

121

processes which produce erotic excitation remain unaltered." Immediately Freud returns to the coprophilic: "The excremental is all too intimately and inseparably bound up with the sexual; the position of the genitals—*inter urinas et faeces*—remains the decisive and unchangeable factor." And then we get a remarkable first use of the phrase that was later to become a celebrated dismissal of women: "One might say here, varying a well-known saying of the great Napoleon: 'anatomy is destiny.' The genitals themselves have not taken part in the development of the human body in the direction of beauty: they have remained animal, and thus love, too, has remained in essence just as animal as it ever was."[3]

If this passage were free association, and it has some of that quality, we could observe a remarkable progression: sexual satisfaction is almost impossible—incest—feces—sadism—feces—(female) genitals are ugly—people are animals. And before the paragraph concludes, *civilization* comes in for a good part of the blame: "The instincts of love are hard to educate; education of them achieves now too much, now too little. What civilization aims at making out of them seems unattainable except at the price of a sensible loss of pleasure."[4]

Let us look closely at the fact that the Napoleon variation of anatomy-as-destiny is used here to explain the impossibility of sexual fulfillment (with civilizing tendencies participating in that failure), and, twelve years later, it was to be used to debase women for lacking a penis. The Freudian view of the permanence of unconscious connections allows us to hypothesize that these two statements are connected, though years apart. By observing this coupling we may see that there is indeed a very deep psychological connection between the debasement of, and lack of fulfillment in, sexuality and the debasement of women. If sexuality is debased and impossible to satisfy, we must have learned those sad facts before we had any notion there was such a thing as civilization. We must have learned them from the mother who raised us and blamed her for our sad human plight. The grand theoretical argument for or against civilization may very well be hiding an intense ambivalence about the mother who was the first to insist that we control our aggression, our feces, and our sexuality. Our initial encounter with "civilization" was a maternal one.

In Freud's argument against civilization, a very subtle theoretical position is being assumed: that incest taboos, the control of sadistic impulses, and the repression of excremental interests are demands made on the psyche from an *external* source—that is, civilization.

But rather than being assumed, this is the precise position that should be questioned. Are incest taboos, for instance, a necessity for society, or for the psyche, or *for both*? Is the psyche perfectly willing and *able* to live with uncontrolled incest acting out, but finds itself impelled toward a more restrained behavior by cultural norms? Or are incest prohibitions a necessity for the psyche itself? "The soul," Emily Dickinson tells us, "selects its own society." The same queries can be made for sadism and anal impulses. If everyone's psyche decided to live without any curb on sadistic urges, is it only society that would fall apart, or would individual psyches themselves become pathological? For myself, the answers seem obvious. Society imposes incest prohibitions, controls aggression, and orders anal inclinations because the psyche's health and survival depend on such regulation. The theoretical split between the psyche and civilization is unnatural. Conceiving of society as external to and oppressive of the psyche, when each are the cause of the other, is related in theory to the concept of the external superego, which imposes its demands on the poor unfortunate ego that has, supposedly, no intrinsic interest in those demands.

Civilization, we must remember, was in Freud's conscious world a masculine achievement—a brilliant, shining accomplishment: the Parthenon resplendent on the crown of the Acropolis; high culture emerging out of the morass of irrational impulses—incest, feces, sadism, ugly genitals. But this kind of theoretical split within the mind will not hold. It is the job of civilization, so the theory goes, to suppress the disruptive irrational. But when the repressed returns and refuses to be contained, we are then told in other essays that civilization itself, not those repressed impulses, is the cause of neuroses, guilt, lack of sexual satisfaction, and the debasement of the love object. Culture is both the best and the worst part of our lives. Ambivalence almost seems a pale word to describe such a schism in thought.

One important theoretical elaboration of the notion that civilization is repressive of sexuality is the logical, but inaccurate, inference that people who are less "civilized" will be sexually freer and find more erotic satisfaction than those who are burdened with the task of carrying civilization's light. This reverse racial and class prejudice has a long history: Jews have been the object of it in medieval and modern Europe, and Black people, especially in the United States, have been equally honored. Freud, we are not surprised to learn, was an upholder of such views. In the *Introductory Lectures* he makes his point about the necessity of sexual repression for civilized existence by telling a fable of a caretaker's daughter and a landlord's daughter who, though intimate friends in childhood, are forced to go separate ways in adult life due to their discrepant social situations. The landlord's daughter submits to the demands of education and morality and ends up repressed and conflicted about sexuality, whereas the caretaker's daughter, free from such encumbrances, can lead a life full of erotic satisfaction.[5] That Freud could believe such a patent absurdity—that the "lower classes" were sexually free and satisfied—may illuminate a severe flaw in the theory of sexual repression and civilization. "Among the races at a low level of civilization, and among the lower strata of civilized races, the sexuality of children seems to be given free rein. This probably provides a powerful protection against the subsequent development of neuroses in the individual."[6] If one really believes that—and it is my view that Freud did not—one's only response to civilization should be: "Tear it down!" Did Freud, or does anyone, truly believe that Beethoven's last quartets and Goethe's *Faust* are worth the neuroticization of most of humankind? To uphold such a proposition and then to continue to admire civilization would be an identification with the aggressor of almost suicidal proportions. Within the theory expounded by Freud, civilization is a scapegoat. It is being blamed for the repression of sexuality and the general neurotic condition of humankind, in order not to see that more fundamental psychic conflicts are involved, conflicts that even the "lower classes" and "primitive races" cannot escape.

Lower-class people may or may not have much culture that represses their sexuality, but they cannot avoid having mothers, and it is within the basic nurturing situation that these conflicts over sexuality and aggression first arise. In Freud's argument against civilization, his indictment indicates that it: (1) Represses incest and sexuality (including masturbation), making sexual fulfillment impossible; (2) represses the instinct of aggression, making conflict inevitable; (3) forces us to control our feces, which we don't wish to do; (4) is helpless in the task of separating sexuality from sadism; (5) seems oblivious to our wishes and insists on imposing its demands on us; and (6) makes us unhappy and neurotic. But are not these things precisely those that, unconsciously and sometimes consciously, we blame our mothers for? The manifest content of the theoretical argument is over civilization; the latent content, the hidden quarrel, concerns the inevitable conflicts involved with nurturing and the women who do it.

Freud's thinking on the question of whether civilization depends primarily on the repression of sexual or aggressive instincts followed the general pattern of his thought in these matters. In the early part of his psychoanalytic life, sexuality occupied the central position; later, aggressive drives became a primary concern. In 1910 he remarked that: "The light thrown by psychology on the evolution of our civilization has shown us that it originates mainly at the cost of the sexual component instincts."[7] And even as late as 1924: "Psychoanalysis has shown that it is predominantly, though not exclusively, sexual instinctual impulses that have succumbed to this cultural suppression."[8] With the writing of *Civilization and Its Discontents* in 1930, however, Freud came to face most directly the reality of human destructiveness: "In all that follows I adopt the standpoint, therefore, that the inclination to aggression is an original, self-subsisting instinctual disposition in man, and I return to my view that it constitutes the greatest impediment to civilization."[9] Having seen the darkness, he was able—at the age of seventy-seven—to make the necessary theoretical correction in *New Introductory Lectures* (1933): "It has become our habit to say that our civilization has been built up at the cost of sexual trends. . . . Well, what we have come to see about the sexual instincts, applies equally and perhaps still more to the other ones, the aggressive instincts. It is they above all that make human communal life difficult and threaten its survival. Restriction of the individual's aggressiveness is the first and perhaps the severest sacrifice which society requires of him."[10]

There is an inherent logical flaw in the whole concept that civilization, or anything else, could be erected on the basis of the suppression of *the* instincts. At whose behest are the instincts repressed, and for whose benefit? No instinct can be suppressed except if it is in the interest of another instinct to do so. First, there is the problem of power itself. Nothing in the psyche is as powerful as the instincts; how then could they be kept from satisfaction by anything except the needs of another instinct? Second, there is the question of why a part of the psyche that is not instinctual (ego? superego?) would require the non-satisfaction of an instinctual drive, except to satisfy some other instinctual need. The proposition that civilization requires the repression of instincts—in general—will not hold. When, however, Freud ultimately arrived, after 1920, at the theory of two opposing instincts in the psyche—death-aggression countering libido-love-Eros—the whole question of repression was clarified. It is easy to comprehend why Eros (an instinct) would repress aggression (the other instinct) for love's sake. Similarly, it would be in the interest of aggression to repress the drives toward Eros. The history of the world becomes, then, a fateful struggle between love and hatred. And civilization, in so far as the term is used positively, represents the gradual triumph of Eros over destruction. In certain passages in *Civilization and Its Discontents*—but, notably, not in all—this is precisely Freud's formulation.

Freud did raise this whole question of oppositional instincts as early as 1912: "For what motive would men have for putting sexual instinctual forces to other uses if, by any distribution of those forces, they could obtain fully satisfied pleasure? They would never abandon that pleasure and they would never make any further progress. It seems, therefore, that the irreconcilable difference between the demands of the two instincts—the sexual and the egoistic—have made men capable of ever higher achievements, though subject, it is true, to a constant danger, to which, in the form of neurosis, the weaker are succumbing today."[11]

The problem with "ego instincts" is that, despite several attempts by Freud and the heroic efforts of Heinz Hartmann, nobody has ever successfully demonstrated their existence. The reasons for the advance of culture cannot be discovered by looking in that direction. There must be something in the nature of sexuality and aggression themselves, or something in their complex relationship to each other, that produces these intricate developments of culture.

Until Freud arrived at the point, in *Civilization and Its Discontents*, of explaining civilization only in terms of a conflict between the opposing instinctual forces of love and aggression, he had some very harsh—and then some hopeful—things to say about cultural progress. In 1912: "the curb put upon love by civilization involves a universal tendency to debase sexual objects." And: "Thus we may perhaps be forced to become reconciled to the idea that it is quite impossible to adjust the claims of sexual instinct to the demands of civilization; that in consequence of its cultural development renunciation and suffering, as well as the danger of extinction in the remotest future, cannot be avoided by the human race."[12] In 1915: "society has allowed itself to be misled into tightening the moral standard to the greatest possible degree, and this has thus forced its members into a yet greater estrangement from their instinctual disposition. . . . In the domain of sexuality, where such suppression is most difficult to carry out, the result is seen in the reactive phenomena of neurotic disorders."[13] And in 1930: "my intention to represent the sense of guilt as the most important problem in the development of civilization and to show that the price we pay for our advance in civilization is a loss of happiness through the heightening of the sense of guilt."[14] This last demonstrates that, even by the time of *Civilization and Its Discontents*, Freud's new insights about the nature of the instincts had not yet succeeded in resolving his ambivalence about the civilizing process.

These pessimistic positions could not be maintained, however, and in the essays of 1915 and on civilization quoted in the last paragraph Freud had some hopeful things to say about cultural advance. As bad as things are now, civilization may yet produce a happier social life in the future. Intellectually, the two positions are irreconcilable. Freud clearly did not believe—could not believe—what he had written negatively about civilization, and needed to take it back—at least for the moment: "On the other hand, the maintenance of civilization even on so dubious a basis offers the prospect of paving the way in each generation for a more far-reaching transformation of instinct which shall be the vehicle of a better civilization."[15] And "this struggle between the individual and society is not derivative of the contradiction—probably an irreconcilable one—between the primal instincts of Eros and death. It is a dispute within the economics of the libido . . . and it does admit of an eventual accommodation in the individual, as, it may be hoped it will also do in the future of civilization, however much that civilization may oppress the life of the individual today."[16] How this amazing transformation is to be accomplished, Freud does not even begin to tell us. Obviously, civilization was not as bad for people as he had often portrayed it.

When writing so negatively about the *permanent* effect of civilization on sexual pleasure, Freud was repressing, among other things, his own vast historical knowledge. In the condemnation of cultural progress, he is extrapolating from his own particular Victorian, sexually repressive society to the whole course of civilization. Such an ahistorical approach might be excusable in a medical man with no interest in, or knowledge of, history, but history was one of Freud's obsessions. He knew, for instance, a great deal of classical history and must have been perfectly aware that historical eras of much less sexual repression existed than in nineteenth-century bourgeois Europe. He had more than sufficient knowledge to observe that periods of greater and lesser sexual repression come and go—that early empire Rome, as example, was a period of formidable sexual license, especially as compared with the relatively stable society of the Republic. Such information, unlike the Minoan-Mycenaean world, was not hidden under hills of rubble. No one could read even a modicum of Roman history without becoming aware of it. But never once, in all his discussion of civilization and the repression of the sexual instincts, does Freud give any hint that he may have knowledge of complex historical phenomena beyond the immediate situation of the culture in which he lived. It may be reasonable to conclude from all this evidence that something more than civilization and its relationship to sexual repression was being discussed in these circumstances, that there was a hidden conflict—with the nurturing mother, as has been postulated here—projected onto the problem of civilization, and that this conflict forced Freud into taking stands he really did not believe: intellectual positions that would sound reasonable to people with the same hidden conflicts. And thus the intellectual problem of "Eros and civilization" persists into our time.

In regard to the question of civilization, as in so many other matters, Freud's thinking underwent a radical change in the latter part of his life, as he began to look directly at the aggressive drives. When the human inclinations to dominate, degrade, and destroy other people are seen with an unclouded perception, civilization's problems with sexuality almost pale into insignificance. In *Civilization and Its Discontents* the great cosmic struggle for Freud is between the instincts of destruction, which, untrammeled, would make human life unbearable (both on the personal and on the social level), and civilization striving to control those inclinations. From a villain that causes guilt, debasement of the sexual object, and neuroses, civilization is elevated to heroic status—the only thing standing between human society and death:

> I may now add that civilization is a process in the service of Eros, whose purpose is to combine single human individuals, and after that families, then races, peoples and nations, into one great unity, the unity of mankind. Why this has happened, we do not know; the work of Eros is precisely this. These collections of men are to be libidinally bound to one another. Necessity alone, the advantages of work in common, will not hold them together. But man's natural aggressive instinct, the hostility of each against all and of all against each, opposes the programme of civilization. . . . And now, I think, the meaning of civilization is no longer obscure to us. It must present the struggle between Eros and Death, between the instinct of life and the instinct of destruction, as it works itself out in the human species.[17]

What happened that produced this profound reversal? Had Freud, like many great men before him, merely become wiser as he got older? It is more likely, I submit, that the grounds of the unconscious, hidden conflict about women and sexuality shifted as Freud aged, that some internal oppositions were resolved which made possible the statement of the problem—and its solution—in a more consistent and perceptive manner. When the poet Sophocles, who lived to be over ninety, was asked how it felt to be no longer the man he was (that is, to have sexual imperatives quiescent within him), he replied that he felt as if a great burden had been lifted off of him. In his earlier writings Freud wrote as if both sexuality and civilization were burdens human beings had to carry: sexuality incapable of fulfillment, civilization only making difficult matters worse. As the oppressive aspects of sexuality were lifted from Freud, he could perceive that the human species would come to extinction, not, as he had previously written, from conflicts over sexuality, but from uncontrolled destructiveness. Previous to this, the inability to separate aggression from libido had made it impossible to think clearly about either.

Freud had insisted, from early on, that all erotic acts contained elements of aggression, that sadism was a permanent problematic for sexual satisfaction. After his discovery of the fundamental importance of the destructive drives, he recognized that in any adult circumstance, in a similar manner, one could not find such a thing as pure aggression. "Luckily the aggressive instincts are never alone but always alloyed with erotic ones."[18] No one need argue with either of these proportions: every erotic act contains some aggressive element; every aggressive act is mixed with Eros. None of this, however, approaches the crucial question of degree. How much aggression is included in an erotic act? To simplify and put into numbers, for the purposes of illustration, things that cannot be numbered: a world in which every erotic act includes 5 percent aggressive experience is a far different world than one in which all erotic encounters are 50 percent aggressive. A person living in the latter situation would suffer from severe psychopathology; someone with only a small amount of aggression to deal with would find himself or herself fortunate. And then there would be all the people in between, those, to continue the statistical analogy, at the 15 or 20 or 25 percent mark. For them, the aggression within sexual experience would begin to become problematic and possibly to interfere seriously with sexual satisfaction. To know exactly how liberated or unliberated a society—or a group within society—may be, it is necessary to know exactly how much aggression still adheres to the average sexual experience.

And the aggression inevitably alloyed with sexual experience is not, as Freud tended to emphasize, primarily sadism, which takes pleasure in the infliction of pain on the other. For the average near-normal or neurotic person it is not sadistic inclinations that debase the sexual experience but anger. Anger that one is dependent for pleasure on another; resentment that the partner is not sufficiently providing; discontent that one cannot keep one's deepest feelings to oneself; indignation that, at a time of intense need, one has to pay attention to another person; for heterosexual women, anger that their sexual needs must now be fulfilled by a breastless, sullen, aggressive, penetrating male; and for heterosexual men, rage that the mother of reengulfment, from whom one imagined—as an adult—one was free, should be reincarnated in the lover-wife. And also a very deep primitive anger, the origin of which no one has yet illuminated. *Postcoitus tristum* is a depressive affect caused by the inability to direct the anger aroused by sexual experience anywhere else but at the self. Sadism is a problem for the few, but anger within sex is a universal human affliction.

Expecially for men. The great conflict over separation and individuation that is played out between a little boy and his mother[19] haunts the adult erotic life of men. Anger and rage are the midwives of individuation and separation, and anger toward women continues to be almost universally expressed by adult men in the mechanisms of degrading, debasing, dominating, or merely putting down.

These conflicts, when unresolved, are always projected onto theoretical discussions and onto the value system of society. The problem of civilization and the instincts—as a theoretical question—cannot be untangled as long as erotic experience is conceived of as including an inordinate amount of aggressive imperatives. On the social level, there is no question that the sexual repression and domination of women is a crucial mechanism by which men express their anger at women and sexuality in general. If we look for a moment at the late nineteenth-century situation in which Freud grew up, we can easily see why he might conclude that "civilization" was increasingly repressive of sexuality, but it is important—when regarding that sexual oppression—to ask *cui bono*? For whose benefit were such repressive institutions erected? Every social institution or norm must satisfy some human need, at least for those empowered in society. What human needs were gratified by such tyrannical forms? Were they a response to the demands of libido, sexuality, or Eros? Clearly not. The repression of sexuality is never undertaken for sexuality's sake, but only in the interest of the aggressive drives. To comprehend the suppression of sexuality—at any time in history—we must use the same tools we would employ to understand the slave trade or the concentration camps. The problem of civilization and the instincts is, overwhelmingly, a problem of aggression and the attempt of human culture to control it. Sexuality may be the victim of this great conflict—and many times it is—but it is never the cause.

In order to disentangle the theoretical questions concerning civilization, we must first understand the aggressive drives—their imperatives, the degree to which they can be sublimated and/or repressed, the extent to which they are affected by real-world behavior on the part of parents and society. Second, we must comprehend the intricate relationship between masculine and feminine roles and the playing out of aggressive needs. And third, we must begin to grasp the process by which these internal psychic conflicts are projected onto social norms and institutions.

The most perceptive statement by Freud about civilization, one in which he takes cognizance of all these ambiguities, does not come from his published writings. At a meeting of the Vienna Psychoanalytic Society in March 1909, the minutes reveal that:

> At the beginning of the lecture, a formula came to his mind. The entire development of humanity could also be characterized, from the psychological point of view, by a formula in which two elements stood out: on the one hand, it is a question of enlargement of the consciousness of mankind (analogous to the coming into consciousness of instincts and forces hitherto operating unconsciously); on the other hand, progress can be described as a repression that progresses over the centuries. Our culture consists in this: that more and more of our instincts become subject to repression, for which there are beautiful illustrations, particularly in poetic productions.
>
> When placed next to each other, these two characteristics seem to be entirely contradictory to each other, for with the progress of repression, more and more should become unconscious, and not the other way round. But then comes the liberating thought *that these two processes are the condition for each other*: the enlargement of consciousness is what enables mankind to cope with life in the face of the steady progress of repression.[20]

Freud never elaborated on these ideas, either in his written work or in any other recorded meetings of the society. What seems to be implied in these remarks is, first, that all global statements about civilization being erected on the repression of instincts are inaccurate. Second, in order to understand the process, each instinctual component must be considered separately. Oral libido may have to be repressed, for instance, so that other libidinal inclinations may be fulfilled—to breastfeed a child for five years may make certain individuated experiences impossible. Weaning, therefore, becomes simultaneously a situation of *repression* of orality and *liberation* of the drives for separation and individuation. If one insists on talking of "civilization's role" in such a context, one must say that civilization is, at one and the same time, repressive and liberating of the instincts. The control of anal functions, similarly, may be instituted not merely for repression's sake, but also to allow genital and then adult sexuality to flourish. Certain instinctual impulses must be reined in, otherwise severe damage to the psyche can result: the failure to suppress particular aggressive inclinations makes it impossible to recognize the reality of other people's existence. Unbridled narcissistic inclinations produce the same sad result. A truly "civilized" mode of child rearing would be acutely tuned in to the intricate complexities of psychic development and know when certain instinctual impulses should be contained in the interests of others. It would use the mechanisms of sublimation as much as possible (of anal, aggressive, and narcissistic inclinations), but our optimism must be tempered with the understanding that, in many circumstances, sublimation by itself will not suffice. A certain degree of repression is inevitable. Because we are by no means close to that ideal mode of child rearing, we cannot yet know what degree is the absolute necessity. And each particular circumstance of child raising will present its own configuration. The most penetrating implication of Freud's remarks is the concept that certain instinctual fulfillments are dependent on the suppression of other instinctual inclinations. One cannot say that civilization is built on the repression of instinctual drives and leave it at that, because that mode of thinking ignores the crucial fact that the drive toward civilization is itself derived from instinctual impulses. If it were not, it would be powerless to counter the drives.

This is not to say that society has not, at every point in its history, acted inappropriately and inadequately in regard to this intricate and complex process. Sexuality has been too much repressed; legitimate oral and anal inclinations have been suppressed; aggression has been repressed both too much and too little. Why this has been so—why, for instance, nineteenth-century bourgeois culture was so repressive of female sexuality—these are sociological problems beyond anyone's competence at the present moment. The answers will not come, however, by thinking about the instincts in global terms. Each instinctual component must be considered separately, because society behaves with that kind of discrimination. To call a society "repressed" is to say very little. We must know how it represses or expresses orality, anality, childhood genitality, narcissism, exhibitionism, humor, magic, aggression, masturbation, "feminine" and "masculine" virtues, religion, shame, guilt, individuation, and so on. Every one of these drives or drive derivatives can be, and are, treated in a differential manner by parents and by the culture as a whole. In terms of understanding society—and history—no more important theoretical work remains to be done.

A crucial psychological mechanism for this whole "civilizing" process is sublimation. Repression of any instinctual drive always creates a pathological potential. Sublimation, however, allows for a lowering of the primitive intensity of a drive without risking the return of the repressed. Sublimation is a transforming experience; repression is a psychological mechanism equivalent to incarceration. Freud understood this distinction clearly, but in his discussion of civilization and the instincts he loses touch with his own insight that both processes are possible. When he condemns civilization in exaggerated terms, he is speaking as if culture were capable only of repression. When he praises civilization as the savior of humankind, he has the capacity for sublimation clearly in mind.

Though clear on the process of the sublimation of sexual instincts (that is, the fact that it produces music, art, literature, and so on), Freud left the question of the sublimation of the aggressive drives unclarified. So open was this issue that when Heinz Hartmann began addressing it seriously in the 1940s and 1950s he felt entitled—because Freud's authority did not prohibit it—to use the word "neutralization" for the equivalent process with the aggressive drives. It is of interest that Freud never confronted this question directly, considering how important it obviously is to the problem of civilization and observing that he came very close to making the connection between sublimation of the sexual and the aggressive drives: "It has become our habit to say that our civilization has been built up at the cost of sexual trends which, being inhibited by society, are partly, it is true, repressed but have partly been made usable for other aims. . . . Well, what we have come to see about the sexual instincts, applies equally and perhaps still more to the other ones, the aggressive instincts. It is they above all that make human communal life difficult and threaten its survival. Restriction of the individual's aggressiveness is the first and perhaps severest sacrifice which society requires of him." And here is where we might expect a comment about the sublimation of aggressive drives, how they too can be made "usable for other aims." But we get instead—not surprisingly—our old friend and tyrant, the harsh and punishing superego: "We have learnt the ingenious way in which the taming of this unruly thing has been achieved. The institution of the superego which takes over the dangerous aggressive impulses, introduces a garrison, as it were, into regions that are inclined to rebellion."[21] The clear implication is that the aggressive instincts are *not* capable of sublimation, that only repression will work, and that the superego has the jailer's job. The image of the harsh, punishing superego from which the ego has to be liberated is the final result of this failure to perceive that—with a nonauthoritarian child-rearing process—the superego can also have the function of *sublimating* aggressive inclinations.

The repressive *or* liberating, the simultaneous liberating *and* repressive, work of civilization is done by mothers and fathers—mostly mothers—on a daily basis in the raising of their children. The essence of child rearing is the communication to the child of what instinctual impulses, and their derivatives, are to be expressed, repressed, or sublimated. Most drives will be partly expressed, partly repressed, and partly sublimated. In regard to any specific instinctual impulse, the mix of these three possible modes will vary enormously from one historical era to the next. If we think only of the last two hundred years in the West, there have been prodigious changes and variations in the manner in which, for example, parents have responded to childhood masturbation and bowel incontinence. Every variation in the response to these instinctual problems represents a change in the liberating or repressive aspects of civilization. We must not think of culture and its repressive-liberating role independently of our first educational experiences, as if we come to know civilization only when we are fifteen years old. The very first thing we are taught is whether to express an instinctual impulse or not. The great theoretical problems of civilization—and its discontents—cannot be answered without full reference to the complex and conflicted task of raising children. Augustine's cry "Give me other mothers and I will give you another world"[22] is an appeal to civilization to do its work of liberation.

9

The Split between the Soul and the Body, between Reason and Feelings

"FEAR OF and contempt for feeling," writes philosopher Mary Midgely, "make up an irrational prejudice built into the structure of European rationalism."[1] That fear and contempt has ancient sources. The Apostle Paul pronounces: "It is good for a man not to touch a woman. Nevertheless, to avoid fornication, let every man have his own wife. . . . But I speak this by permission, and not of commandment. For I would that all men were even as I myself [celibate]. But every man hath his proper gift of God, one after this manner, and another after that. I say therefore to the unmarried and widows, It is good for them if they abide even as I. But if they cannot contain, let them marry: for it is better to marry than to burn [with sexual passion]."[2] And in the religion that Paul helped to establish, after a time, the holiest people—monks, priests, hermits, popes—were required, in the ideal at least, to repress completely all sexual feeling. The conflicted interests of the body were sacrificed for the health of the soul.

Behind Paul lies Plato, who first prepared the soil of classical civili-

136

zation in a manner that would, ultimately, prove receptive to the Christian revolution. In Plato, the split between the sweet soul and the degraded appetites of the body—that conception that the social historian of Greece E. R. Dodds has called our worst inheritance from Greek culture—is clearly demarcated; and only reason, free of debased passions, can impose order in a morally chaotic world.

We are talking about repression. Within the fragmented structure that is our psyche, what drives and needs should be suppressed in the interest of other needs and drives? In what direction does salvation and happiness lie? Soul *or* body; reason *or* feelings? So few of the great thinkers and religious leaders of the Western world have said: let us have *both*.

Since the seventeenth century, the philosophical emphasis has not been on the body and the soul, but reason—in opposition to, and as the repressor of, feelings—has been invested with ultimate sovereignty. Because we reason, we know we exist; utilitarian reason alone is the source of moral behavior. The apotheosis of science is merely the last act in this disoriented drama.

Psychoanalysis, we might think, could provide us with a theoretical structure that would explain why reason and feelings—two obvious goods—have been placed in opposition to each other. Why should the pleasures of the mind be put in opposition to the pleasures of the body? No one has really attempted this analysis. Psychoanalytic theory, with its commitment to establishing psychoanalysis as a "science," is itself caught in that fateful split. "These observations," Freud writes, "will, it may be hoped, serve to justify us in extending a strictly scientific treatment to the field of human love. Science is, after all, the most complete renunciation of the pleasure principle of which our mental life is capable."[3] As if there were no pleasure in science. As if a *most complete* renunciation of the pleasure principle could be anything but pathological. Paul would have understood this desire for renunciation. Let us return to him in the attempt to understand what is so terrible about pleasure or the flesh that both must be degraded and repressed.

Before proceeding, however, it is important to make it clear that we are talking about *ambivalence* in regard to this bifurcation of soul/reason and body/feelings. Paul, as Freud reminds us, eloquently established love as the highest virtue. Plato, as well, in the dialogue of *The*

Symposium could create a great hymn to Eros. In fact, I am using that word in this work—following the manner of Freud—in the platonic sense. And Freud, by freeing society from the tyranny of sexual repression, bequeathed to us a freedom that he himself did not possess. Despite these radical advances, however, a certain fear and contempt for feeling still plays a significant part in all three world views. In Freud's case, most particularly, there is his insistence that science, not moral feeling, is his only *Weltanschauung* and that morality begins and ends with the repressive activities of the superego.

There is something filthy, corrupt, sinful in sexual desire and fulfillment. We are not talking of the repression of sexual feelings that have been fused with aggression and, therefore, need to be contained to preserve the fabric of social life. We are speaking of something in the nature of sex itself that appears to make it shameless and depraved. Incest, feces, genitals are ugly:

> For they that are after the flesh do mind the things of the flesh; but they that are after the Spirit, the things of the Spirit. For to be carnally minded is death; but to be spiritually minded is life and peace. Because the carnal mind is enmity against God: for it is not subject to the law of God, neither indeed can be. So then they that are in the flesh cannot please God. . . .
>
> Therefore, brethren, we are debtors, not to the flesh, to live after the flesh. For if ye live after the flesh, ye shall die: but if ye through the Spirit do mortify the deeds of the body, ye shall live.[4]

For Freud, a scientific creature of the twentieth century, the exact same struggle exists, except that for him reason takes the place of God: "But we have *no other means* of controlling our instinctual nature but our intelligence." And it is remarkable that when Freud describes the eventual triumph of reason over instincts, the narrative has a mythic and deeply religious quality. At first, intelligence—like Christ's message—seems ineffectual in the real world, but ultimately—again like Christ's vision—it triumphs through some ineffable power:

> We may insist as often as we like that man's intellect is powerless in comparison with his instinctual life, and we may be right in this. Nevertheless, there is something peculiar about this weakness. The voice of the intellect is a soft one, but it does not rest till it has gained a hearing. Finally, after a countless succession of rebuffs, it succeeds. This is one of the few points on

which one may be optimistic about the future of mankind, but it is in itself a point of no small importance. And from it one can derive yet other hopes. The primacy of the intellect lies, it is true, in a distant, distant future, but probably not in an *infinitely* distant one. It will presumably set itself the same aims as those realizations you expect from your God . . . namely, the love of man and the decrease in suffering.[5]

All this from an essay, one main task of which is to criticize religion for being unscientific. Can a less scientific explanation of how intelligence, which supposedly lacks any instinctual power, will eventually triumph over the most powerful sources of energy within the psyche be imagined? Reason is capable of growing from helplessness to omnipotence in some mysterious, unexplained manner. Absurd. If reason—the intellectual capability—were not fused with libidinal energy—the desires to love and create order, especially moral order—it would remain impotent against the destructive drives and could never triumph over anything. Without Eros, intelligence has as much commitment to morality and an orderly social life as a stick of dynamite, which can either assist in the construction of a bridge or annihilate a village.

Freud was by no means alone in the belief in the ultimate moral power of intelligence and science. It was a shibboleth of the times and to this day dominates our intellectual life. Most people would still rather believe that social morality is to be reasoned out rather than felt. Psychoanalysis, if it is worth its salt as science, should be able to tell us why a whole culture has pursued this mode of defense. What is it that we are defending against when we reify reason and science and set them up as the highest human virtues? Looking at Paul is helpful, because he represents these anxieties and defenses in a more primitive form than those represented in the modern apotheosis of intelligence and science. Paul insists that even the most legitimate, most unsinful, most sanitized sexuality is still detrimental to the highest form of human existence: "He that is unmarried careth for the things that belong to the Lord, how he may please the Lord: but he that is married careth for the things that are of the world, how he may please his wife."[6] The Lord, we must note, is a masculine entity; service to Him is set higher than service to any woman.

We cannot begin to understand this defensive maneuver without first looking at the relationship of aggression to sexuality. Sexuality can be debased and, consequently, repressed—and Paul is using a particular version of the corrupt superego for this purpose—only with the application of aggressive energy to the sexual drives. Then the so-called fusion of instinct occurs, and all the sinfulness of humankind is thrown into the same pot: "Now the works of the flesh are manifest, which are these, Adultery, fornication, uncleanness, lasciviousness, idolatry, witchcraft, hatred, variance, emulations, wrath, strife, seditions, heresies, envyings, murders, drunkenness, revelings, and such like."[7] Despite all this, Paul never contends that sexuality within marriage is a sin, and consequently one cannot speak of these views as pathological. Nevertheless, some very strong anxiety is being defended against here, and the erected defenses make a healthy view of human sexuality most difficult, if not impossible.

It is very difficult to think about the repression of sexuality in sexual terms only, unalloyed with aggressive significance, because there is no repression of anything without aggression; no matter what the objective of repression may be, the energy required to put it into operation is an aggressive energy. Further, most acts of sexual repression serve the interests of domination of one set of people over another. When we observe the repression of childhood masturbation, adolescent sexuality, consenting-adult homosexuality, or the pervasive repression of female sexual activity, in order to understand the causes of such repression we must ask in whose tyrannical interest the repressive acts are undertaken. To begin with children, we can observe thousands of examples: Hans' mother's threat against his penis if he continued to masturbate is one; severe punishment of a child exercising its legitimate sexual curiosity, to see its parents' nakedness, is another.

What causes essentially caring, loving parents to respond to a child's sexuality in an overly aggressive manner? In my view, such activity occurs because it defends against an anxiety in the parents, and aggression is an inevitable defense against anxiety. Anxiety can be aroused by Hans' masturbation for many reasons. The incestuous overtones of the masturbatory activity may be unconsciously recognized by the mother, stirring up her own incestuous impulses toward Hans and memories of her own such desires as a child, which heightens the anxiety about the possibility of acting out such inclinations. Hans' masturbation may remind the mother of her own unresolved problems in that area, activating the anxiety that she may never resolve the conflicts. Any manifestation of infantile sexual activity on Hans' part may flood the parent's preconscious mind with the recollection of all kinds of unresolved conflicts over sexuality—ancient longings that have been, more or less, successfully repressed may take flight again—all of this increasing the anxious questioning of whether the bourgeous order of life can be maintained. The parent may be anxious that Hans' masturbation is a symptom of pathology, that he will become fixated on, and obsessed with, masturbation and will, consequently, do himself psychological harm. And last, Hans' behavior may cause social anxiety, because doctors and friends are hysterically preaching that such activity is dangerous for the child—one does not want to be thought of as an incompetent parent.

Aggressive response to such anxieties is both a defense and symptom. It works defensively, first, because it does repress the action that has aroused the anxiety and creates the illusion that the problem can be solved, either by Hans' renouncing the activity or by the doctor's knife. Second, it punishes the agent who has caused the heightened anxiety, and this, somehow, restores the sense of order in the psyche. Third, though harmful for Hans, for the parent it is an assertive act; faced with the possible reaction of horror and passivity, the psyche chooses to *act*. All these reasons demonstrate the psychological advantages of dominance for the person exercising it.

The act of overly aggressive repression is, at the same time, a symptom. Freud has told us that all symptomatic behavior contains two things: the repression of an instinctual impulse and the hidden satisfaction of the same impulse. By reacting so vigorously, Hans' mother is not only repressing his (and her) masturbatory and incestuous impulses, but she is, at the same time, satisfying them. Instead of ignoring or downplaying Hans' sexual activity, she plunges right into the middle of it; it becomes a struggle between the two of them. She becomes obsessed with it; he is now forced, every time he reaches for his penis, to think of his mother. The two of them become locked into a struggle over Hans' masturbation; she is there between his hand and his penis; she has managed to satisfy, in the distorted and hidden manner of the symptom, her own masturbatory and incestuous wishes.

If we move on to the area of the social repression of sexuality against adults, we see all the same mechanisms at work. The social repression and severe oppression of male homosexuality was at a height from the middle of the nineteenth to the middle of the twentieth century. We are all acquainted with the cliché situation of the policeman who makes the persecution of homosexuals his specialty, including possible arrest and actual physical beating. That enforcer of the law undoubtedly suffers from intense conflicts about his own homosexual inclinations, and the existence of real-live "preverts" who actually do it raises his own anxiety level to an unbearable height. He beats homosexuals as a defensive measure in order to beat down his own homosexual inclinations and, at the same time, satisfies these impulses by the act of physically abusing another man. Here again, anxiety is the cause of the inadmissible, overly aggressive repressive acts. We may assume that society as a whole, though not engaged in the day-to-day acts of homophobic repression, passes laws against homosexuals and persecutes them in job situations for the exact same set of reasons.

Why society changes over history in its attitude toward repression of homosexuality; why, at certain times, homosexual anxiety on the part of heterosexual people is at a height and then significantly lessens; why, consequently, the repression of homosexuality varies enormously from one historical period to another—these are all sociological questions of enormous importance that seem, at least currently, beyond our theoretical competence.

Analogous to these other situations of inadmissible repression is that of the sexual repression of women throughout most of recorded history. This repression also has varied in its intensity from one period to another, but there seem to have been very few periods, if any, when women were not more sexually repressed than men. "Society" is a shortened way of saying "male society," for every society that we know of, certainly since the end of primitive times, has been male created and male dominated. What reason would men (acting together as society) have to repress female sexuality unless there was something in it that raised their level of anxiety? Here, as in the reaction to Hans' masturbation or the existence of practicing homosexuals, it seems most reasonable to postulate that all social repression of female sexuality is a defensive and symptomatic response to the anxiety that female sexual desire raises in men. The corresponding repression of the body and feelings, even in men, and the enthronement of soul and reason are an integral part of this same psychological syndrome.

Dorothy Dinnerstein in *The Mermaid and the Minotaur*, and Karen Horney in her essay "The Dread of Woman" have brilliantly elaborated the intense conflict that men feel about women's—and their own—sexuality and how all feeling consequently comes to be dreaded. Their recognition that masculine anxieties equate strong sexual feeling with the possibilities of extinction has been incontrovertibly confirmed by the theoretical work of Margaret Mahler, who has identified the fear of reengulfment by the symbiotic mother as a fundamental life anxiety, for both children and adults, most especially for masculine members of the species. Masculine anxiety about reengulfment by the mother is more intense than the similar female anxiety because such reengulfment for the male means the loss not only of the autonomy of the ego but the *gender identity* as well. A partially reengulfed woman still experiences herself as a female person, since the mother of reengulfment is female. A partially reengulfed man suffers from intense anxiety about the state of his masculinity. He must erect defenses that reassure him of his maleness. "Does the man feel," asks Horney, "side by side with his desire to conquer, a secret longing for extinction in the act of reunion with the woman (mother)? Is it perhaps this longing which underlies the 'death instinct'? And is it his will to live which reacts to it with anxiety?"[8] And, we may add, which reacts to anxiety with aggression, devaluation, and degradation in regard to women. Dinnerstein elaborates on these insights, recognizing certain social forms and institutions as masculine mechanisms of defense:

> What these deeper roots mean is that in intimate relations between a man and a woman he is in one very important respect more vulnerable than she is: She can more readily re-evoke in him the unqualified, boundless, helpless passion of infancy. If he lets her, she can shatter his adult sense of power and control; she can bring out the soft, wild, naked baby in him.
>
> Men try to handle this danger with many kinds of sex-segregated institutions that they seem always and everywhere driven to create. Secret societies, hunting trips, pool parlors, wars—all of these provide men with sanctuary from the impact of women, with refuges in which they can recuperate from the temptation to give way to ferocious, voracious dependence, and recover their feelings of competence, autonomy, dignity.
>
> But they need other safeguards too. Short of avoiding women altogether,

the best safeguard is to renounce the opportunity for deep feeling inherent in heterosexual love. One way to do this is to keep heterosexual love superficial, emotionally and physically. Another is to dissociate its physical from its emotional possibilities.[9]

Dinnerstein is elaborating splitting as a mechanism of defense. We may add to her list the fateful splits between body and soul, between reason and feeling.

It is unarguable, I believe, that Freud is engaged in the exact same defense mechanism—in order to contain the same set of anxieties—when he denies the power of female sexuality by describing all genital libido as masculine and when he announces that "it is extremely questionable whether the erotic life of women is dominated by sudden mysterious impulses."[10] "God forbid," as a character in one of the Jewish jokes that Freud loved so well, might say in response to this pronouncement.

An adequate psychological theory of morality suffers a permanent injury when it denies the essential role of feelings and emotions in the origins of conscience. The exaggerated emphasis on thinking, reason, intellect, science is a mechanism of defense erected to deal with the dread of women and female sexuality. Freud did not invent this particular psychic intellectual stance; he is merely one representative of a long line of rational endeavor that, when God would no longer suffice, enthroned reason as the ultimate ground of reality and morality.

Even a short history of Western thought on this issue is beyond the legitimate aims of this work and the competence of its author, but it may be helpful to look at the statements of several representative thinkers. Descartes, many argue, stands at the very beginning of the modern world.

The very fact that I thought of doubting the truth of other things, it followed very evidently and very certainly that I existed while on the other hand, if I had only ceased to think, although all the rest of what I had ever imagined had been true, I would have no reason to believe that I existed; I thereby concluded that I was a substance, of which the whole essence or nature consists in thinking, and which in order to exist, needs no place and depends on no material thing; so that this "I," that is to say, the mind which I am what I am, is entirely distinct from the body, even that it is easier to know than the body, and moreover, that even if the body were not, it would not cease to be all that it is.[11]

Who would want to be a brother, a son, a father, a pupil, a spouse of a man who thinks-therefore-he-is? How much more human to be because one feels, or loves, or hates, or expresses joy, or feels sorrow, or even kills. "I kill therefore I am"—that at least has the virtue of authenticity.

Descartes is describing the sense of identity, of individuality, of a separate and unique existence. We know today that the great triumphal struggle for individuation is played out against the threat of reengulfment by the symbiotic mother. Thinking, reason, intellect are the great masculine virtues because they appear to be uncontaminated by the feelings and the body of the mother of reengulfment. What Descartes seems to be saying is that his existence owes nothing to the mother who bore and nurtured him.

Feelings, then, become the villain in this melodrama; the function of reason is to make sure that they remain thoroughly repressed. "Nearly every respectable attribute of humanity," writes J. S. Mill, "is a result not of instinct but of victory over instinct. The aim of education is not simply to regulate these [instincts] but to extirpate, or rather to starve them by disuse."[12] The degree to which splitting and ambivalence, in regard to moral ideals, is possible in one individual is sharply demonstrated by the fact that Mill, as we have noted, was a radical and prophet on the question of feminine equality, though he would undoubtedly have described his position as having been arrived at through the exercise of his reason. Freud, as we have observed over and over again, was intensely ambivalent on this whole subject, but in the balance the weight of his argument came down on the side of reason and the repression of feelings. "The superego may bring fresh needs to the fore," he wrote in his last, and unfinished, work, "but its main function remains the limitation of satisfactions."[13]

The arguments of Descartes and Mill for the primacy of reason are encountered over and over again with Hobbes and Locke, indeed by the whole of the Liberal and Utilitarian traditions. Western thought, in its entirety, however, was ambivalent about the repression of feeling, and in Rousseau it found a great, passionate voice announcing that the sentiments formed the fundamental ground of our morality: "Mandeville sensed very well that even with all their ethics men would never have been anything but monsters if nature had not given them pity in support of reason; but he did not see that from this quality alone flow all the social virtues he wants to question in men. In fact, what are generosity, clemency, humanity, if not pity applied to the weak, to the guilty, or to the human species in general?" It was a theme he elaborated many times in his work:

> Leaving aside therefore all scientific books which teach us only to see men as they have made themselves, and meditating on the first and simplest operations of the human soul, I believe I perceive in it two principles anterior to reason, of which one interests us ardently in our well-being and our self-preservation, and the other inspires in us a natural repugnance to see any sensitive being perish or suffer, principally our fellow-men. It is from the conjunction and combination that our mind is able to make of these two principles, without the necessity of introducing that of sociability, that all the rules of natural right appear to me to flow: rules which reason is later forced to re-establish upon other foundations when, by its successive developments, it has succeeded in stifling nature.

In order to substantiate the primacy of feeling for the moral order, Rousseau found it necessary to attack the grip of reason on Western philosophy: "In a word, it is in this natural sentiment, rather than in subtle arguments, that we must seek the cause of the repugnance every man would feel in doing evil, even independently of the maxims of education. Although it may behoove Socrates and minds of his stamp to acquire virtue through reason, the human race would have perished long ago if its preservation had depended only on the reasonings of its members."[14]

Rousseau obviously would have found the superego, whose primary function is the repression of desire, a monstrous moral faculty. The basic argument between those who champion feelings against those who enthrone reason rests on a fundamental disagreement as to whether human instincts are to be trusted and allowed to flourish, or whether they are fundamentally disorderly and must be contained by reason, force, and repression. Concerning the destructive drives, all would agree that they must be suppressed and sublimated; the disparity in views arises from a fundamental disagreement as to what instrument is most efficient in containing aggression. The advocates of reason, mistrustful of sentiment, feel that only a repressing force can do the job. For Rousseau, the only adequate counter to destruction is to set another instinct against it: libido, love, pity, compassion, Eros: "By reason alone, independent of conscience, no natural law can be established . . . the entire right of nature is only a chimera if it is not founded on a natural need in the human heart."[15]

Symptomatic Behavior

We may best understand the emphasis on reason, repression, and superego as symptomatic behavior if we see it as a compromise between conflicting desires. The symptom, the compromise formation, will contain both the repression and the satisfaction of instinctual needs. The advocates of reason, from Hobbes's *Leviathan* to Freud's superego, are sincerely interested in containing the destructive element in human relations; insofar as this is true, they are on the side of libido and Eros. But they are also fearful of the full expression of Eros—for reasons elaborated earlier—and therefore they must repress Eros *at the same moment* as they contain aggression. They consequently restrain the destructive drives with an instrument—reason, superego, regressive religious and political forms—that, simultaneously, also represses the full expression of Eros. Eros is both satisfied and repressed, but so are the destructive drives: repressed by the imposition of order on society; satisfied when the fulfillment of Eros is denied.

It may be helpful to elaborate on the concept of symptomatic behavior, because it can illuminate many psychological situations that hitherto seem to have no adequate name. How do we describe the sexism that characterizes Freud's thought and the thought of the vast majority of men in his late Victorian society? Is it pathological? Certainly it is not. Even to call it a neurotic symptom seems much too strong. Neither is it, however, vibrant with psychological health. It is the result of an internal instinctual conflict, and men would be healthier and happier if their conflicts and ambivalences about women were of a lesser degree of severity. Sexism is a compromise formation resulting from an internal conflict, a formation that acts exactly like a symptom in that it gives satisfaction to both sides of the ambivalence simultaneously within the same form. It seems helpful to call all such behavior "symptomatic." Though not pathological, and not necessarily neurotic, all symptomatic behavior is problematic and takes a psychological toll from the actor, in most cases because the symptomatic behavior gives too much satisfaction to aggressive impulses; it represents an excess of aggressive acting out. Though not pathological, it is nevertheless harmful to the psyche.

Many, many human activities, on a social or a personal plane, fall into this category of action. I have often wondered how one—from the psychological point of view—diagnoses the cannibalism of a cannibal society, a society in which everyone is a cannibal, where one learns one's cannibalism from one's parents, a society wherein cannibalism has the blessing of the superego. Psychotic? That seems absurd. Pathological? It does not make much sense to describe a whole society as pathological except in a case like Nazi Germany when a massive social *regression* is taking place. Cannibals are not regressing to cannibalism. On the other hand, the act of cannibalism is not radiant with health. "Symptomatic behavior" seems exactly the right description, especially if we include the notion of compromise formation, which involves an excess of aggressive acting out.

And the same for racism in a racist society, or slave owning in a slave society, or warfare in practically all societies. And the same for the sexual oppression of women, or the suppression of homosexuality, or the stringent prohibition of masturbation in children. All of these nonpathological compromise formations include an excessive amount of aggressive satisfaction. All are costly to the psyches of those participating in them. All are capable of being given up when new compromise formations are invented and instituted, ones that contain less aggressive acting out. Plato's insight that the perpetrator of evil is doing harm to himself is an illumination of symptomatic behavior. Social progress may be defined not by the decreasing pathology in society but by the progressive abandonment of the more primitive forms of symptomatic behavior.

The Apotheosis of Science as Symptomatic Behavior

I am not concerned here with the normal, legitimate, pleasurable, world-transforming aspects of the practice of science. I do not deny the concept that the natural sciences have radically changed the world in which we live, that they have been an essential element in the creation of modern society with all its benefits and anxieties. Three theoretical distortions in regard to science are under discussion. First, there is the notion that there is only one kind of truth: scientific truth subject to experimental validation. A slightly less dogmatic rendering of this idea is that there may be different kinds of truth, but scientific truth is supreme. This view allows for the existence of "hard" and "soft" sciences. Second, there is the judgment that science, in itself, can become a *Weltanschauung*, an overriding world view that locates our place within reality and gives meaning to existence. And third, there is the conception that science can provide a ground for morality. God having been dispossessed, science is able to answer all the questions that were previously the prerogative of religion.

Despite the fact that Freud held all three of these positions, it would be a distortion of his theoretical interests to claim that any of them, or even all three combined, provided a major thrust of his theoretical activities. Freud made most of his comments about science *en passant*, as it were, even though he did devote a full lecture in *New Introductory Lectures* to "The Question of a *Weltanschauung*," a lecture that is an argument primarily against religion and secondarily against Marxism, to both of which he opposes a *Weltanschauung* of science. What is significant is that whenever Freud touched on the question of science and world view, he inevitably came up with one of the three irrational views of rationality just outlined. Some of Freud's immediate and later followers, however, have spent much more energy on the attempt to establish psychoanalysis as a science. Among these, in this chapter I will treat only with Heinz Hartmann, because he was also centrally interested in the problem of morality. Beyond the narrow range of psychoanalytic theory, certain distorted views in regard to science play an enormously important role in our current intellectual life, most especially in certain departments of our universities, where the warfare between the numbers gangs and the humanist gangs are, in individual cases, threatening to tear departments apart. Obviously, something more than just a polite intellectual disagreement as to the most productive road to truth is taking place. But let us examine, in detail, each of these rational distortions of reason.

SCIENTIFIC TRUTH IS THE ONLY FORM OF REAL TRUTH

Truth takes many forms: a body in motion will continue to move at the same speed and direction unless an outside force or resistance is exerted on it; the unexamined life is not worth living; we must endure our going hence as our coming hither—ripeness is all; he who does not remember the past is condemned to repeat it; all dreams contain a fulfillment of a wish; it is better to love a child than to hate it; racism is evil; no happy marriage is possible without compromise; for almost all people, life is hard. It is accurate that all of these statements except the first may be subject to legitimate argument, but it is also correct that to live one's life, one needs the nonscientific brand of truth much more than that which can be confirmed by experiment. Despite this, many intelligent people have claimed that they required, to deal with life's problems, *only* the laws established by science. Freud writes:

> It is not permissible to declare that science is one field of human mental activity and that religion and philosophy are others, at least its equal in value, and that science has no business to interfere with the other two: that they all have an equal claim to be true and that everyone is at liberty to choose from which he will draw his convictions and in which he will place his belief. . . . Unfortunately it is not tenable and shares all the pernicious features of an entirely unscientific *Weltanschauung* and is equivalent to one in practice. It is simply a fact that the truth cannot be tolerant, that it admits of no compromises or limitations, that research regards every sphere of human activity as belonging to it and that it must be relentlessly critical if any other power tries to take over any part of it.[16]

It is of interest to note that Freud rarely wrote with such vehemence. Something in the nature of this subject caused him to use words like "pernicious," "cannot be tolerant," "no compromises," and "relentlessly critical." Never had Freudian language been so close to Marxian.

Arguments about *Weltanschauung* obviously bring about the use of that kind of aggressive language. It is important to know why. First, however, it is significant to point out that the argument itself is spurious. Freud had established, at least to his satisfaction, that religion was an untruth that taught lies, which were childish wish-fulfillments: that God exists, that there is life after death. He had never established, in any manner or form, the same condition for "philosophy," whatever that meant for him. In these sentences, it seems to mean every statement about life that is neither religious nor scientific. Having established nothing about the untruth of philosophy, Freud proceeds to lump it with religion as the enemy of science and then declare the latter the only possible champion.

Freud, as we know, was not alone in this childish wish-fulfillment that science could establish an unarguable basis on which life is to be lived. Even the humanist fields of history, sociology, and political theory have joined the great pilgrimage to the altar of science and established themselves as the "social sciences," validating that designation with a few paltry verities of technology that have very little to do with scientific theory. And when challenged by the natural sciences that social, historical, and political speculation can never become truly scientific, the humanist fields—identifying with the aggressor—have invented the notion of "soft" sciences, which do not give the same kind of answers as the "hard" sciences but give valid answers nevertheless. Psychoanalytic, nonscientific speculation has taught us that two very important things in the world are much better hard than soft. Science is one.

SCIENCE AS *WELTANSCHAUUNG*

"In my opinion, then, a *Weltanschauung* is an intellectual construction which solves all the problems of our existence uniformly on the basis of one overriding hypothesis, which, accordingly, leaves no question unanswered and in which everything that interests us finds its fixed place." Having said this, Freud quickly elaborates that the desire to have one view that explains everything in the world is a childish wish-fulfillment. We may say that the belief that any *Weltanschauung*, so defined, is possible, is religious by definition because it involves a positive belief in the possibility of intellectual omnipotence. Having said that, one would imagine that he would announce that psychoanalysis, in the interests of truth and the reality principle, rejects all *Weltanschauungen*. Instead, he declares that psychoanalysis is "quite unfit to construct a *Weltanschauung* of its own: it must accept the scientific one." However, Freud goes on to say that science is unlike all other *Weltanschauungen*: its promise of full knowledge "is relegated to the future"[17]; it is limited to what is known at the moment; science is against all illusion and wish-fulfillment. In essence, the argument asserts that science is not really a *Weltanschauung* as *Weltanschauung* has been previously defined.

In the interest of intellectual consistency, Freud should have rejected any *Weltanschauung* for psychoanalysis and merely confirmed that it was based on the scientific *method*, asserted scientific *truths*, believed nothing that was not *demonstrable*. That he did not do so indicates that he was not entirely free of the search for religious certainty and intellectual omnipotence that he, in many places, argued so passionately against. Having spent a good part of the lecture arguing in opposition to the religious and Marxist brands of *Weltanschauung*, he displays his own ambivalence by reiterating at the end: "Psychoanalysis . . . is a part of science and can adhere to the scientific *Weltanschauung*."[18]

SCIENCE AND REASON AS THE BASIS OF MORALITY

What Freud was incapable of accomplishing was the separation of *Weltanschauung* and morality. It is possible to reject all *Weltanschauungen*, as defined by Freud, and still maintain a consistent moral stance. It is true that in religion the imperative of good conduct arises out of the basic conception of the world: God rules both what is and how we ought to behave. It also may be argued that a dogmatic Marxism makes the perception of the class struggle the source both of understanding the world and of individual behavior. This fusion, however, is not inevitable. One may perceive that racism and sexism and the destruction of the world are evil without having a commitment to any complicated philosophical or religious system.

Science, for Freud, was not only the correct *Weltanschauung* but also provided the grounds of morality. "For science is content to investigate and to establish facts, though it is true that *from its applications rules and advice are derived on the conduct of life.* In some circumstances these are the same as those offered by religion, but, when this is so, the reasons for them are different." Fortunately, we are spared Freud's giving us any example of this mental activity—demonstrating, by the scientific method, that Eros should be preferred to the destructive drives. My guess is that if Freud had attempted it, he would have fallen back on the old, "scientific," utilitarian notion of self-interest and self-preservation. Eros is to be preferred because it fosters the preservation of the world and the self. By what scientific method or experiment, however, can one establish that such interests must override all others? There is no "proof" even that life is to be preferred to death. Carried away by the *Weltanschauung* of science, Freud made assertions that directly contradicted what he had written earlier about the relative strength of passion and reason: "Our best hope for the future is that intellect—the scientific spirit, reason—may in the process of time establish a dictatorship in the mental life of man. . . .* But the common compulsion exercised by such a dominance of reason will prove to be the strongest uniting bond among men and lead the way to further unions."[19] In *Civilization and Its Discontents*, we had been told that "instinctual passions are stronger than reasonable interests"[20] and that the thing that binds men together is "eternal Eros." This earlier formulation is certainly nearer the truth. Reason has been used over and over again to persuade men to destroy each other. The same cannot be said of Eros.

Thirty years after *Civilization and Its Discontents*, Heinz Hartmann, one of the most important, if not the most important psychoanalytic theorist of the period following Freud's death, a thinker in the direct Freudian line, published a book entitled *Psychoanalysis and Moral Values*. As could have been expected, Hartmann maintained a "scientific," "value-free" stance toward any particular moral imperative. Following the lead set by Freud, he observed: "The question of what one ought

---

* The dictatorship of reason, in the interest of moral progress, seems to be the Freudian equivalent of the dictatorship of the proletariat.

to consider good or bad remains outside the limits of my presentation," a credo that was repeated in a summary section later in the book: ". . . psychoanalysis as a science cannot be expected to provide us with ultimate moral aims, or general moral imperatives; these cannot be deduced from its empirical findings."[21] We note that Hartmann does not insist on using the more global word "*Weltanschauung*" but maintains that psychoanalysis cannot approve any "general moral imperatives." This would imply that although psychoanalysis may find no "scientific" evidence that racism, or sexism, or fascism result from psychic disturbance and conflict, it cannot "scientifically" pronounce these formations as immoral.

Earlier in his book, however, Hartmann observes that psychoanalytic theory can explain why people have a need for morality:

> But the factors that bring it about that man is capable of developing directions of a moral nature, ideals or imperatives which are part of his mental functioning—these factors originate in the long dependence of the human child on the adults, in the identifications and object relations that result as a consequence of the child's early sexual and aggressive development. That there exists the experience of the "ought," of a moral "good" or "bad," for the individual is essentially traceable to these beginnings.[22]

Having said this, Hartmann, who wrote as much about aggression as anyone, gives us not the slightest hint that the child might possibly equate "good" with love and "bad" with aggression. To argue thus, obviously, might lead us to statements such as "It is better to love one's children than to be aggressive toward them," a moral imperative toward which psychoanalysis has to maintain scientific neutrality.

Ambivalence will out, however, and at the end of this volume Hartmann makes a remarkable statement for a man of science:

> I am more embarrassed by the incompleteness and, particularly as to some parts of it, the sketchy character, of this lecture. In regard to what a few might well consider my most regretable omission—that I did not try to adduce arguments for or against specific moral directions—I fully explained to you why I had to exclude any such attempt from my discussion. I did not avoid this aspect because I am blind to its importance, but because I realize that it has no place in scientific discourse. It belongs in the *realm* not of science but *of ultimate personal positions*; no scientific psychology,

even if it were perfected beyond what it is today, could take the *place of personal responsibility* in these matters.[23]

The "scientific" purpose of psychoanalysis is to understand the psyche and its functions; the whole range of the psyche, not just a part, is its subject. Where does this "realm . . . of ultimate personal positions" or "the place of personal responsibility" exist? If it resides inside the psyche, then it is a proper area of analysis by a psychoanalytic psychology. Since Hartmann says it is not a proper area of study, it must therefore lie *outside* the psyche, *outside* the sphere of psychological behavior and reaction. What possible source of motivation for Hartmann can be nonpsychological? The religious person has no trouble finding such in divine intervention. I doubt that Hartmann has that in mind. The only other possible nonpsychological source of motivation would be a mystical or metaphysical realm, which is neither divine nor psychological. Here again, one doubts Hartmann's commitment to such a kingdom.

What, in essence, Hartmann is insisting on is a realm within the psyche that cannot be the subject of "scientific" analysis, and it is within this realm that he finds the source of his own moral position. It is a rational absurdity to insist that some parts of the psyche can be subjected to "scientific" inquiry and others parts are not so subject— and that every theorist can make his or her own arbitrary judgment (as Hartmann has done, in this case) as to which parts fit into which category. The objective of such intellectual distortion seems clear: not to subject the ground of one's own morality to investigation. Repressing, therefore, what? Its purpose is to maintain the split between body and soul, between reason and feelings. It is a safekeeping of the heroic intellect from the contamination of the mother.

These subtle bendings of intellectual position in regard to science by no means represent pathological behavior: they do not even give indication of having resulted from any severe internal conflicts. But they are nevertheless the symptomatic resolution of a conflict, and it is a legitimate activity to inquire into the nature of that internal discord. Once we see that the apotheosis of science is not only an intellectual stance but a mechanism of defense erected against the threatening aspects of body, feelings, and maternal preoccupations, we can begin to understand why argument about the role of science can provoke such vehemence, for example, in some of our university departments of social "science." An important quantitative—that is, scientific—sociologist in a top-ranked university was heard to remark, in the 1970s: "We have to increase the number of our quantitative requirements in order to get rid of some of the women in this department."* Civilized argument about the most propitious road to truth is one thing, but when you threaten to take away a man's fundamental defensive resolution of conflict, he will kill many times before he will give it up.

It may be of value to inquire whether the exaggerated emphasis on numbers, technology, and "science" and the sometimes near-hysterical attack on humanism that we have witnessed in the last twenty years of our intellectual life do not owe their origins to the growing demands of women for intellectual and sexual equality. That men become more defensive in their behavior as the traditional modes of domineering over women erode is beyond question. An exaggerated emphasis on science may be as much a refuge from the latest gender wars as the locker room and the exclusive male club. In the history of Western thought, the splits between body and soul, between reason and feeling, have widened and narrowed, demonstrating great variety in the manner and intensity with which they are displayed. To explain these vicissitudes of attitude it may help to relate them to something else going on within the culture. That "something else" could very well be the changes in the relative repression or liberation of women and in the male conflicts and symptomatic behavior that are inevitably responsive to these changes. That intellectual positions are many times adopted not because of their intrinsic worth but in order to contain deep, primitive anxieties—to this proposition all believers in the validity of psychoanalytic theory (scientific and nonscientific alike) can certainly assent. Behind the defensive mask of scientific rationality lies panic-anxiety.

* Arlie Hochschild, personal communication.

PART IV

TOWARD A RECONSTRUCTION OF THE PSYCHOANALYTIC THEORY OF MORALITY

10

Love, Identification, and the Origins of Conscience

IT IS NOT SUFFICIENT to demonstrate that the equation of the superego with the moral capacity of the psyche is theoretically indefensible. Having done that critical work, it is important to begin the attempt to construct an adequate psychological theory of moral development. What relationship, if any, exists between the development of the psyche and the moral capacity? Most important, is morality a necessity for the healthy psyche? In what way, if any, is immorality the cause, or the result, of psychopathology?

The first question that must be addressed is whether the psyche possesses any moral capacity at all. It could be that not only is the superego inadequate, but also that nothing else in the psyche has the power to discriminate between moral and immoral actions. It can be argued that the psyche is morally neutral; it can deal with relative values but not with an absolute morality. Values—views of what constitutes good or bad behavior—exist within all societies and are communicated to children by parents, teachers, mass culture, and so on. These values, so the argument may run, are accepted or rejected by the child for reasons of psychological conflict that have nothing to do with morality. The superego, then, even if a very poor instrument of moral control, may be the only resource we have in this circumstance. This manner of argument would leave us all back with Freud in 1915 pensively wondering why he and his six adult children felt compelled to behave in a morally satisfactory manner.

The opposing argument—the one that will be developed here—insists that the psyche does have the capacity for moral discrimination, that it can differentiate between moral and immoral imperatives, that we are all born with an ultimate capacity for critical moral reflection that goes beyond values. If one wishes to describe that capacity in metaphorical terms, inquiring what "instrument" in the psyche performs that function, I prefer to call that mechanism "conscience" and to oppose conscience to superego as *the* moral agency within the psyche. This argument for conscience will be made *within* the psychoanalytic tradition, using data from Freud and other psychoanalytic theorists who have studied the early development of children. The argument will proceed along lines that suggest that an adequate psychoanalytic theory of conscience already exists, even though, thus far, no one has quite put it together.

The thesis to be advanced here asserts that a healthy conscience is developed in three stages. In the first stage, the rock foundation of conscience is prepared in the basic situation of love and nurturing between parents and the child. The more adequately the child is loved and nurtured the more chance there will be that its conscience will be sound and robust. No 100 percent correlation of these factors is assumed; however, it will be argued that the adequacy of nurturing is one of the most important factors in the development of the moral capacity.

In the second stage of moral development, all children exhibit two basic modes of identification that are crucial for the flowering of conscience. Identification with the nurturer and the provider reveals itself in the universal human inclination—clearly visible in very small children—to give back love in return for love received. The second mode of identification—with the comforter—reveals itself in identification with the victim; its basic attributes are pity and compassion, which Rousseau and even Freud, on occasion, have declared to be the bases of all moral action.

The third stage, necessary for the ripening of a full adult conscience, is that in which the desires to give back love and nurture are generalized to people who are not of one's own kin. The capacity to act lovingly toward people whom one does not even know is essential for the development of a social conscience. This cannot be accomplished without the ability to generalize, to abstract from the particular situation of the family to a larger, universal circumstance. This third stage presents complex sociological and psychological problems that cannot be much illuminated by the study of pre-oedipal or oedipal children; a discussion of its complexities will therefore be left for a later chapter. This chapter will concern itself primarily with the first two stages of moral development: love and identification.

Love and Nurturing

In this endeavor to establish the primary importance of love for psychic health, and for the origins of conscience, the only psychoanalytic arguments to be used come from Freud himself. There is no question that he regarded love-Eros-libido as a fundamental ground of a healthy human existence. Indeed, reading certain passages almost compels one to regard him as an apostle of love. What Freud failed to do, however, was to extend his discussion of Eros into the place of its origin. He refused to see or talk about what is obvious to us today: that love begins for the human child in its relationship with its mother and that every circumstance of love in all of life—whether for people, for things, or for ideas—resonates with this very first experience of Eros.

Freud's greatest gift to humankind was the practice of psychoanalytic therapy, which is made possible only by the existence of the phenomenon of transference: the projection by the patient onto the therapist of intense positive and negative feelings that originated in the patient's psychic past and have remained active and important in the patient's unconscious. "Transference," Freud wrote to Jung in 1906, "provides the impulse necessary for understanding and translating the language of the unconscious; where it is lacking, the patient does not make the effort or does not listen when we submit our translation to him. Essentially, one might say, the cure is effected by love. And actually transference provides the most cogent, indeed, the only unassailable proof that neuroses are determined by the individual's love life."[1] In that same year, when speaking at a meeting of the Vienna Psychoanalytic Society, Freud touched upon what was to become a fundamental concern of psychoanalytic therapy: who can or can not be helped by psychoanalysis and why. "The translation of the unconscious material into consciousness is performed with the help of the transference. The core, therefore, is effected by means of conscious love. In hysteria and obsessional neurosis, part of the libido is mobile and treatment can start with this part. In paranoia, however, this chance is not available because of the regression to autoerotism. There is no faith in the physician because there is no love. The patient, just like the child, believes only whom he loves."[2] A patient must have achieved a certain degree of psychic health before he or she can be aided by psychoanalytic therapy; a patient incapable of love cannot be successfully treated.

Ten years later, in 1916, Freud expanded his understanding of the transference situation to include all education, but in this instance we already see creeping into his thought the confusion between love and punishment that was to mark much of his later work. "Let us say that the doctor, in his educative work, makes use of one of the components of love. In this work of after-education, he is probably doing no more than repeat the process which made education of any kind possible in the first instance. Side by side with the exigencies of life, love is the great educator; and it is by love of those nearest him that the incomplete human being is induced to respect the decrees of necessity and to spare himself the punishment that follows any infringement of them."[3]

This insight that the love of the patient for the doctor re-created a child's love for its parent was deepened after psychoanalytic theory began to pay attention to the very beginnings of psychic life—to the infant-mother symbiotic world. In articles published in the 1950s, Ida MacAlpine,[4] Phyllis Greenacre,[5] and René Spitz[6] demonstrated that the basic situation of psychoanalytic therapy re-creates the primitive situation of infant and mother. The patient lies down on a couch; his or her movements are limited, like a baby in a crib; he or she can symbolically call out to the doctor, but the doctor, like the mother, may or may not come (that is, may or may not answer). The patient cannot even see the analyst, as the baby in the crib cannot see the mother. External stimuli are reduced to a minimum; like the infant's world, the amount of visual and audio stimulation is severely limited. The patient comes to the doctor seeking help and, at least during the precious fifty minutes, has the complete sympathetic attention of another person—fulfilling every infant's dream of the omniproviding mother. Spitz claims that the "fundamental rule" of psychoanalysis—to say whatever comes into one's head—is itself a re-creation of the infantile experience. "It corresponds closely to what the infant does when he manifests, without selection or inhibition, by movement or sound, by silence or agitation, the processes of his own organism of which he becomes aware."[7]

Freud had great problems thinking about the infantile situation. In creating the methods of psychoanalytic therapy, however, his unconscious triumphed over his resistance. He re-created the ambience of the mother-infant world and was not fearful to call the process of cure "love." It may be that the mechanisms that make the psychoanalytic process work are identical to those that create conscience in the child's psyche. If the patient incapable of love (that is, transference) cannot be cured, it may be that the identical thing can be said of the patient incapable of conscience. It will be, most probably, the same patient.

It is not conscience, however, that causes parents to love their children or a child to love its parents. Parents love their offspring, first, because it fulfills a biological necessity: a completely unloved child, if it does not physically die, would become a psychological catastrophe. The species could not survive should parents not love and nurture their progeny. No parent is completely loving toward a child; nor is any parent completely devoid of affection. Nurturing is always a matter of degree. The imperative to love one's children is powerfully supported, additionally, by what Freud called the compulsion to repeat. There is a tendency to think about the compulsion to repeat in its negative aspects only: having been battered as a child and grown to parenthood, a person will most probably batter his or her own child. The compulsion to repeat, however, operates with the same power in regard to beneficial behavior: having been nurtured, one desires to nurture. Basic love is not the result but the foundation of conscience. Conscience becomes important in situations of conflict, when love is challenged by instinctual forces in opposition to it.

Love, being so important, so powerful, and so pleasurable, would reign supreme in the world if it lived alone in our psyches. The drives toward hatred and aggression, the desires to dominate, degrade, and destroy other human beings are the primary hindrances to loving behavior. The most important human situations are those in which loving and aggressive desires are in conflict. Conscience becomes crucial in situations of moral conflict, of ambivalence toward a person or group of people—as in Huckleberry's dilemma or the story told by Coles's informant. If one has absolutely no desire, for instance, to domineer over people subordinate to one, there is no need to appeal to conscience to assist in sustaining mutuality. However, if one is tempted—as everyone is tempted—to mistreat subordinates, and if one's ultimate desire is to maintain a moral stance, the resort to conscience is inevitable. *Conscience is the primary mechanism in the psyche whereby conflicts between basic love and aggression are resolved in a moral (that is, loving) manner.* The capacity to make such resolutions, the ability to deal with aggression in a productive way—these faculties are essential for psychic health. Immorality, conversely, is the resolution of such ambivalent conflicts on the side of aggression. All immoral behavior—fascism, racism, child seduction, wife-beating—is aggressive. That psychoanalytic theory which refuses to equate moral behavior and psychic health (Hartmann's)[8] still recognizes that the failure to handle aggression leads to pathology. But the theorists do not identify immoral behavior as an illegitimate satisfaction of the aggressive drives. There is always a potential psychological danger in the acting out of illegitimate aggressive inclinations; immorality and aggressive satisfaction can never be uncoupled. Immoral behavior may not be a manifestation of psychopathology, but it is always symptomatic and problematic for the psyche. Any movement from an immoral to a moral stance is always in the direction of increasing psychic health, because it always represents a diminution of aggressive acting out.

Freud lost his way in his thinking about morality when he ignored the powerful need of the child (and the adult) to return nurturing for nurture given. He takes no cognizance of the child's desire to please the parents—for its own sake—and says that prior to the birth of the superego, the child is controlled *only* by punishment and fear of the loss of love.[9] He does not conceive that the desire to love back can also be a powerful impetus toward socially acceptable behavior. His emphasis, in his discussion of the compulsion to repeat, is primarily on its negative aspects. The desire to please the parents is not the same thing as the anxiety that they will cease to love if one does not satisfy them. The distinction is crucial. The hallmark of nonauthoritarian child rearing is that it emphasizes the longings to reciprocate love in preference to the threat of punishment. Freud is correct when he sees the threat of punishment underlying superego imperatives—but this is yet another indication that we need to go beyond the concept of the superego to discover the sources of morality.

The great conflict between Eros and the aggressive drives dominated Freud's thinking in the latter part of his life. He spoke very little about the basic human drive toward destruction (that is, aggression) until he was over sixty years old. The modern index to the *Introductory Lectures on Psycho-Analysis*, originally published in 1916–17—lectures that are a very lengthy summary of Freud's thought to that date—contains only two references to aggression. From the end of World War I until his death in 1939, the aggressive drive was a major preoccupation for Freud. As it became clearer and clearer to him how pervasive and how powerful was the human inclination to destruction, he obviously began to ask himself how it was that human destructiveness had not succeeded in totally dominating personal and social life. How is it, he must have wondered, that any healthy personal life or stable society is possible, given the strength of the destructive drive? As a result, Freud began to talk about love and its power in personal and social life in a manner he had never before engaged in. He continued pessimistically uncertain whether Eros would succeed in triumphing over Thanatos, but he remained convinced that it was neither reason nor intelligence nor science—nor the superego—that would contain the destructive drive. Only Eros could serve humankind in that struggle.

In *Group Psychology and the Analysis of the Ego* (1921), Freud attempts to discover what it is that holds any society together. He proceeds to give us a brilliant discussion that distinguishes with great clarity between sexuality and love:

Libido is an expression taken from the theory of the emotions. We call by that name the energy, regarded as a quantitative magnitude (though not at present actually measureable), of those instincts which have to do with all that may be comprised under the word "love". The nucleus of what we mean by love naturally consists (and this is what is commonly called love, and what the poets sing of) in sexual love with sexual union as its aim. But we do not separate from this—what in any case has a share in the name "love"—on the one hand, self-love, and on the other love for parents and children, friendship and love for humanity in general, and also devotion to concrete objects and to abstract ideas. Our justification lies in the fact that psychoanalytic research has taught us that all these tendencies are an expression of the same instinctual impulses; in relations between the sexes these impulses force their way towards sexual union, but in other circumstances they are diverted from this aim or are prevented from reaching it, though always preserving enough of their original nature to keep their identity recognizable. . . .

We are of the opinion, then, that language has carried out an entirely justifiable piece of unification in creating the word "love" with its numerous uses, and that we cannot do better than take it as the basis of our scientific discussions and expositions as well. By coming to this decision, psycho-analysis has let loose a storm of indignation, as though it had been guilty of an act of outrageous innovation. Yet it has done nothing original in taking love in this "wider" sense. In its origin, function and relation to sexual love, the "Eros" of the philosopher Plato coincides exactly with the love-force, the libido of psycho-analysis. . . . and when the apostle Paul, in his famous epistle to the Corinthians, praises love above all else, he certainly understands it in the same "wider" sense. But this only shows that men do not always take their great thinkers seriously, even when they profess most to admire them.[10]

Freud is bending the truth, of course, in his indication of the public relations problems of psychoanalysis. There was no "storm of indignation" from the public about Freud's emphasis on love in this discussion; it was Freud's insistence on the overwhelming importance of sex that had the citizens angered at him from the beginning. Including love in the definition of libido, and implying that love of mankind and of abstract ideas were manifestations of _instinctual energy_ were certainly radical notions, and Freud was clearly uncomfortable in setting them down. It was not the general public, however, but only the small group of those concerned with psychoanalysis who might create an uproar.

Love, Identification, and the Origins of Conscience

Freud's most powerful investigation of the aggressive drive and its potential for destroying the whole civilized world as we know it was set down in *Civilization and Its Discontents*. Within this essay, Freud speaks ardently and ambivalently both for and against civilization. The work also contains some of Freud's most impassioned discussions of love. No healthy human being can look undistortedly at the worst things people can do to each other without becoming frightened, without seeking aid from those forces in the psyche that can, possibly, tame destructive impulses. The brilliant clarity with which Freud perceived why man is wolf to man, "*homo homini lupus*," made the discussion of love inevitable.

> I may now add that civilization is a process in the service of Eros, whose purpose is to combine single human individuals, and after that families, then races, peoples and nations, into one great unity, the unity of mankind. Why this has happened, we do not know; the work of Eros is precisely this. These collections of men are to be libidinally bound to one another. Necessity alone, the advantages of work in common, will not hold them together. But man's natural aggressive instinct, the hostility of each against all and of all against each, opposes this programme of civilization. . . . And now, I think, the meaning of the evolution of civilization is no longer obscure to us. It must present the struggle between Eros and Death, between the instinct of life and the instinct of destruction, as it works itself out in the human species.[11]

It must be emphasized that Freud writes that civilization is in the service of Eros, and not vice versa. The superego, when it enters this picture, is certainly subsumed under civilization. In the hierarchical ordering of love-conscience and civilization-superego, it is important to observe that Freud, in this instance at least, gives the highest priority to love. An exact connection between love and conscience was never made by Freud, but he did come very close to doing so in an essay *Why War?* published three years after *Civilization*. There he does use the crucial word "identification." It is identification with other human beings that enables conscience to generalize concerns of love and nurturance to those who are not kin. Freud writes:

> If willingness to engage in war is an effect of the destructive instinct, the most obvious plan will be to bring Eros, its antagonist, into play against it.

Anything that encourages the growth of emotional ties between men must operate against war. These ties may be of two kinds. In the first place they may be relations resembling those towards a loved object, though without a sexual aim. There is no need for psycho-analysis to be ashamed to speak of love in this connection for religion itself uses the same words: 'Thou shalt love thy neighbour as thyself.' This, however, is more easily said than done. The second kind of emotional tie is by means of identification. Whatever leads men to share important interests produces this community of feeling, these identifications. And the structure of human society is to a large extent based on them.[12]

The superego is not mentioned; that instrument, steeped in the threats of punishment and castration, with its own commitments to aggression, is of no value in preventing war. We know, and I am sure Freud would readily agree, that when the decision is made to launch the missiles that will permanently blacken the sun, the superego, with its corrupt imperatives to save the world from communism or capitalism, will give the command. Without the power of love, identification, and conscience we would long ago have lost our world.

Though Freud had no shame in talking about love and Eros as more than just manifestations of raw instinctual libido, he hardly mentions or analyzes the great source of a healthy relationship to Eros: the mother-infant dyad. Freud knows that only love and identification can save us, but he does not speculate on what will determine whether humankind will, ultimately, choose Eros or Thanatos. He does not reveal to us what we now know with certainty: that the determination between Eros and Thanatos, between love and destruction, goes on in a thousand ways every day between a child and its primary nurturer(s). The experiences of infancy are ultimately played out in Hiroshima and Auschwitz, and antithetically in the lives of moral leaders such as Gandhi and Martin Luther King. So much of the world's misery results from the fact that when politically empowered, he who cannot identify with his fellow human beings becomes a killer. The capacity to make these crucial identifications is fundamentally dependent on the quality of the nurturing that a child receives. The truth of this assertion is supported by everything we have learned about the essential human processes of identification with the nurturer and the comforter. We must accept Freud's emphasis on Eros as leading us toward a recognition of the role of the mother in the origins of conscience, but we must also understand that the use of this abstract mythological personage both reveals and disguises simultaneously. It reveals the importance of love for human survival on both the personal and social levels, but it also hides from us the fact that Eros is nothing more, and nothing less, than an abstract, symbolic, and sublimated representation of the mother who nurtured us.

Identification

In the very first year of a child's life it begins two psychological activities that are essential for psychic development and psychic health: it starts to return love to those who love it, and it accomplishes this by the mechanism of identifying with the nurturer. Though we can talk about these two processes separately, in reality there is no unyoking them—there is no identification with the nurturer without loving back, and the child does not conceive of returning love without having first identified with the nurturer. The whole process results from the fact that no healthy human being takes in food, love, or care without ultimately expressing the desire to give the same to someone or something else. "The counterpart of the passive fantasy of being suckled," writes Ruth Mack Brunswick, "is the active oral fantasy of suckling. . . . One must never lose sight of the fact that every passive fantasy acquires its active counterpart, and that this play of interchanging roles is one of the chief characteristics of childhood."[13] Spitz describes several of those delightful circumstances, familiar to all parents, when the infant first endeavors to feed the mother back. At seven months and sixteen days: "The mother, holding the child in her lap, is feeding the child from the bottle and introduces the nipple into his mouth. The child accepts it, sucks, *and at the same time pushes his finger into the mother's mouth.*" At thirteen months and three days: "There are no problems with his drinking milk from a cup, but when he is offered cake, noodles, etc., he is more interested in offering these to his mother than in eating them himself."[14]

We are all under a powerful psychological compulsion to do unto others as was done to us. The feeding of the mother by the child is the prototypical activity of a psychological mechanism that is immensely important in personal and social life. One crucial result of giving back nurturing is that it ultimately makes possible the perception of the reality of other people. If the nurturer remains for the child merely an omniproviding machine, serious psychological disorders must result. The child who never adequately learns to nurture back will know only how to take love and, grown to be adult, will be accomplished only in using other people for its own purposes. Rousseau has beautifully described the *auspicious* resolution of this development:

> A child's first sentiment is to love himself; and the second, which derives from the first, is to love those who come near to him, for in the state of weakness that he is in, he does not recognize anyone except by the assistance and care he receives. At first the attachment he has for his nurse and his governess is only habit. He seeks them because he needs them and is well off in having them; it is recognition rather than benevolence. He needs much time to understand that not only are they useful to him but they want to be; and it is then that he begins to love them.[15]

At first, the child exhibits an almost indiscriminate drive toward identification. Just as the infant, at a certain point in the oral stage, insists on putting into its mouth everything that its hand can master, no matter whether the object is beneficial or harmful—a promiscuous mouthing—just so Spitz describes a veritable orgy of identification beginning in the sixth month of life:

> From my observation of infants, I have gained the impression that at this age, between six and eighteen months, the wish to identify is so strong and plays such a major role in object relations, as well as in the need for mastery, that the child identifies indiscriminately with any behavior of the love object he is able to appropriate. It is as if the mechanism of identification at its inception would go through a phase of nondifferentiation. It is indulged in by the child for identification's sake, as it were. It is used for object relations, as well as for mastery, for defense as well as for attack. Perhaps this indiscriminate way of appropriating *everything* that is available from the love object—things, gestures, inflections, actions, attitudes, etc.— explains the origin of identification with the aggressor.[16]

Love, Identification, and the Origins of Conscience

Three basic modes of identification—all of which are crucial for the development of conscience, all of which are operating with significant effect in the first two years of life—have been distinguished by Rosalind Gould: identification with the provider or protector (the nurturer), identification with the aggressor, and identification with the victim.[17] It is essential to look at each in detail. Before that, however, we may observe that identification with the nurturer and the aggressor are in conflict with each other, and it may very well be that conscience is the psychological form whose function it is to resolve such conflicts.

IDENTIFICATION WITH THE NURTURER

The undifferentiated drive toward identification is undoubtedly responsible at first for the imitative behavior the child exhibits when feeding the mother. As development proceeds, however, the healthy child learns to discriminate between the various modes of identification, and feeding back becomes loving back. John McDevitt writes:

> Due to the infant's immaturity, the first internalizations or incorporations are in the form of merging or primitive global imitations. Later, as his developing nature permits, the child takes over from his parents those selective identifications that are essential elements in the development of his object relations. Identifications contribute to the development of the self and of psychic structure. They also modify and enrich object relations.

What McDevitt is describing is one of the processes leading to the development of psychic health. There is no sound psyche without the capacity to "modify and enrich object relations," and there is no healthy conscience without this same capability. A well-functioning ability to identify with the nurturer is essential for both health and conscience:

> Furthermore, by actively showing care and concern for the doll, the child repeats the same behavior and emotions that the mother has shown toward him and begins to develop the *capacity* and means of *actively expressing* comforting and loving *feelings* toward others. Donna, over the next two and a half years, frequently demonstrated the same care and concern toward younger children and a favorite playmate that she had shown toward her doll.[18]

There is no question, in my view, that temperamental (constitutional and genetic) factors greatly influence this process of the origins of conscience. We are talking of various capacities: to identify, to discriminate, to prefer (for whatever instinctual reasons) identification with the nurturer rather than identification with the aggressor. As to capacities, individuals differ enormously. Despite the existence of these differences, however, the mode in which the child is nurtured cannot help but significantly influence its ability to identify with the nurturer and to deal productively with the need for aggressor-identification. That better-than-adequate nurturing will reinforce the power to identify with the provider is obvious to anyone who has thoughtfully raised a child or who has observed the psychic development of small children. Gould, on the basis of her observations, succinctly concludes: "A child who experiences essentially positive nurturing in its first year of life will acquire . . . distinctly associated schemas of a 'conscience' by about age two."[19]

Taking cognizance of all these observations of children, and recognizing the intimate connection between adequate nurturing and concern for *others*, we may wonder what psychological conflict causes thoughtful psychoanalytic theorists to make an absolute separation between psychic health and morality. The therapist, writes Hartmann, "in his therapeutic work . . . will keep other values in abeyance and concentrate on the realization of one category of values only: health values." This stance is required by the theoretical observation that announces that "psychoanalysis as a science cannot be expected to provide us with ultimate moral aims, or general moral imperatives; these cannot be deduced from its empirical findings."[20] Such ambivalence about morality most probably has its origins in an ambivalence about the source of that morality. Splitting in regard to mothers and women generates splitting in regard to morality.

No claim is being made here that, from the adult point of view, a child of two experiences imperatives from a fully developed conscience. It is equally true, however, that not even the most avid supporter of the primacy of the superego in the area of moral development would claim that a child of five has attained a fully developed superego. A two-year-old's conscience is as much a conscience as a five-year-old's superego is a superego. And no significant conflict between superego and conscience is possible until adolescent or adult years. Such conflict entails a challenge to the corrupt values of the superego, a challenge that necessitates the subjection of the values of parents and/ or society to criticism. Only in adolescence does the psyche become potent enough to generate such a critique.

Not only human beings, but even animals, it appears, find the basis of "social action" in a repetition of the nurturing situation. Midgley tells us that "As soon as the [care of the young] became current (chiefly among birds and mammals, though teleost fishes and certain reptiles did some of the pioneering), it provided an excellent repertory of gestures that could be used to soothe anger, to beg for help, and in every way to oil the wheels of society. . . . *it is at this point—long before the emergence of primates—that nature ceases to be Hobbesian.*"[21]

Freud, most probably, would have found this mode of reasoning unacceptable in the 1920s when he introduced the superego to the world as the representative of humankind's "higher nature." It is not surprising to discover, however, that in his younger days he had made the exact same connections that are being made here. "This path of discharge," he writes to Wilhelm Fliess at the turn of the century, in a letter that formed a part of *The Project*, "thus acquires the highly important secondary function of *establishing human contact*, and it is the early helplessness of human beings that provides the *original source of all moral motives*."[22] It is probably no longer possible to ascertain whether, at that time—as in later years—Freud would have said that this first human contact was provided by the father.

IDENTIFICATION WITH THE AGGRESSOR

Identification with the aggressor is a psychological process whereby the child incorporates into itself real or imagined aggressive behavior on the part of people in its environment, usually its caretakers, and thereupon acts the part of the aggressor, either in reality or fantasy. Having swallowed the aggressor—or merely certain aggressive attributes of a caretaker—the child may make either itself or some other person the victim of its aggressive behavior and fantasy. This psychological mechanism is of crucial importance in the life of adults as well; we are all familiar with the aggressor-identification aspects of brainwashing experiences, or concentration camp inmates who became surrogates for their masters. And adults exercise the same option as children, victimizing either themselves (masochism) or other people (sadism, immorality), or, most probably, doing some of each. Anna Freud[23] explicates identification with the aggressor as a mechanism of defense used by the ego to resist dissolution. A child who, for instance, having been nurtured by a caretaker, finds itself being brutally beaten by that same person faces the serious possibility of loss of ego cohesiveness. The child's defense against this threatened dissolution is to incorporate the aggressor-caretaker into itself, saying, in effect: "I am not a child being beaten, I am an adult who beats children." That such a child grows up to be a child beater itself is a well-established phenomenon. Without question, the mechanism of identification with the aggressor is crucial to all immoral behavior, whether of a personal or social dimension: child beating, racism, sexism.

Whether Melanie Klein is correct, or not, that such psychological incorporations are already operative in the first or second month of a child's life, there is no question that identification with the aggressor is manifest in the child's behavior by fifteen months and is an important psychological attribute by the end of the second year of life. Long before the superego comes on the scene, the ground is fully prepared for all future moral and immoral behavior.

The degree to which the child's personality and character are ultimately constructed of aggressor-identification elements is crucially important for the health of the psyche and the happiness of the individual. The extent of aggressor-identification is determined by three factors. Of first importance is the degree to which real aggressive behavior exists, from caretakers, siblings, and others in the environment—child-beating or molestation are only the most dramatic ways of being aggressive toward a child. Second, all children, even the most beneficially nurtured, have conflicts about aggression springing from *internal* causes. The child's autonomous aggressive feelings are projected onto the caretakers, demonstrating to its satisfaction that it is *they* who want to harm the child, not the child who entertains destructive fantasies about its nurturers. In this circumstance, dissimilarities in temperament and psychological constitution can make a significant difference. Independent of the environment, all children differ in the amount of aggression they have to deal with and in the various capacities they possess to sublimate, repress, displace, and contain aggressive drives. A child with strong aggressive inclinations and small capacity to deal with them is fated to incorporate a large degree of aggressor-identification mechanisms, regardless of how beneficial its environment may be.

The third factor determining the degree of aggressor-identification, the one we find significantly operative in the average "normal, neurotic" adult, is a combination of the first two factors. A slightly aggressive action on the part of the caretaker is exaggerated to catastrophic proportions by the projection of internal conflicts within the child, with the result that the parent appears to be much more aggressive than he or she really is. The mother becomes a witch, the father a castrator. This exaggerated, distorted view of the aggressor is then incorporated, resulting in serious identification-with-the-aggressor activity and fantasy.

Spitz discerns the initial manifestations of identification with the aggressor in the first half of the second year of life, when the child starts saying "No, no!" to itself in a role-playing game.[24] Even here, however, we can observe the identification-with-the-aggressor process already modified and "humanized" by an identification with the nurturer. The prohibiting parent undoubtedly engenders aggression from the infant who does not wish that its desires should be thwarted. Reinforced by the process of projective identification just described, the child conceives that the parent has established the prohibition as a result of the parent's anger. As a defense against the parent's, and its own, wrath, the child identifies with the aggressor and internalizes the prohibition. Should we observe a child shouting "No, no!" to its doll or stuffed animal, and then severely whacking it, we easily postulate identification-with-the-aggressor behavior. But this is not what Spitz perceives; he observes the child in a role-playing *game*. Anyone who has watched children carefully knows that in such games sternness and soothing behavior are mixed together; a good proportion of identification with the nurturer is combined with aggressor-identification. We may, in fact, postulate that such a compromise is exactly the point of the game. The child, angry at the prohibiting parent and yet recognizing, unconsciously and not too clearly, that the parent has erected the prohibition for the child's own good—that it is another extension of caring activity—creates the game of "No, no!" in order to integrate this conflicted situation into its psyche. Identification with the aggressor, unalloyed with any nurturing virtues, is a dangerous activity. The game of "No, no!" is a manifestation of psychic health and represents a very different situation from one in which the parent is actually cruel to the child who, regardless, is compelled to internalize such behavior.

Though identification with the aggressor has been described as a "defense mechanism," too much use of that defense is an indication of pathology. Gould insists that children can be categorized as displaying a primary identification with the aggressor or with the provider/protector, and that those in the former category already display signs of psychic disorder:

> The struggle to be good in children who manifest a predominant identification with aggressor is discernably different than in those with a predominant identification with provider. Within limits, the aggressor-identification case may serve to bind the separate strands of do's and don'ts experiences, and play a major role in governing the child's good behavior in reality. But the intrapsychic resultant is, in effect, the installation of an internalized opposition, and at the extreme a persecutory enemy of one's me-self, rather than its guardian. As such, it will tend to be more subject to projection (or re-projection), and as a directive influence on behavior, relatively inconstant.... Several interrelated cognitive affective features have been noted, as consequences, in some of the study children manifesting prominent (but not unmitigated) identification with aggressor:
>
> (a) self-condemnation tends to be global rather than limited to the specific bad act;
>
> (b) magical thinking, in areas apperceptively associated with aggression and power by the child, tends to persist despite other developmental advances in thought and reasoning;
>
> (c) a relative sense of unsafety or fluctuating certainty is arousable in such circumstances, beyond expectable developmental limitations;
>
> (d) both the creative range and defensive utility of fantasy appear constricted thereby, as is also the child's ability to develop some trust in his own impulses as good or controllable.[25]

Identification with the nurturer is so essential for psychic health because it is the only effective defense against destructive drives and identification-with-the-aggressor symptomology. "A major reason," writes Gould, "for a fundamental relation between positively charged protector-provider experiences in infancy . . . is that these generate an elemental capacity for empathy and remorse-anxiety in the child for the primitive destructive impulses which . . . are not uncommon in early human development."[26]

This momentous struggle between aggressor- and nurturer-identifications has a fundamental impact on the origins of both conscience and the superego. A healthy conscience depends on the triumph of nurturer-identifications and containment of aggressive manifestations. "The point is," remarks Gould, "that identification-with-aggressor does not a conscience make. Rather, it tends to stimulate and magnify . . . anticipated consequences, sealing off primitive aggressive imagery and related magical thinking from developmental reality-testing and impulse-driven modifications."[27] The superego, on the contrary, has identification with the aggressor as both midwife and primary means of support. Without the capacity to identify with the aggressor, the superego would be forced to go out of business. Spitz recognizes this when he considers "this form of identification with the aggressor, in which the child plays the mother's role and applies the prohibition to himself, as one of the primordia which will go into the later formation of the superego."[28] And Freud's description of the birth of the superego—as we have seen—reads like the most apt illustration of the identification-with-the-aggressor process. "The superego is . . . not simply a residue of earliest object-choices of the id [towards mother and father]; it also represents an energetic reaction-formation against those choices. Its relation to the ego is not exhausted by the precept: 'You *ought to be* like this (like your father).' It also comprises the prohibition: 'You *may not be* like this (like your father)—that is, you may not do all that he does; some things are his perogative.' This double aspect of the ego ideal [superego] derives from the fact that the ego ideal had the task of repressing the Oedipus complex."[29] And when the Oedipus complex is "smashed to pieces" by the threat of castration and the male child renounces his oedipal goals, giving up the desire to possess the mother sexually, in effect he is castrating himself into psychological impotency in order to preserve his anatomy intact. Essentially *he identifies himself with the father's supposed aggres-*

sive intentions toward him. What role does identification with the nurturer play in this grisly drama of the birth of the moral function? In Freud's narrative, a very insignificant role, if any at all.

IDENTIFICATION WITH THE VICTIM AND THE COMFORTER

In discussing the mechanism of identification with the victim, it is important to establish immediately that I am *not* talking of a masochistic identification with a person destined to be defeated in life's struggles. I am speaking of a *distanced* identification that allows one the expression of pity, compassion, and solace without having to *become* the victim. Rousseau believed that such capacity is the very basis of moral life:

> Thus is born pity, the first relative sentiment which touches the human heart according to the order of nature. To become sensitive and pitying, the child must know that there are beings like him who suffer what he has suffered, who feel the pains he has felt, and that there are others whom he ought to conceive of as able to feel them too.
>
> But when the strength of an expansive soul makes me identify myself with my fellows, and I feel that I am, so to speak, in him, it is in order not to suffer that I do not want him to suffer. I am interested in him for love of myself, and the reason for the precept is in nature itself, which inspires in me the desire of my well-being in whatever place I feel my existence.[30]

Hegel was referring to the identical psychological process when he talked of the recognition of self in others. And Freud, early in his psychoanalytic life (1905), even before he had seriously begun to think about the aggressive drives, recognized that identification with the victim was a primary counter to destructive impulses: "Cruelty in general comes easily to the childish nature, since the obstacle that brings the instinct for mastery to a halt at another person's pain—namely a capacity for pity—is developed late."[31] The German word translated as "pity" is even closer to the concept being elaborated here: *Mitleiden* means suffer with, the capacity to suffer with.

We now know, from careful observation of children, that the capacity to suffer with develops quite early in the child's life, many years before the superego makes its dramatic appearance on the psychic stage. Manuel Furer describes "a significant step forward in development" of the child when, around fourteen to eighteen months, he or she first expresses consolation or sympathy toward the mother and, in many cases, verbalizes the feelings by saying "I'm sorry." "The child is conscious of harm that he or someone else or something else has done to a person whom he loves; he is able to feel along with the person . . . and then to express to the object his sympathy or concern."[32] Furer describes such behavior as "identification with the comforter," wherein the child steps into the place of the parent who has previously comforted it. What keeps this mechanism of identification with the victim from being an expression of masochism and passivity is precisely the fact that an identification with an active, powerful parent is essential to the expression of compassion.

What is so important in the development circumstance Furer describes is that multiple capacities for identification come together in this one experience. First, the child recognizes (not consciously) that the parent is not omnipotent, that he or she also can feel pain, as the child knows it can. Second, the child comes to see that it can give pain in the same way that it has known the parent could. Third, the child becomes aware that one can give pain to someone loved. And fourth, the child must identify with the comforting, nurturing aspects of the parent who has given love and pain and controlled its own anger toward the child by emphasizing love.

Furer does not distinguish in this article between the circumstance where the child is the cause of the parent's pain and that where something else is the cause. We can imagine if a parent falls down, cuts him-/or herself, and begins to cry, a child of eighteen months could respond as Furer describes. From the psychological point of view, however, that would be a far different thing than the case where the child, either through defiance or misbehavior or indication of distaste for, or displeasure in, the parent, is itself the cause of the parent's discomfort. In such circumstance, the child can arrive at the point of saying "I'm sorry" only after it has renounced its own anger, its own pleasure in the parent's suffering. (The story that Robert Coles reports about school integration provides remarkable confirmation of this, including the pronouncement of the exact same words, "I'm sorry.") The arrival of the child's capacity to resolve a situation of ambivalence toward the parent in the direction of love and comfort is, most certainly, a critical developmental step. This resolution cannot be achieved without the adequate sublimation of aggressive drives, and that sublimation, in turn, cannot be accomplished without an adequate identification with the victim and the comforter.

What is so powerful in the mechanism of identification with the victim is that it *transforms an identification with the aggressor into an identification with the nurturer*. Faced with another human being in a hapless situation, two primitive negative modes of responding are inevitable. First, one perceives the victim as a loser in life, one destined for failure; a slight feeling of terror that the same could happen to oneself creates the need for distance, and one withdraws, announcing, in effect, "He is not me." Second, one responds with aggression; the victim is a perfect vehicle to carry one's aggressive needs to satisfaction; he cannot hit back. Aggression also helps maintain the barrier between oneself and the unfortunate one. This mode of response to another's failure and suffering is beautifully illustrated by a custom in certain societies: if a man's wife deserts him, instead of offering him compassion and solace the remaining male members of the village proceed to despoil the man's hut of everything that is in it.

The only positive alternative to these negative responses is to identify with the victim's pain and suffering and to offer pity and compassion—in effect, to play the role of nurturer toward someone in need. Margaret Mahler tells the story of the child Teddy, who consistently alternated between these two fundamental modes of reacting to others' suffering:

> Teddy's reactions to another child's crying . . . were interesting to observe. He just would not bear to hear another child cry. This seemed somehow to stimulate his aggressive defensiveness; unprovoked he would attack other children. His undeniable awareness of separateness and vulnerability seemed, however, to have given rise to a new capacity for empathy, which was expressed in positive ways as well. Teddy, who often showed this aggressive reaction when he heard another child cry, at other times reacted quite sympathetically to the moods of other children. For example, he would bring his own bottle to Mark when Mark was crying, or else he would approach Harriet with great sympathy and interest on a day when she was in an obviously low mood.[33]

Love, Identification, and the Origins of Conscience

We must ask why it is that some people—if not most people—are incapable of an adequate identification with the victim. We may then begin to see that such inability results from failure to handle problems of aggression, failure to get "good enough" nurturing, failure to separate adequately from the symbiotic mother. If we see such matters in this light, we may start to perceive that moral action and psychic health are intimately related to each other.

In summary, the capacity to identify with both the nurturer and the victim is essential to both conscience and a healthy psyche. This conclusion never could have been reached by a psychoanalytic theory restricted to oedipal and post-oedipal life. The fundamental weakness in Freud's theory of morality and the superego is that it ignores the pre-oedipal life of the child. It is of interest to observe that every one of the analysts whose work is used in this chapter has worked with children in the pre-oedipal stage. Freud became intensely aware, late in his life, of the importance of that stage of psychic development, and he did attempt to evolve new insights about female sexuality from that perception,[34] but the theory of morality and the superego was left undisturbed. It is only in the last thirty-five years that a new generation of analysts, trained in the observation and treatment of children, has come forward with theoretical insights that enable us to construct a much more adequate theory of moral action. McDevitt has succinctly described the crucial importance of the earliest years of a child's life:

> Identifications with a mother's loving care foster the very beginnings of love and concern for others. I am suggesting a developmental progression in which the human bond, trust and confidence, mutual love, and altruism have their roots in the preoedipal mother-child interaction and the internalizations that result from this reaction.[35]

It is no exaggeration to state that the whole structure of society is ultimately dependent on an adequate identification with the nurturer. Talcott Parsons, whose concern for abstract, obtruse social theory seems to be as far away from the mother-infant dyad as thought can be, has nevertheless explicitly made the connection between nurturing and the very possibilities of culture: "Culture . . . is a system of generalized symbols and their meanings. In order for the integration with affect, which constitutes internalization, to take place, the individual's own affective organization must achieve levels of generalization of a high order. The principal mechanism by which this is accomplished appears to be through building up of attachments to other persons—that is, by emotional communication with others so that the individual is sensitized to the *attitudes* of the others, not merely to their specific acts with their intrinsic gratification-deprivation significance."[36] Reward and punishment alone will not do it, Parsons is saying. The superego, whose main weapons are the giving of satisfactions and chastisements, cannot a culture make. Without conscience human beings could never come together in any kind of stable society. Freud knew full well that it was Eros which held society together, but he would never have argued that our first experiences with Eros are in the oedipal predicament. Without identification with the nurturer and with the victim—left only with identification with the aggressor—the fabric of the social world as we know it would be torn asunder. Conscience—the ability to reconcile aggressive/loving conflicts on the side of order and Eros—is our only secure defense against our impulses of destruction, impulses toward both ourselves and the world we live in. Morality is an absolutely necessary condition of psychic health.

11

The Capacity and the
Need for Idealization

ALL HUMAN BEINGS have a capacity for idealization: the ascription of attributes of perfection, beauty, excellence, and power to self, parents, siblings, loved ones, children, ancestors, nation, the political and economic system under which one lives. Beyond capacity, we have the *need* to give expression to this potential. The word "need" implies that there is an energy operating that fuels this faculty for idealization. What kind of energy I cannot say, but failure to use sufficiently the psychic capacity to create ideal images results in an impoverishment of the psyche. Idealization is an essential activity contributing to psychic health.

Many readers, when working through this chapter, will respond: "Oh, that's the ego ideal," reflecting the tendency of psychoanalytic theory to turn all psychic capacities into instruments, structures, or departments of the mind. Superego is one such metaphorical structure, and in response to that kind of metaphorization I myself have countered superego with conscience, seemingly another such structure. Some also contend that we have, somewhere, an ego ideal, an additional psychic instrument. This structuralization of the mind could go on forever, if we turn every psychic capacity into an instrument. The capacity and the need for identification could be called "the interego" and the capability of abstracting and generalizing these identifications could be designated "the omni-ego." The necessity and capacity to create symbols, accordingly, could be characterized as "the symbol-ego." With so many different egos, we would begin to wonder where the ego itself has gone. The truth is, of course, as Jacob Arlow—as orthodox a Freudian as there is—has said, the ego does not exist in the way we conceive of the liver or the heart existing. The ego, as Arlow wryly comments, "resides within textbooks and monographs on psychoanalytic theory."[1] "Ego" is a metaphor that brings together in one symbol the various capacities that the psyche possesses to think rationally, to order the world, to test reality, to preserve existence, to balance and compromise alternatives, and so on. For some reason we have a need to think of all these various, but related, psychic capacities as being under the direction of one particular structure of the mind, a structure that is supposed to serve certain basic psychic functions and have its own "interests." Such a structure does not exist. What do exist are the various needs and capacities of the psyche—any of which may be in conflict with any of the others, regardless of whether they belong to the same exclusive structure "ego" or to other "structures."

Up to a certain point, these metaphors—ego, superego, id—are extremely useful in our attempt to understand psychic conflict, and their continued use is theoretically legitimate, provided we do not forget that we are describing things metaphorically, not actually. When we read in Freud that "To the ego, therefore, living means the same as being loved—being loved by the super-ego, which here again appears as the representative of the id,"[2] we are in the world of drama and myth, not of "science." There are nonetheless many truths to be discovered in those realms, and therefore there is no reason to repress the metaphorical mode of talking about the psyche, provided we continually bear in mind what mode of discourse we are actually using. Ultimately, understanding may require the use of many different modes of discourse.

I have found the metaphorical use of the word "superego" useful in this work even though I recognize that we are only talking about the psychic capacity to internalize permanently certain values given by parents and society. I have also spoken of "conscience" as if it were an instrument, not just a capacity, as if it were *the* moral instrument in the psyche. The designation "superego" has a long, clear history, and there is a high degree of agreement as to what it means. If a writer contends, for example, that Western culture suffered in the nineteenth century from too much superego and suffers now from too little, one may agree or disagree with the contention, but it is quite clear what he intends to say. Freud described the superego, its workings, and its origin at great length.

"Ego ideal" carries no such authority or history. Very few theorists would even agree as to its meaning, its date of birth, its relationship to the superego, and so on. For my purposes there is no reason to metaphorize the psychic capacity to create ideals, and theoretical clarity is aided by leaving it as it is. I talk of a mode of psychic action, not of a structure.

If one were to use the metaphorical mode, one could say that the ego ideal is the heir of the narcissistic position, just as the superego is the heir of the Oedipus complex: "He is not willing to forego the narcissistic perfection of his childhood; and when, as he grows up, he is disturbed by the admonitions of others and by the awakening of his own critical judgment, so that he can no longer retain that perfection, he seeks to recover it in the new form of an ego ideal. What he projects before him as his ideal is the substitute for the lost narcissism of his childhood in which he was his own ideal."[3] In Freudian terminology, the ego ideal, whose birth precedes that of the superego by several years, is ultimately incorporated into the superego after its establishment at the end of the Oedipus complex: "The superego is also the vehicle of the ego ideal by which the ego measures itself, which it emulates, and whose demand for ever greater perfection it strives to fulfill."[4] What this metaphorical mode of description of structures and instruments misses is a certain dynamic understanding of what really occurs. The intense, all-consuming narcissism of early childhood must be given up if the psyche is to remain healthy, but nothing that important psychologically is ever merely abandoned; it must be transformed, sublimated. The psyche's capacity and need for idealization is the mechanism by which the narcissistic view of the world is transformed into a more mature, more developed position. The ego ideal does not replace the narcissistic mode; a more transforming, more sublimated, more distanced mode of idealization replaces a primitive one. One finds ideals in others, in things, in art, in ideas, and not merely in one's self. One is no longer the only beautiful, perfect thing in the world, but beauty and perfection can still exist. They do not have to be abandoned—a point made succinctly and dramatically by Hartmann when he writes that "the setting up of the ego ideal can be considered a rescue operation for narcissism."[5]

This capacity for idealization, although it deals fundamentally with perfection and beauty, also concerns itself inexorably with power. The more primitive conceptions of omnipotence are also transformed into ideal conceptions of potency. In the first stage of omnipotence, the child imagines itself as all-powerful. This position cannot be totally abandoned but is transformed and sublimated by the transfer of omnipotence to the parents and ultimately to the gods, so that they now provide the safety and security that was previously supplied by self-omnipotence. An idealized view of how powerful and protecting the parents are is essential at a certain stage of psychic development; we can see how important this conception is for religion.

Though it is essential to move beyond the narcissistic position and beyond the very first grandiose transformations from narcissism, it does not follow that the ultimate aim of the healthy psyche is eventually to eliminate—in the interest of science or the reality principle or whatever—all the idealizations of childhood. Such a situation would, itself, be pathological. Speaking of that mythological time after the structure "superego" has incorporated the structure "ego ideal," Edith Jacobson writes: "The superego, this unique human acquisition, becomes the one area in the psychic organization where, by virtue of a reactive reversal of aims, the child's grandiose wishful fantasies can find a safe refuge and can be maintained forever to the profit of the ego."[6]

To illuminate exactly what happens, this descriptive mode of one psychic structure incorporating another is unnecessary. I have spent so much energy in this book making the point that the superego is corrupt by definition, because it internalizes immoral values of the parents and the culture, that I am afraid sight has been lost of the fact that the metaphorical superego also incorporates many, many *moral* values:

honesty, loyalty, love of family, friendship, democracy. The average, normal parent constantly emphasizes for the child the validity of certain idealized views of the world. "You are a wonderful, beautiful, brave, intelligent, capable child!" "Your parents are all-loving, all-caring, all-providing, all-protecting people!" As the child matures, it is told, with emotion, that it is a wonderful country in which we live, a marvelous religion that we practice, beautiful music or art or scenery that we pursue. It is not to be wondered that, at the end of the Oedipus complex, when the psyche engages in an extraordinarily intense period of internalization of parental values, idealized values should be among those taken in. We need no notion of a structure called "ego ideal" to explain the process.

This capacity and necessity for idealization is of unequaled importance for morality and the exercise of moral action, and by adding the concept of ideal values to our argument, we advance the discussion of morality far beyond the mother-infant dyad into the world of adolescence and adulthood, where idealized values play an enormously important role.

In the beginning, the two objects of idealization are the self and the parents. As the child grows, uncles, aunts, older brothers and sisters, teachers, sports stars, rock singers, political figures of the past or present are added to the list. Once a child achieves adolescence, it is even possible to glorify immoral behavior. An adolescent son in a slightly criminal family could idealize his father, for instance, as a brilliant corrupter of politicians. For the young child, however, this kind of corrupt idealization is impossible; he idealizes only those aspects of the parents, or parent surrogates, that are loving, beautiful, or powerful. Power, though also wanted for its own sake, is primarily the source of protection, security from harm and anxiety. In essence, the small child idealizes the parents for doing what parents are supposed to do; he sees them as wonderful—not "good enough"—parents. "There is no doubt that this ego ideal is the precipitate of the old picture of the parents, the expression of admiration for the perfection which the child then attributed to them."[7] Aggressive, corrupt, uncaring, selfish, pathological behavior is not idealized; it is, in fact, severed from the glorified image of the parents, creating the split—in Melanie Klein's metaphor—between the good mother and the bad mother. This glorified, idealized image of the good mother (parents) is suffused with actions that are intimately intertwined with the origins of morality: loving, caring, pitying, protecting, encouraging. Such an idealized image is essential for psychic health; the child who lacks it remains extremely vulnerable to pathology.

This capacity and need for idealization immediately becomes integrated with the various processes of identification, and the more the child identifies with the good, idealized images of the parents, the greater are its chances of following a normal road of psychic development. Spitz succinctly defines identification as "the attempt to *be* as the love object *is*."[8] The difficulty, as discussed before, is that the love object is also seen as aggressive and unloving, and identification with the aggressor is an ever-present danger. Identification with an idealized, loving object is essential for overcoming this situation of conflict. Klein writes:

> For I assume the ego develops largely round this good object, and the identification with the good object shows externally in the young child's copying the mother's activities and attitudes. . . . A strong identification with the good mother makes it easier for the child to identify also with a good father and later on with other friendly figures. As a result, his inner world comes to contain predominantly good objects and feelings, and these good objects are felt to respond to the infant's love. All this contributes to a stable personality and makes it possible to extend sympathy and friendly feelings to other people.[9]

It is interesting to observe how simply and naturally Klein's discussion shifts from the description of psychic health to an image of moral behavior. Psychic health is directly dependent on a capacity for sublimation, both of the more primitive sexual impulses and of aggressive drives. "It is a well-known fact," writes Hartmann, "that disturbance of identification often leads to disturbance of sublimation."[10] If adequate sublimation is dependent on adequate identification, which in turn is dependent on adequate idealization, then we are correct in finding the origins both of a sound psyche and a robust morality in this same psychic mechanism. Freud, not surprisingly, had seen the connection between idealization and morality and expressed it in the very letter to Putnam that opened this work: "So one could cite just my case as a proof of your assertion that such an urge toward the ideal forms a considerable part of our inheritance. . . . if one had the means of studying the sublimation of instincts as thoroughly as their repression, one might find quite natural psychological explanations."[11] The superego, however, especially as described by Freud, is not an instrument of sublimation but one of brutal repression. The correct vision of the origins of moral sentiments was lost when the superego took center stage as the moral structure *par excellence.*

Klein, in defining the path to psychic stability, focuses on some contradictory psychological mechanisms. The problem that must be overcome is that the child experiences both intense affection and intense rage toward the primary nurturing parent, usually the mother. The mother, in her turn, is never 100 percent loving toward the child; aggression always occupies too great a space, even in "good-enough" nurturing. The child feels its own rage as coming from itself and also projects much of it onto the mother, disavowing its internal origin. The child also both perceives and denies that the mother could be aggressive toward it. All this fuels the mechanism of splitting, wherein the "good breast" and the "bad breast," the image of the "good mother" and the "bad mother," are sundered from each other: the imago of two *different* mothers now exists in the psyche. After this splitting has been accomplished, Klein tells us, psychic health ultimately demands that it be reconciled and healed. The mother must be seen as *one* person with good and bad qualities; the child must come to accept that both loving and destructive impulses come from itself. Failure to cure this split results in psychopathology, the degree of which is directly related to the extent of the unreconciled fissure within the psyche. On the other hand, however, as the quotation just given indicates, a stable psychic development also requires the preservation and enhancement of the imago of the idealized good parent or parents. The average healthy person can accomplish both these operations, can both incorporate the bad mother and still preserve an idealized image, and at times of crisis can productively regress to the world of the idealized, good, caring, omnipotent mother.[12] In serious illnesses, for example, especially those that ultimately turn out satisfactorily, there is a healthy glorification of the doctors and nurses who—in this primitive part of the mind—have brought about the cure.

This inevitable splitting of the image of the parents inescapably influences the whole process of identification. The "bad parents" invite identification with the aggressor; the "good parents" invite identification with the comforter, nurturer, provider. Splitting makes both these forms of identification necessary. The mature psyche that can reconcile this split and yet maintain the glorified imago of the good parent can also accomplish a rather difficult, but necessary, psychological task, that which Jacobson has designated "selective identification." This latter process means, simply, the psyche's deciding to be like the parents in certain respects and unlike them in others. The child may become identified with the parents in caring about music but reject identification when it decides not to be interested in sports. A child may decide to identify with his parents in the process of becoming extremely ambitious but decline identification when deciding *not* to become a doctor. One can identify with the parents when they demonstrate that they feel loving and caring (within the family) is important and yet refuse identification when they express aggression against people who are not within the family: Jews or Blacks or poor people. In situations where the parents give an ambivalent message, the child may internalize the parents' ambivalent stance, but the psychologically mature child has the option of selecting one aspect of that ambivalence and identifying with it while rejecting the other. When told that all men are created equal but women are not the equal of men, a child has three essential options: internalize the contradiction, emphasize the aggressive valence, or identify with the moral stance. To accomplish the latter, the child will make use of the parents' ambivalent relationship to equality and will emphasize the internalized, idealized image of the good parents that has been preserved intact: "But it was *you* who told me that all people are created equal." Jacobson asserts that this faculty for selective identification is essential for the establishment of the child's separation and individuation; the extent of its use, therefore, becomes a measure of psychic health:

> Moreover, the selectivity of identifications increasingly expresses the child's rebellious struggle for the development and maintenance of his own

independent identity, since it means: "In this respect I like you and want to be like you, but in other respects I don't like you and don't want to be like you; I want to be different, in fact myself."[13]

All this has great implications for the theory of morality and the superego. The more primitive (and pathological) the process of superego formation is, the more castration anxiety plays a role at its birth, the more it will reflect the exact image of the parents' value system, with all its contradictions and gross immoralities. The more mature and developed (the healthier) the process of superego formation is, the greater will be the child's options and freedom to select the values it finds conducive to its own view. It is at this point that moral progress becomes possible. At this moment the role of conscience is crucial, because *conscience, we can now see, is inexorably intertwined with the imago of the idealized "good" parent—compassionate, loving, nurturing, powerful.*

No claim is being made here that a child of four or five has made discriminations in its superego about how racist, sexist, or egalitarian that structure (if it is a structure) is to be. But there should be no question that a fateful decision has been made about how harsh and punishing, as opposed to how loving and nurturing, the incorporated parents are to be experienced. The story of little Hans dramatically demonstrates the transformation of a harsh, punishing, castrating superego into one of freedom and promise—in a very young child. There is no doubt but that there was a radical change in Hans' view of the world, how much good and how much evil it contained. The critical question for the superego is how much or how little its contents reflect the idealized image of the good parents; how much of a part is played by identification with the aggressor, as opposed to identification with the nurturer; how much of a role conscience plays in its function. Here, the role of child rearing is of vast significance. Authoritarian child rearing and a harsh and punishing superego are of a piece; they are the cause of each other. A mode of child rearing that fundamentally rejects the temptations to tyrannize over children will produce a far different system of values. The story of little Hans, his neurosis and his cure, is a parable of the transition from nineteenth- to twentieth-century child rearing. It is, over and over again, the struggle between Eros and destruction.

It is no exaggeration to say that the whole fabric of society is dependent on capacities for identification and idealization—that, without these, no social system would exist. The great tradition of sociological analysis created by Durkheim, Weber, and Parsons has laid great stress on the value system within culture and within society. A system of shared values—decisions, sometimes ambivalent, sometimes clear-cut, as to what actions and attitudes are considered legitimate and which illegitimate—is at the core of any social system, and no social change is possible without a corresponding change in the system of values. The sharing of these values is made possible by the mutual identification of people with each other, and this in turn is made possible when people recognize—not necessarily consciously—that they share the same *idealized* views of the world. "Social feelings," Freud says, "rest on identification with other people, on the basis of having the same ego ideal [that is, superego]."[14] All value systems consist, in good part, of idealized values. No society has ever been erected on the proposition that we are all thieves together in this thing. Even the utilitarian notion that society can consist of a series of justly balanced "interests" is a psychological impossibility, because human nature dictates that *ideals*, not only values, are essential for society.

In the later years of his life, when he was free to look, undisguisedly, at human destruction, Freud saw clearly that the only weapons humankind has in the effort to preserve society are Eros, identification, and idealization. One way to prevent war, Freud says, is to encourage identifications and the community of feeling, emotions that represent, to a large degree, the foundations of society.[15] The fundamental human problem, however, is that bad, destructive, pathological values are capable of being shared and idealized. People can experience intense identification with each other because they partake of the same evil intentions. The superego in Nazi society was entirely dependent on this tragically ironic psychological mechanism. One powerful reason that makes it almost impossible for human society to eliminate warfare from its repertory of social action is the fact that warfare appeals profoundly to certain identifications and idealizations. A country never feels so united, people never experience such closeness to others in society, corrupt idealized images of masculine power and courage never ring so plausibly, as when the trumpets blare, the banners unfurl, and the young men march off to their death.* If the rituals of warfare were incapable of idealization, such slaughter would long ago have disappeared from the world. One symptomatic resolution of the conflict between the imagos of the "good" parent and the "bad" parent is to emphasize identification with the aggressor and then idealize the aggressor's actions, as a way of satisfying the repressed Eros. The "good" parent, then, does "bad" things. A fascist society is impossible without this particular psychological maneuver.

The great problematic within the concept of idealization, therefore, is that idealization, just as the superego, is capable of corruption. Corrupt idealized values are incorporated into the superego as easily as moral values. Conscience remains our only defense against moral anarchy.

The dependency of idealization and identification on basic love, affection, Eros is as true for society as it is for the individual psyche. Without emotional affect, there can be no value system. From a certain point of view, therefore, *all* values are idealized values because we learn them from people whom we love. The community of feeling is a manifestation of sublimated Eros. In order to get to the plane of social action, consequently, the psyche has to traverse a four-step process: basic love and nurturing, identification, idealization, and incorporation of values. From the point of view of morality and psychic health, the problematic lies in the fact that, at each stage of development, the process of adequate resolution may break down, resulting in symptomatic or pathological compromise formations that feebly attempt to resolve conflicts. Basic love and nurturing, to begin with, is a situation fraught with ambivalence; the drives toward destruction play too great a role in this drama. Identification also becomes problematic because the parents themselves most often carry pathological and/or morally corrupt values. Idealization suffers from the deep conflicts surrounding the problem of splitting. And the incorporation of values is fundamentally dependent on the capacity to generalize from the family to society as a whole, and this process presents its own multifarious possibilities

---

* This powerful insight into the nature of warfare I owe to Kurt Thompson, a graduate student in the sociology department, University of California, Berkeley.

and conflicts. The intellectual and moral problem of how we get from the mother-infant dyad to a society of over 200 million people making moral decisions every day is, thus, prodigiously complex. In the following chapter an attempt will be made at least to sharpen the questions that must be asked if we are ever to understand that fateful process.

12

Moral Contradictions in Adult Life

W HEN "in the middle of life's journey" I became intensely occupied for a period of ten years, locally and nationally, with the politics of peace and arms control, several circumstances in regard to moral action were particularly striking. First, it was startling to discover that there were many people in Washington, most particularly members of Congress, who approached the issues of the war in Vietnam, the cold war, and arms control primarily from a moral perspective. True, everyone desired to be reelected, but one could observe many elected officials who were far ahead of the voters of their districts on these issues, with their positions many times placing them at electoral hazard. During those years (1969–79), several of the finest members of the Senate and House went down to defeat because they would not compromise their commitment to a rational peace.

Equally unanticipated was the observation that there seemed to be so little correlation, within individuals, between the morality of public issues: peace, racial matters, civil liberties, concern for the disadvantaged; and moral behavior on the private level: personal honesty, treatment of subordinates, attention and concern with one's own family. I leave on the side the questions of alcoholism and driven sexual behavior because, from the psychological point of view, these problems seem to be of a different order than those of day-to-day relationships with people around one. I was not surprised to find as many alcoholics and sexual libertines on the "dove" side as on the "hawk" side, but I had naively expected that those who fought for racial equality, peace in Southeast Asia, and so on, would, in general, treat their subordinates with more respect, take fewer bribes, and be better spouses and parents than those whose political positions were opposite. It turned out not to be true. Politically admirable and courageous individuals would treat their staffs with contempt, neglect their families (particularly their children), and avail themselves of all kinds of illegitimate money. An adequate psychological theory of morality (conscience and super-ego) is obliged to try to explain such behavior, because, in all its variations, it is prototypical of the world. Novelists, for instance, delight in bringing it to our attention.

Nor is it necessary to travel all the way to Washington to observe the phenomenon. Typical is the individual in, let us say, a church or a synagogue who is a model of communal concern: always volunteering and working hard, visiting the sick, chauffering children whose mothers are indisposed, giving charity even when it involves some personal sacrifice. And yet that same person, on the political level of action, can easily vote a racist, elitist, militarily aggressive politics. This same kind of intense splitting on moral issues is observed in the equally typical example of the psychiatrist acutely interested in the welfare of his or her patients, to the point where the pleasures of a weekend or a vacation may be interfered with, who yet severely neglects the psychological needs of spouse and children. Everyone is able to give of themselves in some areas of life and not in others.

An archtypical example is patriotism, which can involve a genuine love of one's country and all the people in it, and even a willingness to die for its interests, combined with an intensely aggressive stance toward those who are outside the boundaries of Eros. It is a question of moral boundary setting. No healthy individual lives alone; everyone of any achieved maturity has a moral concern with a group of other people. Even the most politically reactionary individual is truly concerned for the welfare of some group, be it only white millionaires. No society, or subgroup within society, is possible without Eros: "We will try our fortune, then," Freud writes, "with the supposition that love relationships (or, to use a more neutral expression, emotional ties) also constitute the essence of the group mind. . . . Our hypothesis finds support in the first instance from two passing thoughts. First, that a group is clearly held together by a power of some kind: and to what power could this feat be better ascribed than to Eros, which holds together everything in the world? Secondly, that if an individual gives up his distinctiveness in a group and lets its other members influence him by suggestion, it gives one the impression that he does it because he feels the need of being in harmony with them rather than in opposition to them—so that perhaps after all he does it '*ihnen zu Liebe*' ["for their sake," "for love of them"]."[1] The love remains in the group; aggression is directed outside.

When we observe, then, that even a Nazi behaves morally toward, has a true concern with, and a strong sense of loyalty to other Nazis ("Himmler believed and preached that the whole SS was based on the principle that 'we must be honest, decent, loyal and comradely to members of our own blood and nobody else.' ")[2]—observing this, we come to realize that the moral or immoral life of an adult is never a question of presence or absence but always of wider or narrower *limits*. The crucial question is: Where is the boundary of moral action drawn? The deeper question: Why is it ever drawn at all? When we found the origins of conscience in more-than-adequate nurturing and predicted that a child well nurtured would grow up with the desire to cherish others, we did not then ask: How many others? One's own kin? All those of a particular religious faith? All white people? Everyone, regardless of race or religion, in one's particular country? All people? It is a long way from good nurturing to a morality that can include all people. Clearly, there are many more steps in the development of an adult conscience than the very first one of basic love and caring. Let us make an attempt to discover what the further stages of moral development, and the psychological conflicts entailed in those steps, might be.

The relationship between the post-oedipal superego and pre-oedipal experiences of nurturing and aggression must leave a definite mark on adult moral conflicts; traditional psychoanalytic theory makes a contribution toward understanding those relationships. In this work, I have been so intent on rendering a critical judgment on the theory and the nature of the superego, so determined to demonstrate that the superego is corrupt by definition, that there has been almost no discussion of the fact that the superego also incorporates the *moral* imperatives of the parents and society. And more than just moral imperatives: the specific attitudes of nurturing, consoling, encouraging are ultimately internalized into the superego "structure." "Not only the prohibitions of the parents," writes Hartmann, "but also their love survives in the relation of the superego with the ego."[3] This is a view ultimately based on Freud's notions of the superego; in terms of emphasis and amount of discussion, a minority view, it is true, but one that Freud adhered to nonetheless. "If it is really the superego which, in humour, speaks such kindly words of comfort to the intimidated ego, this will teach us that we have still a great deal to learn about the nature of the superego. . . . And finally, if the superego tries, by means of humour, to console the ego and protect it from suffering, this does not contradict its origin in the parental agency."[4]

Freud's ultimate view of the superego, which I accept as valid, is that at the end of the Oedipus complex there is an intense period of incorporation of the values of the parents. Commands and imperatives that had previously seemed to come (and most times did come) from outside—and therefore were "not myself"—now appear to come from inside and are, certainly to a much greater degree than before, "myself." There is a merging of values and self. These values, as has been argued here at length, can as easily be immoral as moral, as easily corrupt as wholesome. All the loving, caring, comforting, encouraging, idealizing actions of the parents—with which the child has identified—now become internalized and structured in a way they were not before. The same is true of all the destructive attributes of the child's reality. It is apparent, therefore, that the superego is not only corrupt by definition but also morally wholesome by definition, which inevitably results in the fact that the superego is eternally *in conflict with itself.* If we use nonmetaphorical language, which abjures the structures of the mind, we may say simply that internalized immoral values and imperatives are eternally in conflict, within the psyche, with internalized moral values. The psychic stance, vis-à-vis morality, is inevitably ambivalent.

One prevalent symptomatic way of resolving this conflict, one readily available compromise formation that gives satisfaction to both sides of this ambivalence, is a form of splitting whereby the loving, nurturing aspects are lavished on certain people—"my people"—and the destructive, corrupt imperatives are unleashed onto others. Whether this splitting is as flagrant and as primitive as that advocated by Herr Himmler, or whether it is a common, ordinary, grass-snake variety of patriotism as demonstrated, for example, by the absurd but hardly tragic or catastrophic Falklands war between Argentina and England, it is still the same splitting mechanism demonstrating its power to resolve conflict. The English have a love feast with each other while they collectively beat up on the Argentinians. From similar motives, the truly morally committed senator fights for peace and civil rights while simultaneously degrading his staff and ignoring his children. This intense conflict within the superego relates directly to a more primitive conflict over the basic nurturing situation itself; we shall return to that aspect of the problem later.

Freud's analysis of the nature of the superego also contains a particular problematic in regard to structural analysis. Freud's last model of the psyche sees it as a structure composed of three parts: ego, id, and superego. *All* psychic action is subsumed under one of these three sections; all neuroses are the result of a conflict between one component part of the mind with another; ego versus id, superego versus ego, and so on. Structurally speaking, however, the situation is slightly confused. Freud does not discuss the matter in these terms, but from his description of these component parts it appears that the ego and the superego are themselves structures—analogous to the heart and the lungs—whereas the id clearly is an unstructured source of energy. The ego, within which structure we find various psychic mechanisms such as reality testing, mediation between id and reality, calculation of means and ends (rationality), the instinct for survival, and so on—this ego nonetheless does not incorporate into itself any previously formed psychic structures. With the superego, this is not the case. The ego ideal is a psychic structure predating the birth of the superego, and it is incorporated into the superego once the latter is formed: "One more important function remains to be mentioned which we attribute to this superego. It is also the vehicle of the ego ideal by which the ego measures itself, which it emulates, and whose demand for ever greater perfection it strives to fulfill. There is no doubt that this ego ideal is the precipitate of the old picture of the parents, the expression of admiration for the perfection which the child then attributed to them."[5] The ego ideal, in an adult, then becomes a structure within a structure, like the Bureau of Indian Affairs inside the Department of the Interior.

The Bureau of Indian Affairs may have "interests" that are at variance with the main "interests" of the Interior Department as a whole. Is the same true of the ego ideal within the superego? This kind of conflict is referred to in present-day psychoanalytic theorizing as "intrasystemic conflict," that is, conflict within the system superego.

The metaphorical mode of describing the psyche is useful when it gives us insight into actual conflicts in adult life. It is my contention that the picture of an ego ideal structure incorporated into a superego structure does not illuminate moral conflict but obscures the real source of conflict, and that may possibly be the reason such a cumbersome picture was constructed in the first place. Moral conflict results from the fact that we have incorporated into our psyches attitudes toward others (patriotic jingoism, as an example) that claim to be right and legitimate but are, nevertheless, immoral. And we know them to be immoral—though that knowledge is probably only unconscious—because we have incorporated other attitudes, all of which may be subsumed under the one heading "Eros," that pronounce a negative judgment on any acting out of the destructive drives. Two things are essential to bring a child to health and to lay a satisfactory foundation for psychic development: the child must be adequately nurtured and it must be taught to control, in some manner, the most primitive aspects of the aggressive drives. Through identification with and idealization of the parents, the child comes to regard these two attributes of its upbringing as "good" and their opposite as "bad"—the beginnings of conscience, as I have used the term. As the child matures into an adult, it learns to equate what is good with what is moral and what is bad with what is immoral. No matter what kind of immoral attitudes (racism, sexism, jingoism) it is ultimately taught and which it ultimately incorporates, there always remains a part of the psyche that knows that only loving attitudes and the control of aggression are truly moral. We may remember that it was Freud who told us that "the normal man is far more moral than he knows."[6] We do not need the notion of ego ideal to explain ambivalence within the superego; all we need is the knowledge of the inescapable conflicts resident within that partly corrupt "moral instrument."

In addition to moral contradictions originating within the psyche, it is also true that we cannot think of the ultimate moral contradictions of adult life without being cognizant of the role of society in establishing social norms. The overwhelming majority of people eventually end up with a superego and a moral position almost identical to, or only slightly changed from, that of their parents. When these people do differ from their parents' value system, the change usually reflects the path that social values have traversed in the twenty to thirty years between generations. If society has become less racist and sexist, we would expect to find most people moving in that same direction, while attempting to remain compatible with their parents' values. Once the intense period of adolescent revolt and idealization are over, there seems to be a very powerful psychic tide compelling a person to imitate his or her parents. The transition involved in becoming adult—career, marriage, parenthood—seems to be so treacherous that it allows, in most cases, for very little selective identification. The compulsion is not merely toward imagos of adult behavior but also toward specifics within the system of values. In the attempt to become a mother or father, one feels compelled to behave like one's own mother or father.

And it is here that we observe most keenly a great contradiction between psychic health and morality. I have been told of a psychoanalytic patient who came from a family with strong anti-Semitic attitudes. Having rejected those values in adolescence and having attended a liberal Ivy League school, this young person found herself in psychological difficulties while attending a professional graduate school, and went into analysis. As the analysis began to "take" and the desires for some kind of reconciliation with the parents became vivid, the young woman commenced to feel and express anti-Semitic feelings (the analyst was not Jewish, which negates the possibility of this being a negative transference manifestation). The moral conflict manifested resulted from the young woman's desires to get back in touch with the positive (loving, nurturing, idealizing, moral) attributes of her relationship with her parents; the all-powerful need for identification necessary for this process indiscriminantly incorporated aspects of the parents that directly contradicted the loving, idealized view of them. In the ultimate interest of Eros, an attitude of aggression was legitimated. A lesser good was given up for a greater; the Jews were sacrificed for the parents' love and approval.

I was not told whether the patient ultimately came to the point where she was healthy enough to reject that particular aspect of her parents' value system and still feel reconciled with the idealized image of the "good" parents. The experience is described here in order to demonstrate the kind of moral conflict that most people are subject to as they attempt to become adults in a world of corrupt superegos. Freud recognized that, for most people, there was something healthy in the desire to be like the parents, regardless of their values. That moral contradiction did not bother him; he merely endorsed an unreconcilable split between morals and health. Writing to Putnam in June 1915: "The unworthiness of human beings, including the analysts, always has impressed me deeply, but why should analyzed men and women in fact be better. Analysis makes for integration but does not of itself make for goodness. I do not believe, as do Socrates and Putnam, that all vices originate in a sort of obscurity and ignorance. I feel that one puts too great a burden on analysis when one asks that it realize each of one's dearest ideals."[7]

The superego, as ultimately constituted, incorporates two different sets of values: familial and social. Parents teach a child, first, how they think it is appropriate to behave in family situations: with mother, father, siblings, near relatives. Authoritarian or egalitarian, loving or aggressive, generous or stingy, exuberant or depressed, optimistic or pessimistic, anxious or reasonably calm, separated or engulfed, frightened or free. All of these value decisions are independent, to a greater or lesser degree, of Jews, Blacks, women, slaves, warfare, imperialism, capitalism, democracy. The parents, however, have opinions that they communicate to the child on all these social issues, and no one-to-one correlation exists between these two different moral systems. More-than-adequately-loving parents in a slave society will still teach their children the legitimacy of that institution.*

---

* I do believe that there is a direct correlation between the mode of child rearing and social institutions—that, for example, one cannot have a democratic society when all children are swaddled, given out to wet nurses who are partly the practitioners of infanticide, and are not taught the values of separation and individuation. Also, I do

The child incorporates—or rejects—both these sets of values, or aspects of each set. In the metaphorical usage, the superego of an adult is the precipitate of a private and a public world of values. The concept of the superego becomes, then, from the theoretical point of view, a crucial point of contact and intermingling between the theory of the psyche and the theory of society. In the sociological theories of Durkheim and Parsons, "the social role of moral norms" plays a crucial part, and the theory of the superego is a precise link between personal and social morality. "This concept of the superego," writes Parsons, "forms one of the most important points at which it is possible to establish direct relations between psychoanalysis and sociology."[8] What Parsons does not elaborate upon, and what is essential to acknowledge if we are to understand the system of moral norms within society, is that the superego—for all the reasons just amplified—is in a constant state of conflict within itself: eternal war between corrupt and honorable, moral and immoral, rages within it. The system of moral norms that controls society is, in its very nature, racked with ambivalence. The cannibal is ambivalent about acting out his cannibal fantasies[9]; the slave owner in a Christian society never, unconsciously, reconciles his tyranny with his conscience*; the Nazi both admires and despises the Jew he exterminates.

In summary, to achieve even a reasonably adequate adult life a person must be properly nurtured as a child. Such nurturing, through the mechanisms of basic love, identification, and idealization, results in an image of the world as good and loving—the basis of what I have been calling "conscience." The society in which one lives legitimizes and certifies as correct certain social actions that are aggressive, immoral, and contrary to the loving view of the world we carry within us. The superego of an adult, therefore, represents not only the moral attributes of the psyche but is itself a compromise formation that attempts

---

believe that children who are told that if they touch it again, the doctor will come and cut it off, do not grow up and have the courage to march in the streets against a war in Vietnam, against the police with their truncheons and tear gas. That is a subject, however, much larger than this book, although I have attempted in chapters 3 and 4 to touch upon the connection between changes in child rearing and changes in society at large.

* Eugene Genovese, personal communication.

to reconcile—with greater or lesser degrees of success—the various moral and immoral imperatives within society and the psyche.

All of this, by itself, gives a rather forlorn picture of the possibilities of moral progress, especially when we recall how important the approval of the parents, and the internalization of their values, becomes at the entrance to the adult world. Two important psychic mechanisms, however, have yet to be discussed, mechanisms that represent crucial stages in the development of the moral sense. In adolescence, especially late adolescence, moral questions become subject to the psychic capacity to generalize and to abstract. In addition, received morality may be greatly transformed by the psychic need to question parental authority.

Generalization and Abstraction

I am postulating five crucial steps in the development of adult morality: basic nurturing, identification, idealization, generalization and abstraction, and questioning parental authority. The first three primarily concern infancy and childhood; the two last become important in adolescence, late adolescence, and early adulthood. Each step or stage is subject to conflict, and the primarily healthy or pathological resolution of conflict in early stages will affect subsequent ones. Failures of basic nurturing will negatively influence identification and idealization. These last two are intimately related to each other; poor identification can either result from or cause inadequate idealization. In general, a felicitous experience of nurturing, identification, and idealization will result in a vigorous moral capacity. The course of adolescence, the occasion when moral questions are consciously addressed for the first time, will be profoundly influenced by these childhood experiences, but adolescent history is by no means completely determined and has an autonomy of its own. Moral positions at that time will be acutely influenced by actual political and social experiences (most dramatically, the war in Vietnam, the integration of the schools, the efflorescence of feminism, the rise of Naziism); by current activities of the parents, in the areas of work, marriage, and political or social action; and by certain skills, talents, and interests of the particular adolescent, attributes that have an independence of childhood experience.

No transition can be made between family experience and society; no transformation of identification with the nurturer into a genuine concern for the disadvantaged; no erection of a system of laws, values, and morals—none of this is possible without the capacity to generalize the experiences of childhood and to recast them by means of a high level of abstraction. Freud writes: "In the course of development the superego also takes on the influences of those who have stepped into the place of parents—educators, teachers, people chosen as ideal models. *Normally it departs more and more from the original parental figures; it becomes, so to say, more impersonal.*"[10]

Parsons, one of whose major interests was this capacity for abstraction, commented: "Culture . . . is a system of generalized symbols and their meanings. In order for the integration with affect, which constitutes internalization, to take place, the individual's own affective organization must achieve levels of generalization of a high order." The importance of this faculty for psychic health is revealed in his discussion of the father symbol.[11] Arguing from the point of view of the male child attempting to resolve oedipal struggles, Parsons comments that it is not necessary for the child to become (as an adult) *his* father, but *a* father. Becoming his father, actually taking his father's place, is much too risky and a psychological impossibility. But a child can generalize the notion of fatherhood, based on the specific reality of his own father and other fathers he has known, and then incorporate that abstract image. In the land where there is only the father, only one can exist; but in a world of fatherhood, there can be many fathers. Without this capacity for generalization and abstraction, psychic health is impossible, and many have noted the crippled capacity for abstraction exhibited by psychotic patients.[12]

Equally essential is generalization for the establishment of an adult moral position. "To prevent pity from degenerating into weakness," writes Rousseau, "it must . . . be generalized and extended to the whole of mankind. Then one yields to it only insofar as it accords with justice, because of all the virtues justice is the one that contributes most to the common good of men."[13] In essence, good nurturing, idealization, and identification are transformed into the concept of justice through the capacity for generalization.

Why, however, do some adults extend their experience of good nurturing to "the whole of mankind" and others stop this process of generalization short at the boundary of religion, or race, or class, or country? The ambivalences and conflicts surrounding nurturing, identification, and idealization undoubtedly play their role, and I will look at that later, but here I would like to suggest something of a different order. Human beings differ profoundly in their capacity to generalize and abstract. Just as some have a greater capacity for physics or mathematics or music or baseball than do others, so, correspondingly, some have a greater potential for generalizing and abstracting moral considerations. We say that someone has a talent or a gift or even a genius for chemistry or basketball; equally so, we can observe individuals with a talent, gift, or genius for moral generalization. For such people, moral action becomes a necessary condition of existence. Just as Titian could not live without painting, as Freud could not live without confronting the irrational, just so people like St. Francis or Gandhi or Eugene Debs could not live without forcing moral issues to the highest level of generalization.

Ordinary people, lacking talent and genius, nevertheless differ in their capacities for intellectual and artistic accomplishment, for sport, or for manual achievement. Moral generalization is also such a skill, and, in adolescence, just as some discover they must have music or sport or an intellectual life, so others discover that they cannot and will not live without attention to moral ideals. The experiences of infancy and childhood undoubtedly influence the final adult outcome, but the unique quality of personality should not be underestimated. It may indeed be that the fundamental difference in approach to moral issues, for instance, between J. J. Putnam and Freud ultimately comes down not to childhood history or even to cultural diversity but to differences in the individual need and capacity to generalize moral considerations.

This absolute necessity to generalize and abstract moral ideals is the principal portal through which reason enters moral discourse. Philosophers, like composers and mathematicians, have a gift and a strong need to exercise capacities for generalization and abstraction. It is the abstract nature of their thought, and not the subjects dealt with, that makes the works of many philosophers so difficult to comprehend, even for the intelligent, educated lay person. Abstracting and generalizing represent one essence of the reasoning capacity. Because these capacities are essential for the attainment of an adult moral position, it is no wonder that many have mistaken reasoning as the *source* of our morality, especially when deep psychological conflicts (discussed in chapter 9) are propelling the individual toward the same intellectual position. That ultimate morality is not an either/or proposition as regards emotions and reason, but a both/and circumstance, seems a reasonable hypothesis, a view lent support by the statement of Rousseau just cited, where he argues the necessity to generalize the feeling of pity.

No argument is being made here that the moral stance is in any way dependent on a general intellectual capacity. At most it may be a necessary, but hardly sufficient, condition of moral action. We need no Gallup Poll to inform us that there is absolutely no correspondence between intellectual capability, or degree of education, and a truly moral political and social position. One dinner party among the elite will enlighten us. If reason were the source of our morality, we would expect to find the most moral people among those most capable of reasoning. Here again, we need no extensive social research to determine the truth or falsity of that proposition. What is being argued is that some people have a talent or a gift for morality, and that for such a heightened morality to exist, a good heart is not enough. In order to care for "the whole of mankind," one must have a particular capacity to generalize moral experience, which is a far different thing from the general capacity to reason. Everyone has that morally generalizing capability to some degree or other, but it is enormously vulnerable to the pressures of parents and the society in which one lives. It may be encouraged or discouraged, encouraged in some areas and discouraged in others. Without the keen support of parents or society, for most people any desire to generalize moral experience ends up as one factor in some ambivalent compromise formation. A factor, nevertheless, that should not be underestimated. For every individual, the degree to which he or she has a need and capacity to generalize moral experience is a significant component in his or her final adult moral position.

TOWARD A RECONSTRUCTION

Questioning Parental Authority

At a meeting of the Vienna Psychoanalytic Society in 1906, Freud touched upon a subject that was not destined to be very important in the corpus of his theoretical work; he rarely returned to it: "The capacity for independent judgment ... is acquired only when the human being begins to question parental authority."[14] In the years since Freud's death, the problems of independent judgment and the questioning of parental authority have occupied practically no space in the books and the journals of the psychoanalysts, even though independent judgment is a goal most patients in analysis wish to achieve, and one that almost all analysts have set for their own lives. Whether independent thinking and critical regard for parents are requirements of psychic health or not, they are certainly necessary to the self-esteem of any self-conscious member of current society. To be told that one is incapable of judging things for oneself, independent of parental opinions, is an insult to anyone over the age of fourteen. Achieving the goal of autonomous judgment is, obviously, no simple task, but one full of ambivalences and conflicts. One might have expected much more theoretical effort devoted to explicating the process. For a theory of moral development, it is essential to understand that no fully mature, adult moral stance is possible without a critical review of parental values. And no moral progress is possible without the exercise of the same psychological capacity.

Of adolescence, we have been told by psychoanalytic theory that one of its primary goals is to separate sexuality from incest, to transport sexual desire to an exogamous situation—away from the household. One must leave home in order to become a sexual adult. Adolescence, as William James has told us, is not only the time when a person becomes interested in sexual fulfillment, but also the occasion when powerful interests in music, history, politics, and so on, first arise. And powerful interests in morals and a moral system, we may add. Might there be a connection between the necessity of a nonincestuous sexuality, an independent interest in the intellectual "goods" of this world, and the capacity to question parental authority? It would be surprising

208

to discover that there was no connection. Autonomous sexual activity is, undoubtedly, more important to psychic health than independence of judgment and lifestyle, and more people obviously achieve an adequate degree of sexual autonomy than they do the latter; but yet, if maturity admits of degree, independent of the notion of health, the most mature situation must be that in which independence of judgment and action suffuses all areas of living.

Independence of judgment, I hasten to point out, does not denote a kind of extreme individualism wherein one has no "need" of, or regard for, other people. Autonomous judgment means simply the ability to think for oneself, reasonably free of the pressures of parents and society. "A consummation devoutly to be wished," but one impossible, as Freud has told us, without a critical response to parental authority, and one that very few people truly achieve in their lives.

As independence of judgment is a great human virtue, what effect, we must ask, will a superego, come to power over the ruins of an Oedipus complex smashed to pieces by the threat of castration, have on the possibility of achieving such integrity? Clearly, a profoundly negative effect. It is a remarkable tribute to the vitality of the human psyche that, in the midst of an authoritarian, harsh, punishing, threatening child rearing, any rebellious soul managed to reach the heights of autonomous thought and action. It is no wonder that the great symbol of such effort became the suffering Prometheus, his liver devoured nightly as punishment for daring to challenge parental authority. Freud himself, one such Promethean figure, demonstrates the ambivalence of his age. His own capacity for independent judgment becomes the very oxygen of his life, but his image of moral authority—the superego as a garrison in a conquered city—if true, would make it almost impossible for anyone else to aspire to that autonomy. Once again, we see the importance of the fact that the Oedipus complex should end on a note of triumph rather than despair.

Moral autonomy—the capacity to subject received values to critical judgment and to disavow inherited immoral values—is the final stage of the development of a system of moral values. Moral autonomy depends on the capacity for independent judgment in all areas, not just morals. And independent judgment requires the ability to challenge parental values without an intense fear of retribution—castration, in the psychoanalytic system of metaphors. Such capabilities do not appear by accident. A child must be educated to them, by parents and society. Only a superego primarily loving, encouraging, and idealized can provide a ground for such autonomous behavior. The fact that very few adults achieve this position does not surprise us in a world where our chief anxiety remains, year after year, whether the people in the "most advanced" nations will allow the planet to live. The quality of the superego is determined by the quality of child rearing and by the moral state of society. We return to where we began: the possibilities of moral development are revealed only through social evolution— only through history. The capacity to transform the value system of the parents is the crucial element that makes moral progress a real possibility.

Within the process of transformation of parental values we can observe how essential is the idealized view of the parents. In truth, we can successfully challenge the parents' or society's value system only with weapons provided by those agencies themselves. A society wherein all men are created equal can become a society with an insistent demand for female-male equality. Morally ambivalent and contradictory parents who have been nurturing and loving toward their children will provide an ideal image of equality that can be used to disavow inherited hierarchical values. We can observe how dependent each stage of psychic development is on the satisfactory resolution of the conflicts of previous stages. The more satisfactory is the internalized idealized view of the parents, the more possible it is to challenge the moral contradictions in their value system. The movement from a primarily authoritarian, oppressive mode of child rearing to a truly liberal, caring, enlightened mode has enormous implications for the possible transformation of society.

Summing Up

Five stages in the development of an adult moral sense have been postulated. Each stage generates its own particular conflicts and ambivalences, providing, in each situation, therefore, the possibilities of pathological outcome and immoral imperatives. To conclude this section of the book, it may be helpful to look at the five circumstances and the problematic in each. It is only a cursory look, but it demonstrates nonetheless how hazardous is the road to a truly moral condition:

STAGE	PROBLEMATIC
1. Basic love	Aggression, splitting, ambivalence
2. Identification	Parental unavailability, immoral values, identification with the aggressor
3. Idealization	Splitting, idealization of bad values
4. Generalization	Separation anxiety, society, incapacity
5. Questioning parental authority	Psychic inability, separation anxiety, fear of retribution

BASIC LOVE

Primitive rage makes it impossible to have an unconflicted experience of basic nurturing. Not only is the mother the original source of all love, compassion, comfort, and protection, and not only is she the original object of the child's desires to return love for love received, this same mother is also the original object of a fierce, unsublimated, unrepressed aggression; and even beyond this, through the mechanism of projection, the child imagines that the mother is also, at times, consumed with rage toward the child. Splitting is the first mechanism of defense erected in the attempt to contain this impossible situation. As the disjointed view of the mother begins to give way to the concept of one person with both loving and aggressive aspects, ambivalence becomes the characteristic mode of mother-child interaction. That ambivalence toward the first nurturer-destroyer is never healed, though love or aggression, to greater or lesser degrees, may predominate in the ultimate compromise. Conscience is born and tempered in this fiery furnace. To a greater or lesser degree of intensity, everyone remains ambivalent, throughout life's course, about the dictates of conscience. We became partisans of the war between Eros and destruction at our mother's breast, with the capacity to battle on both sides. Conscience is the finest hero and the greatest casualty of that war.

211

IDENTIFICATION

"To *be* as the love object *is*."[15] To be, nevertheless, as the hated object is. Identification is morally neutral. Identification with the aggressor is a fundamental problematic, if not *the* fundamental problematic, for the moral life. Both projection of the child's destructive inclinations and an accurate perception of the parent's ambivalences provide sufficient energy to fuel the identification-with-the-aggressor process.

The necessary accomplishment of *positive* identifications may be crippled, additionally, by the unavailability of the parents. Psychological and emotional unavailability or actual physical distance at crucial times will distort the normal process of identification with nurturing, comforting, protecting. In most traditional child rearing, the father has been inaccessible as a primary image for identification until much too late in a child's life. This has had grave implications for the moral sphere, creating, on the social level, an enormously costly split between a feminine world of caring and nonseparation and a masculine one of individuation, ambition, and destruction.[16]

IDEALIZATION

Idealization comes into the world as a necessary aid to the process of splitting. Only by separating out the negative aspects of the nurturing parents is it possible to preserve an imago of a benign world. A subsequent introduction of reality becomes necessary to see the mother or the father as *one* person. A high degree of negative introjects makes this process impossible without producing a pessimistic or cynical view of the world as essentially bad. Some people suffering from severe psychopathology never heal the basic rift. For most ordinary people, sentimentality ("Gee, Mom!") attempts to smoothen over a fissure that will not close. The most difficult task, and the one most essential for the development of the moral life, is to preserve, in a vibrant form, an idealized image of the parents, while simultaneously allowing for reconciliation with a real, whole person.

Idealization, like its twin, identification, may act in a morally neutral manner. Any action or any person that excels may be idealized, no matter what the moral content of the activity may be: Caesar, Napoleon, and Hitler are heroes to some people. The acting out of unresolved conflicts over nurturing and aggression plays a crucial role in determining negative idealizations. Equally important is the question of who and what the parents are. In the attempt to reconcile with inadequate or mediocre parents, or even with an inadequate or mediocre society, idealization is particularly subject to corruption.

GENERALIZATION

Any psychic activity that begins in earnest in adolescence must be profoundly influenced by the manner in which earlier psychic conflicts were resolved. Problems with nurturing, identification, and idealization must cast a dark shadow on the adolescent experience. Beyond that, however, everything is not fully determined by age fourteen, and the adolescent ordeal does have a certain autonomy. Generalization demands moving out and beyond the family experience. Separation anxiety now becomes a factor in limiting the moral field. Any breakaway from the kinship system creates anxiety, and one cannot generalize one's moral experience of good nurturing to humanity as a whole without leaving the restricted boundary of the kin. Such separation anxiety may very well explain the phenomenon of the person who leads a reasonably moral life within the restricted boundary of church, class, or race, and yet takes deeply hostile positions against those beyond the pale. When we recall Margaret Mahler's observations that there is an intense return of stranger anxiety during the crucial rapprochement stage of the separation-individuation process,[17] we can see the psychological logic in setting up those outside the kin as "other" and then directing aggression at them. One maintains a moral stance only within the confines of the symbolic family. We have to keep "others" at a distance because their existence raises the level of anxiety.

Generalizing moral experience to larger and larger units of humanity is also greatly inhibited by the state of society in which the adolescent finds himself or herself. In ancient Greek society, not one major voice of a philosopher, historian, playwright, or politician spoke out against the institution of slavery; this in a culture that produced the very beginnings of moral philosophy in the West. Even in regard to lesser matters, it is the rare young adult in the 1980s who can resist the enormous social pressures that are currently herding our young people in the direction of money values. Here again, problems of separation anxiety play a role. To maintain an autonomous moral position in the face of powerful social pressure requires a high degree of tolerance of the disquietude of separation. Most people lack that psychological capability.

QUESTIONING PARENTAL AUTHORITY

Every circumstance, personal and social, that conspires to make the end of the Oedipus complex a catastrophe, and to institute a harsh and punishing superego, makes this last step in moral development less possible. Every unresolved psychic conflict that takes away a child's freedom contributes toward the same paralysis of spirit: separation anxiety, the sense (usually accurate) that "they" really do not want one to separate, fear of retribution if one does leave, all manner of neurotic guilt feelings, all perceptions of the parents' inadequacies and inner shame, grandiose notions of parental power, severe castration anxiety, absence of a secure sense of self-worth and esteem. The list is as long as the tale of human woe one wishes to tell. In essence, without the power to be a psychically autonomous and caring person, there is little chance of arriving at a place of moral autonomy. Our morality is as vulnerable and as fragile as the psyche wherein it dwells.

Sensitive to all these possibilities of moral disability, it is remarkable that any moral life has been realizable and even more remarkable that we have witnessed a goodly number of triumphs: the abandonment of cannibalism, human sacrifice, and infanticide; the termination of slavery; the creation of the ideal of human equality; the institution of democratic society. Something equally powerful, or even a slight bit more powerful, than the destructive drives must be working within us. When we consider all the lethal land mines scattered on the field that leads to a moral life, it is unimaginable that we have no guide helping to take us through. Nothing should convince us of the power of Eros more than the contemplation of how difficult—even, from a certain viewpoint, impossible—a moral life seems to be.

Cognizant of all the evil humans have committed against each other, it is still to be remarked that so many people are capable of achieving the high level of moral compromise that, for example, makes a viable democratic society possible. Considering the power of the destructive impulses, the fragility of the psyche, and the hazards of child rearing, it is extraordinary that even one individual could transform and generalize the experience of basic nurturing into a love of humankind as a whole. And yet hundreds of thousands, maybe even millions, of people have done so. Freud has said it as powerfully as anyone: "Civilization is a process in the service of Eros, whose purpose is to combine single human individuals and after that families, then races, peoples and nations, into one great unity, the unity of mankind." The process itself remains mysterious: "Why it has to happen, we do not know." But the actuality is unarguable: "the work of Eros is precisely this."[18] *

* Upon rereading this penultimate chapter, I have become aware that I have reconciled myself with Freud—the ambivalent contradictory parent—by resorting to the idealized image of him, which I have extracted from his work. I have used Freud's own emphasis on Eros to argue against the flawed theory of the superego in the attempt to transform it into a truly moral instrument. Without the capacity for idealization, even this limited psychic transposition would have been impossible. On the much larger scale of social action, the same psychic mechanism is essential for moral progress.

PART V

CONCLUSION: TIME PRESENT, TIME FUTURE

13

Some Reflections on a Fundamental Change in the System of Values

THE MOST IMPORTANT symbolic structure determining the nature of a society—what it can and cannot do—is the system of values. The value system tells us whether ambition is to be prized or despised, whether sexuality is to be enjoyed or repressed, whether poor people are to be degraded or ambivalently regarded, whether God, the gods, or magical spirits exist or not. One cannot have a capitalist system without a capitalist system of values. In a society that regards lending of money for interest as usury and sinful, capitalism is impossible. Similarly, a nurturing society is impossible without a nurturing system of values. A culture that concerns itself almost exclusively with those who are shrewd, psychologically daring, or fortunately born cannot be, or become, a nurturing society. Clean or dirty; conscientious or lackadaisical; exuberant or repressed; democratic or fascist; slave or free—the system of values is the ultimate authority by which judgment is made between these momentous alternatives.

Like the psyche, the system of values is always in a state of conflict.

The values themselves may be conflicted, the result of profound ambivalences. In addition, society may be acutely divided on questions of value. The legitimacy of abortion splits our society today, as does the question of the extent to which the welfare state should be paralyzed or dismantled. Irreconcilable differences about the system of values can result even in civil war, as the history of this country has shown. Disparate opinions on slavery, the nature of the Union, and the bourgeois versus the aristocratic life propelled hundreds of thousands of men to kill each other.

It is not a simple task to discover exactly what the values (probably conflicted) in a society are or have been. Historians conduct a sublimated form of warfare against each other over questions of how sexually repressed the nineteenth century was, or how equal with men were aristocratic women in twelfth-century Provence, or how much commercial interests contributed to the expansion of the Roman Empire. Similarly, no two sociologists can agree about the current state of the value system in our own society. Exactly how narcissistic, racist, selfish, sexist, or paranoid about Russia are we as a people today?

And today is continually resigning in favor of tomorrow. *Change* is always an essential element in any value system. There may have been certain times in the history of the world when there were only minuscule alterations in values. Perhaps the "Dark Ages" in Europe or the Byzantine Empire exhibited such relative stability. Possibly "primitive" societies produced only extraordinarily slow alterations in values. Be that as it may, in the Western world—which is the locus of this book—and certainly since the twelfth century, transformations of the value system have been continuous and prodigious. Every fifty-year period presents us with a significantly different view of the world. And in this century the pace of cultural change has taken a quantum leap. Even a superficial reading of history instructs us that the most erroneous form of social forecasting is that which projects the persistence of current values into the future, along some predictable line of development. Who among the social prophets, in the midst of the "repressed" Eisenhower years, told us that the cultural turmoil of the 1960s was in the making? And who in the vortex of that "Green Revolution" had the wisdom to inform us that, within fifteen years, the United States was to become the land of Yuppies? We have as yet no sociology ade-

220

quate to the task of informing us what even the next twenty-five years will look like. Intelligent speculation about real possibilities represents the current limit of our understanding.

The great sociological and historical task is to explain *why* the values in society are transformed in a particular manner. Why does one country develop from monarchical rule into a democratic state and then revert to fascism, whereas another changes from monarchy to democracy and remains a stable, free society? How do we explain the origins of the feminist movement and the extraordinary vicissitudes it has gone through in its 350-year history? Obviously, no attempt is made here to resolve this kind of question. What is being emphasized is that, in all such discussions, what we are always talking about are changes in the value system of society. What value do we give monarchy, democracy, fascism, or gender equality? And why does that value change in the way it does from one historical period to another?

Social theorists have taken two fundamental approaches to explain alterations in the system of values. One approach insists that the value system has no autonomous existence; it is completely dependent on changes that occur in other areas of social action. The other view looks for contradictions, conflicts, and ambivalences within the value system and sees change as the result of these inconsistencies either being worked out or exacerbated. Orthodox Marxism is the most powerful representative of the first theoretical stance; it regards almost all the values in society, certainly the most fundamental ones, as completely dependent on power relations as defined in the economic sphere. Changes in the system of values result from changes in the mode of production and in the relations of production (who controls the economic power in society). The sociological tradition of Durkheim, Weber, and Parsons, on the other hand, emphasizes the autonomous nature of the value system and looks for contradictions, or repressed possibilities, within it to explain transformations of values. The truth, as in most either/or situations, lies in the capacity to combine both theoretical approaches. Certainly nothing of social importance in the twentieth century can be understood without comprehending the nature of capitalist society. But with equal certainty, that understanding is necessary, but hardly sufficient, to comprehend permutations in the system of values. Other symbolic formations—religion, morality, ideology, the expression of aggression—play a role equal to, if not greater than, that of economic power.

One significant contribution a psychoanalytic sociology can make to this discussion is the recognition of the autonomous developmental capacities of the psyche and the role they play in social evolution. Every theory of psychology—whether that of Freud, Jung, Piaget, or Kohlberg—rests on two basic assumptions. First, that there is such a thing as human nature that all people share. The theories may differ as to what that nature is, but they all agree that human psychological universals exist. Second, a universal human psychology must rest on a universal human biology, for it can have no other foundation. We are, as Cassirer has said, an *animal symbolicum*—a symbol-making animal. The analysis of our animal nature gives us biology; our symbol-making nature gives us psychology.

Crucial for my argument is the fact that the moral impulse is a psychological fact and therefore rests on a biological base. Freud saw this with great clarity. The narrative of the birth and development of the superego (the moral capacity for Freud) is a description of *instinctual* (that is, biopsychological) development. The evolution of the moral impulse is an absolute given of human nature. The great human problem, of course, is that the immoral impulse—the instincts of aggression; the need to dominate, degrade, and destroy others—is also a psychological fact that rests on a biological base. Once Freud perceived this with brilliant clarity, it became apparent to him that the course of civilization—the history of humankind—was played out under the great struggle between Eros and destruction. The history of the world—and future history—can be comprehended only by keeping this fateful dichotomy in mind.

As I have argued from the very beginning of this book, it is essential to understand that the value system in society is not identical to the moral system. The value system always represents a very complex compromise between the drives of morality (Eros) and the destructive drives. The norms of society may insist, as they did in ancient Greece, that it is just to own slaves but that they should be treated well by their masters—a perfect resolution of conflicting needs. If the value system within society always includes many elements of morality, the crucial question becomes one of degree. To what degree does the system give

222

satisfaction to moral impulses and to what degree to their opposite? Moral progress, then, can be defined as an increase in the degree to which moral needs are expressed within the system of values. In essence, the critical question remains: How much tyranny and how much equality does society regard as legitimate? History reveals enormous variety in the answers to that question.

There are many things within a value system that have nothing to do with morality, even though there is a tendency for people to make "value judgments" about almost every aspect of social norms: whether ties and jackets are required for dinner in restaurants; whether baseball or football is our most popular sport; whether science or "superstition" is to predominate in our intellectual life. From the psychological point of view, certainly from the cognitive developmental view, a commitment to science can be seen as a "more advanced" stage of development. Freud argued the same about rationality versus religion, maintaining that the belief in God represented a more childlike view of the world than scientific atheism. The moral dimension, however, is much more complicated. Many believers in scientific rationality and atheism are great supporters of tyrannical social forms (the Nazi leaders were remarkable in their atheism, and with Stalinism atheism itself became a mode of tyrannical oppression). On the other hand, many religious people have been in the forefront of the moral political struggles of the last twenty-five years. It was of great interest to observe, during the great challenge to the war in Vietnam, that among middle-class, middle-aged activists the two most important groups were (1) former old-style left-wing atheists and (2) religious leaders.

Psychological development and moral development, in all their intricate detail, cannot be equated one with the other. Similarly, the evolution of society does not represent an exact parallel with the unfolding of moral possibilities. With those reservations, however, it does seem important to note that, although moral concerns have always played an important role in social transformations, starting with the seventeenth century and certainly since 1800—and without doubt today—*moral questions are at the very center of social conflicts, at the very center of the issues that concern the transformation of the system of values.* Racism, sexism, the care or neglect of the disadvantaged, the domination of industrial over nonindustrial countries, the ravagement of the environment, the ultimate destruction of the world—these are all moral questions. And with the exception of a few items of scandal, airline crashes, or unique sporting activities, these issues dominate the front page of our newspapers and determine the outcome of our elections.

What role moral issues have played in past history is an open question. Whether, for instance, they contributed anything to the struggles that brought an end to the Roman Republic and the establishment of the Empire in the first century before Christ is uncertain. But there is no question that they completely infuse our political life. How this has come to be is beyond the scope of this work, but the fact that it has happened leads us to seriously consider the idea that morality is a driving force in history, certainly in the history that we are living. All technocratic tinkering with society in the attempt to solve our basic social problems is doomed to failure. The moral problems of racism, sexism, and the criminal neglect of our economically disadvantaged will be solved only by moral solutions, only by a transformation in the system of values that will pronounce intolerable the existence of these unconscionable forms. True, we may survive, as we have until now, without resolving these issues. Survival is one form of human existence. Even survival becomes problematic, however, when we consider how tremendously the hydrogen bomb has raised the cost of immoral or irrational behavior.

It is a brave soul who would offer, under the current conditions of American society, even a faint-hearted optimistic prognostication as to where, as a people, we are going. The welfare state is under severe attack, and, one by one, we are abandoning the hopes we had of eliminating the underclass—and the wretched life it leads—from our society. Articles appear in the *New York Times* comparing a now-typical New York experience to Calcutta, where after encountering what at first looks like a bundle of rags on the sidewalk and then discovering that it represents a person asleep, one does not know whether to walk around, call the police, or cry out in anguish. We seem unable to discover any other cure for inflation except to maintain a hard-core 7 or 8 percent unemployment, with percentages as high as 15 and 20 percent among certain ethnic groups. The tragic human cost of that economic "solution" does not make the front page.

Instead of heading toward possible cure—as might have been imagined fifteen years ago—the cancer within our society that is racism, intimately related to problems of underclass and unemployment, remains a permanent malignancy in the body politic. About gender equality we are enormously ambivalent. Great strides have been made in the past twenty years, but a persistent, malicious sexism and the sustained strength of the forces of reaction perpetuate a legitimate anxiety that in this area, as in the problematic of racism, continued moral progress is by no means guaranteed.

And to make flagrant matters even worse, that group of people from whom, in a democratic society, one can look to for the energy to invigorate moral progress—thoughtful, caring folk who have the capacity to look beyond their narrow individual interest and exercise the virtue of citizenship; people of the order of those who created the abolitionist movement, gave us child-labor laws, fought for women's rights, put an end to the war in Vietnam, and challenged a racist society—such people, we are told by social analysts, are so mired in narcissism, radical individualism, and me-tooism that they are spiritually exhausted.* Another group of potential citizens is so battered by the current destruction of bourgeois marriage that it has all it can do to try to hold some form of decent life together.

In the center of all this how can one talk of, much less hope for, a fundamental change in values in the direction of moral progress? In the midst of our despair we have lost touch with the one thing that gives us some occasion for optimism: the sense of history. It is essential to understand that such fundamental changes of values have occurred in the past. And that human beings have recovered from situations far worse than ours. The extraordinary moral progress of the last four hundred years in the areas of child rearing, sexuality, freedom from slavery, democracy, and social equality is not illusory, no matter how deep the trough we may be in at the moment. There is both a remarkably grand story and a nightmare to be extracted from the reading of history. Both interpretations are true. It is an easy task to recount that nightmare. Far more difficult, yet equally profitable, is it to examine whether there is not also a moral narrative that our species has to tell.

* The most important and persuasive analyses are in Christopher Lasch, *The Culture of Narcissism*, and Robert N. Bellah et al., *Habits of the Heart*.

Changes in the system of values are not random or arbitrary. There is a certain logic determining these transformations. The developmental path of the psyche and the moral dimension within that progression significantly help determine the course of history.

It is important to recognize that the act of postulating a psychological paradigm for social evolution by no means rests on the assumption that moral progress is inevitable. Moral progress in society is no more inevitable than psychic maturity for the individual, though both must be seen as inherent human possibilities. We are born with the capacity to achieve psychic health. Similarly, all human societies have developmental potentialities. Possibilities and inevitabilities, however, are two different orders of human experience. And nothing in the postulation of a psychological developmental course precludes stagnation and regression. A psychological evolutionary theory, unlike the biological theory of evolution, must include the possibility of regression as an essential element. Both individuals and societies, under circumstances of severe strain, are subject to regressive behavior. Moral progress *and* moral regress define our humanity. Neither the Nazi experience nor the comparatively mild regressive mode of the moment negate a theory of *potential* social evolution.

Many different degrees of change characterize transformations in the system of values. *Minor changes* go on every day; certainly over any five- or ten-year period. In the modern world views on education, work, sexuality, consumption, leisure, and so on vary greatly from one ten-year period to the next. In addition to these minor shifts in values, *major changes* can be observed throughout history: the elimination of slavery, a ten thousand–year institution; the erection of the welfare state; the sexual revolution of the last thirty years. Even major changes can be institutionalized without changing the fundamental nature of the value system. Slavery is discarded and the welfare state erected without eliminating racism or horrendous economic disparities. *Fundamental changes* in the value system cannot be made without affecting the entire system of norms. Such a fundamental change is analogous to a radical shift in the scientific paradigm. The whole world becomes a different place. If we travel from the medieval society of the year 1000 to the beginnings of the modern world of 1600, it is almost as if we have been transported to a different planet. Barring natural or social catastrophe, by 1600 modern society as we know it was inevitable. In 1000 such a development was inconceivable. Elemental changes in values, such as the institution of democracy or the validation of gender equality or the establishment of a nurturing society, cannot be accomplished without radical reverberations throughout the whole system. Such fundamental changes make the world unrecognizable from the viewpoint of previous history.

The existence of such revolutionary transformations of values legitimates the theoretical notion of definite and specific stages in the evolution of society. Each stage is made possible by a system of values that is elementally different from those of the previous or following stages of development.

It is understandable that, even among those social theorists who support the concept of developmental stages in society, each theorist will draw his or her historical map differently. My viewpoint—as open to argument as anyone else's—sees five stages in the last three thousand-year history of the West:

1. The classical-pagan world, beginning with Homer and the rise of the Greek city-states, c. 750 B.C., and ending with the conversion of the Emperor Constantine to Christianity in c. A.D. 312.
2. The world of the Christian fathers of the Church, which ends in c. 1100.
3. The high Middle Ages and the transition to the modern world, from c. 1100 to c. 1600. This period, so crucial for our own, includes the three great "renaissances"—that of the twelfth century, the Italian, and the Northern—and the Protestant Reformation.
4. The modern world, beginning in 1600 and extending somewhere into the nineteenth century, perhaps even until the end of the century. This is the world of liberalism, capitalism, democracy, "class struggle"—the world of Marx, Nietzsche, and Freud.
5. The present era, which I characterize as the Age of Ambivalence.

Theoreticians have grown into the fashionable habit of describing our current situation with the prefix "post." We live, we are told, in a post-modern, post-industrial, post-Freudian, post-class-struggle, post-ideological society. It seems, apparently, that we have put most everything behind us. Everything, that is, except our intense ambivalence about almost every moral issue in our society. We are not living, certainly, in a post-ambivalent world.

It becomes immediately apparent that there are huge overlaps in these historical periods. No one year defines the revolution in values; the culture does not suddenly erupt in 1100 and immediately enter a new world. The exact dates for each stage of society are illustrative and possibly arbitrary, but the hypothesis that we have witnessed, in the West, five fundamentally different systems of value since about 750 B.C. seems to me a reasonable one. Even should the truth eventually settle on the number three, or seven, or ten, it would not contradict the essential point about radical transformations in values. Think of the world in about 750 B.C., A.D. 312, 1100, 1600, 1848, and 1980. It is almost miraculous that one species could invent so many fundamentally different ways of looking at, and living in, the world.

Again, in the middle of one historical period, circumscribed by its particular system of values, the changes in values that are to occur in the following period are unimaginable. If one had said to any thoughtful person in England in 1550 that the time would come when the great lords of the realm would be politically irrelevant, when bankers would rule the world, and when every person in England would vote on the question of who should lead the country, at the least the epithet "utopian" would have been uttered with scorn; at the worst, the cry of "lunatic." Just so today, if one has the temerity to announce that the time will come when we will abandon the fierce competitiveness that now characterizes our society and that people will regard their work as a mode in which they can, among other things, be of service to society—if one were to utter such an outlandish proposition, the identical labels of "lunatic" and "utopian" would be the probable response.

Still more can be learned from the history of the changes in fundamental values. Such alterations take an enormous amount of time. A great deal of time may elapse from the moment when a fundamental transformation of value is first seriously proposed until it is generally adopted by the culture. In the fourteenth century John Wycliffe was almost brought to his death for espousing views that ultimately became the foundation of the Reformation. He escaped such a fate and died of natural causes in 1384. Jan Hus of Bohemia was not that fortunate. He was executed in Germany in 1415 for similar beliefs and pro-

228

nouncements. It was not until 130 years after Wycliffe's death that Luther nailed his ninety-five theses to the door of the castle church in Wittenburg and permanently changed the history of the world. I have commented upon how long the feminist revolution has been in the making. We wrong the moral potentialities of our society when we take a small historical trend, one of perhaps eight or ten years, and project it into the future, declaring: "That is where, as a people, we are going." The sixties gives way to the seventies, which give way to the eighties, and, taken all together, they are only thirty years. And *no one* has the wisdom really to know what even the nineties will bring us, much less the century to follow.

We are, nevertheless, the most self-conscious people that has ever lived, and we have a greater possibility of self-understanding than any culture that has gone before us. Psychology has given us an instrument of inward human understanding, imperfect but more powerful than anything from the past. And the disciplines of history, anthropology, and sociology have brought us tantalizingly close to a real understanding of society. It would not be amiss, therefore, to attempt to comprehend the contradictions and potentialities of our culture, which might then give us some indication of where society might go should we decide to lift ourselves out of our current malaise.

The purpose of this historical discussion is to force us to view our own time in as large a historical perspective as possible. We are riding an evolutionary process, and the only way we can even begin to know where it is taking us is by understanding the past. No fundamental change in values has ever occurred until the old order has lost its vitality. Cultural systems, which are primarily dependent on the system of values, become exhausted. They lose their flexibility, their capacity to respond to change, and their potentiality for growth. When this occurs, they no longer speak to people with authenticity. They no longer give people a true sense of purpose in life. No individual, no culture lives a satisfactory life without a deep sense of meaning: the sense that existence, somehow, somewhere has a purpose.

When this state of moral exhaustion predominates in a culture—if the culture is not destined to collapse—a new, more vigorous meaningful system of values begins to be constructed within the shell of the old society. The result is a period of moral and value transition in which the voices of both the exhausted prophets of doom and of the new era yet to be born are simultaneously heard in the land. These periods of transition assume a definite character: the evils in society are clearly perceived, but practically no one has any real intention of ending them. "With the gradual relaxation of discipline," Livy writes, "morals first gave way, as it were, then sank lower and lower, and finally began the downward plunge which has brought us to the present time, when we can endure neither our vices nor their cure."[1]

Livy was writing at the nodal point when the depleted Roman Republic gave way to the Empire of Augustus, which did succeed in transforming values and re-creating a sense of purpose in social life. The transition from republic to empire was a major alteration in values but did not represent a fundamental change in the value system. The values of the empire did not fundamentally contradict the mores of the classical, pagan world. In the third century A.D. that classical world came to its final crisis. Spiritually exhausted; producing no major poet, playwright, philosopher (possibly Plotinus is an exception), or visual artist; politically throwing up one mediocre or despicable emperor after the other: all virtue seemed relegated to the past. Except within the Church. Here the fresh vision of the world, a radically new system of values, was being created, and the people who carried it were educating themselves for power. But who in the year 250, amid all that gloom, would have predicted with any kind of certainty that the "miracle" of the fourth century would take place?* In such a period of spiritual malaise, to many thoughtful people the world appears as a dark—and doomed—place.

Northern Europe in the fourteenth and fifteenth centuries presents us with a similarly conflicted time of transition. While Italy was busying itself with the pre-Renaissance and the full Renaissance, northern Europe was suffering from a "post-Renaissance" depressive mood. The awakening of the twelfth century was the first crucial event in the process that ultimately made modern Europe possible. It established, once

---

* Peter Brown, an eminent historian of the early Church, writes in his review of Robin Lane Fox's book *Pagans and Christians*: "Such a religion might survive. It was unlikely to triumph." The members of third-century society knew "nothing of the future." "The conversion of the Emperor Constantine to Christianity ... was 'an entirely unexpected event.'"[2]

and for all, that Roman Catholicism was to be a religion of *this world*, that there was to be a flexible coming and going between the monastary and real-world seats of power, that the old split between Caesar and Christ was no longer viable. Ultimately this meant that the Church was committed not only to castigating, but also to changing, the world. The Reformation of the sixteenth century finds its origins in the 1100s.

In the thirteenth century a momentous struggle ensued between the forces of reaction intent on keeping reason, and especially the influence of Aristotle, alien to the world view of the Church, and those who wished to admit reason and reconcile it with the principles of faith. Despite the fact that some of the doctrines of Aquinas—the great proponent of the progressive view—came close to being declared heretical, his synthesis of reason and faith ultimately prevailed, and he was canonized fifty years after his death. The triumph of his synthesis assured developmental progress and kept the Church from becoming a dead hand opposed to all evolutionary change.

Contrary to what one might expect, these two centuries of spiritual progress did not immediately result in a period of optimistic expectations. Exactly the opposite took place. The 1300s were a time of pessimism and gloom. It is very difficult even to speculate why this was so. The Black Death certainly contributed to the dark mood, but there were also deeper causes. Possibly rising moral expectations that could not be fulfilled contributed to the sense of hopelessness. For whatever reason, social turmoil was at a height. The peasant revolts of the fourteenth century represent the most important and widespread struggle of lower-class people against established power to take place between the slave revolts of Roman times and the French Revolution. When the season of revolt was over and all the rebellions crushed, however, the peasants had won very little for themselves.

By the end of the century a deep moral dissatisfaction with the Church became evident. Wycliffe, Hus, and the thousands of their followers signified an attempt to construct a new system of values within a culture spiritually wasted. And here again, who could have known, after Hus was burned alive, when—if ever—his views would prevail?

I assume by now, even with this too hurriedly told history, that it has become apparent that I believe we are living in a similar time of spiritual exhaustion, where the old set of values no longer authenti-

231

cates our lives and gives them meaning and where we are still helplessly unable to embrace a new system that would radically redefine the relation of people to each other. "Western civilization," wrote André Malraux in 1949, "has begun to doubt its own credentials."[3] Today that doubt is almost complete.

Nothing illustrates this sense of transitional malaise better than the current moral disarray of the Democratic Party in the United States, the party responsible for almost all the important social legislation of the twentieth century, the party that brought some degree of moral responsibility to our economic lives. The New Deal, the Great Society of Lyndon Johnson, the charismatic energy of the Kennedy brothers—all of this does not sell anymore to the electorate. We must discover, therefore, what will sell. We will convince the people, announce the leading candidates, that *we Democrats* can best teach the country how most effectively to compete with Germany and Japan—as if the transformation from moral spokesman to technocrat could restore the sense of purpose that most people find lacking in their lives. The "moral" rationalization of the "new" politicians is that the only way to help the economically disadvantaged is to make the pie bigger so that the middle and upper classes do not have to pay anything more for the project of reconstituting our society. To which one feels compelled to ask: With the pie (per-capita income adjusted for inflation) over two and one-half times as large as it was in 1940, why does the poverty level remain around 20 percent and why are more people than ever sleeping in the streets?

Our VCRs, our Bloomingdales, and our cocaine have not yet succeeded in making us happy. What makes us imagine that even more goods will accomplish that task? And yet the candidates who speak most clearly for genuine equality have no chance of a national victory. We too, it seems, can tolerate neither our vices nor their cure.

How can anyone be anything but pessimistic in the face of our pervasive moral ambivalence and paralysis? Where is the energy to come from to effectuate a fundamental change in values, a change that seems essential if we are to survive as a viable culture—or possibly even survive at all? First, we have to think about the numbers. Clearly, no one generalization speaks for all, or even a majority, of the people in American society. (I talk only of the United States because it is what I know something about, but it does seem that the whole of the Western world is suffering from the same spiritual malaise, for much the same reasons.) Twenty years of active political work and teaching have convinced me that, allowing for certain cyclical variations as one decade succeeds another, 20 to 25 percent of our citizens today are ready to put an end to racism, poverty, sexism, missile madness, and the fierce competitive nature of our society. One finds such people among those who stay socially and politically active: community organizers, environmentalists, feminists, and those working for racial equality and against nuclear madness.* And there remain a large group of people who live only private lives but who are willing to support, with both their money and their votes, the moral transformation we are talking of. Exactly how large this constituency is has not been determined, as far as I know, but it definitely is large enough to indicate that the notion of "utopian" is no adequate critique of this analysis. It is no longer a question of inventing a new value and moral system that would be appropriate to our needs. That agenda has already been set, and hundreds of thousands are, even in these conflicted times, working for its institutionalization. In a democracy, however, one needs a majority. And how are others to come to this position?

Even the most cynical, amoral observers of human nature would probably agree that people want to be happy, that unhappy people are dissatisfied. It is one of the crucial arguments of this book that human beings cannot be happy if they severely repress the basic human need for idealization in their lives. When we observe people behaving as if life had no meaning, no authenticity, no self-definition, no legitimacy, we can be sure that idealization plays very little role in their existence and that happiness must elude their grasp. The pursuit of material goods has no ideal dimension to it. The pathetic quality of narcissism is revealed in its foredoomed attempt to satisfy the need for idealization with acts of consumption and adornment. Idealization, as discussed earlier, is a healthy transformation of primitive narcissistic needs. The movement, therefore, from meaning to material goods, from authenticity to adornment, from idealization to narcissism can

---

* In *Habits of the Heart*, especially part 2, "Public Life," Bellah and cowriters give a vivid presentation of the moral potentialities still remaining in our society.

only be profoundly regressive and unsatisfying for the human condition, no matter how passionately it may be pursued. If self-centered pursuit and neglect of all others could truly make people happy, we would have an unsolvable philosophical problem. But we have no such problem because our current, temporary worship of wealth is, as Shakespeare said of lust, "an expense of spirit in a waste of shame." It can never restore meaning to life, and only meaning makes happiness possible.

The nonutopian hope, then, is that the moral regeneration of our society will happen for the same reasons it has occurred in the past. Those who made the Christian Revolution of the first four centuries of our era; those who created the great Reformation in the fourteenth, fifteenth, and sixteenth centuries, were not absolute self-sacrificing martyrs working only for the happiness of others. Their basic need was to restore meaning to *their own lives* in a culture that could no longer provide it. And nothing has more power to transform the world.

Anxiety, Defense, Immorality

There is no assumption of inevitability in this speculation about moral transformation. At most one can argue only what such a transformation might look like, *if* it were to occur. First, the bomb has to be held off long enough to give us time to work this sociological miracle. That in itself is clearly problematic. But second, even should the world decide to remain in existence, no argument from history can convince us that, because such fundamental transformations have occurred in the past, they are destined to happen in the future. One must remain agnostic in regard to the inexorable character of the evolutionary process. Instead of taking the progressive step, humankind may decide to regress into an authoritarianism designed to contain both freedom and anxiety. Many of the great anti-Utopias of this century—*Brave New World, 1984*—have explored this possibility. We may also perpetuate ambivalence for several hundred years, dancing on the edge of the momentous decision, indecisive whether to leap for freedom or plunge backward in panicked retreat, and actually doing neither.

Uncertain as we are in regard to the future, we can nevertheless attempt to understand what factors may determine the outcome. Specifically: What keeps people from joining this projected moral revolution? It seems obvious that a society without poverty, racism, sexism, and nuclear destruction would be so much happier a place to live in that it is important to try to understand why the vast majority of people reject the steps necessary to achieve this goal. The usual answers to this question name selfishness, greed, ignorance, and evil (human destructiveness) as the hindrances to moral progress, and there is no question of their importance, but here I would like to emphasize the essential significance of anxiety in fostering both conservatism and immorality. Not only is anxiety a problem in itself, but I believe that we can better understand selfishness, greed, even narcissism, and certainly destructiveness as mechanisms of defense against anxiety. As social and personal anxiety increase, the need to defend against them grows stronger and stronger, and people are more and more tempted to resort to certain mechanisms of psychic behavior that, somehow, do succeed—at least temporarily—in containing possible panic.

One of the oldest saws in the world proclaims that we should eat, drink, and be merry—for tomorrow we die. If we are unusually frightened of death, or of anything else, says the proverb, then some delicious take-out pasta and a good bottle of wine can do the trick. If it could be established that our culture is suffering from an unusually acute period of anxiety—as I think it can be—then the Yuppie phenomenon as well as the intense increase of narcissistic, self-centered behavior would become more comprehensible. One knows from everyday observation that people in unusual states of anxiety cannot care much for others and must look intensely to themselves. Whatever works to hold the self together in such circumstance is resorted to. And, traditionally, certain mechanisms have aided this attempt to keep anxiety from accelerating to panic:

1. Oral regression to food, drink, or drugs.
2. Narcissistic regression to sleep, adornment, and consumption.
3. Intensely looking out for number one, because "nobody else will take care of you if you don't watch out for yourself."

235

4. Conservatism in lifestyle and politics in the attempt to keep the world from changing so fast.

5. Aggression toward others—creating victims within society and finding enemies without: the paranoid defense (authoritarian regimes are particularly adept at this maneuver).

Every one of these defense mechanisms is in prominent evidence within our culture today. The Yuppies and the narcissists—not necessarily the same people—represent the first two modes. All those young people graduating from law and business school, intent on making $100,000 a year by the time they are thirty, have adopted the third maneuver. Conservatism has been the significant political stance for ten years now. And the paranoid chorus has been conducted from the White House itself since 1981.

The level of anxiety within society is not constant but fluctuates enormously from one historical period to another. Certain times exhibit unusual states of anxiety and, consequently, unusual mechanisms to deal with that anxiety. In society, as with an individual, things are not always what they seem. Take the Eisenhower years, for example. The accepted observation pronounces the 1950s a conservative time in dress, lifestyle, politics, and religion. Church attendance was at one of its highest levels in the history of the United States. Women stayed home and raised large families while their husbands struggled through "the rat race" during the week and barbecued in the backyard on weekends. The very picture of a repressed, stable society, moving backward to traditional values or, at the least, repressing any impulse for change.

Despite superficial appearances, however, revolutionary things were happening in that society. More people than at any other time in our history, in a remarkably short amount of time, were picking up and leaving the ethnic, family neighborhoods where their families had lived for two to four generations and were settling down in the suburbs among people whom they did not know. Italians, Irish, Jews left the inner-city neighborhoods where they had associated almost exclusively with "their own kind" and proceeded to live in the new and more intense melting pot of suburbia. No wonder they flocked to the churches and synagogues to reinforce their kinship ties. People who had lived for several generations in such close family context that mother and grandmother could look into one's pots to see what was for dinner or into the baby's diaper to determine how it was doing—such people broke those close family connections and went out on their own. All of this represents a breaking of family and kinship ties of an extraordinary order. Those who made that pilgrimage to the non-kinship suburban world maintained their ground, did not retreat to the old kinship structures, and made a life separated and individuated from ethnic neighborhoods. Such breaking of kinship attachments—no matter how progressive it may be psychologically—generates an inordinate amount of separation anxiety, which in turn creates the need for complex defenses against that anxiety. And conservatism in dress, lifestyle, and politics may represent exactly those defenses. In one part of their lives they had taken a revolutionary step, and they compensated for that by trying, in the other parts of their lives, to have the world turn as slowly as possible.

It was both a revolutionary and a conservative time. Psychic balance was maintained by a complex trade-off. The great problem for psychic development and for social evolution is that many advances—new modes of living together that are in the human interest—bring a heightening of anxiety. First, they do so because they represent change, which always generates fear. But, of even greater importance, they do so because they separate us more and more from earlier modes of attachment and defense. Psychological and moral advances demand of us that we give up previous defensive modes. Nothing is harder for human beings. Men have used the various forms of sexism to defend their fragile masculine identity. When one asks a man to give up sexism, one is not just appealing to him to welcome half of humankind as his equal. One is also insisting that he take the enormous risk of losing his own gender identity. It is no wonder that he is willing to do almost anything else before assuming that hazard. The great moral and developmental advances of abandoning sexism and racism vastly increase the level of anxiety within society. That is our great psychological and political problem.

We live in just such a time of intense anxiety. At least four fundamental factors make this situation inevitable. First, no matter how much it may be repressed from consciousness, the very real threat of nuclear annihilation affects everyone's feelings about the future. When the future is not secure, the level of anxiety must rise. There was a time, for instance, when one could soften anxiety about death with the thought that one's children and grandchildren, at least, would continue to live after one. That compensation is no longer available. And those children represent the first generation in the history of the world that has to recognize that there may indeed be no future. We are only beginning to comprehend the psychological damage created by such an enormity in the "real world."

We have, second, the anxiety generated in both men and women by the demand for equality for women. I have discussed the distress that men feel on this account, but it may be important to add that women have their own anxiety about demanding equality. The old unequal system was a mode of defense for women as well as men, as has been elaborated by several current theorists, most perceptively by Dorothy Dinnerstein.[4] And here we are face to face with one of those great ambiguities of cultural and moral development. The abandonment of the tyranny of men over women—an undeniable moral good—significantly raises the level of apprehension in society, causing people, both men and women, to take up modes of defense (narcissism, conservatism) that are the exact opposite of a moral good. Especially is this so in this time of transition when everyone seems to be profoundly ambivalent on the question, so that we can neither finally resolve it in a moral mode nor make it go away.

And to make a problematic matter even worse, feminist demands, and the failure of men and women to meet them, have created a situation of such acute ambivalence that relationships between the genders are under tremendous strain. The old stable bourgeois patriarchal marriage has been sundered. Yet a new form of marriage, based on true equality, has been achieved by very, very few people. The result is a family system in almost total disarray. Whereas in the past getting married signified security, today it represents one new cause for anxiety. (Will it hold? And for how long?) Women and children, as has been usual in history, are the primary victims. By the end of 1986 more than 25 percent of all American families were single-parent (that is, mostly mother-led) households.[5] No one claims that a single parent cannot raise a child lovingly and healthily, but such a situation is a sociological disaster. Disorder is the prime cause of anxiety. We may be laying an intolerable burden on our children.

The fourth major cause of distress in our society is our failure to deal with the subtle genocide that is racism. Here again we are caught in an ambivalent bind. Equality between races is on the agenda, and year after year we vote it down. By our refusal to solve the problem we manage to raise the level of our anxiety. Angered at Black people, both because they have the "arrogance" to demand equality and also because they are associated in the minds of most white people with crime in the streets, we reduce welfare and food stamp payments, cease building housing for low-income groups, and enforce a 15 to 20 percent unemployment rate. This results, quite naturally, in an increase of the feeling of moral malaise on the part of whites and more political activity by Blacks, which in turn raises the level of anxiety to an even higher pitch.

Considering, then, the burden of fear under which we are living, one must say that narcissism and conservatism are comparatively mild defensive mechanisms. One profound reason for hope is that we have not yet resorted to—nor do we seem to be heading toward—the more potent and dangerous social modes of defense against excruciating anxiety: authoritarianism and fascism. We remain, in regard to these fundamental moral issues, pervasively ambivalent. Our world could go either way.

To Love and to Work

If we combine the theoretical description of symptomology given by Christopher Lasch and Robert Bellah—narcissism and radical individualism—with these observations on anxiety and defense; if we add to this picture the outrageous aggression practiced against women, Black people, and the economically disadvantaged, and keep in mind the paranoid system of international politics that keeps us constantly on the brink of world destruction, building so many missiles in our search for "security" that our enemy—and ourselves—can no longer sleep at night; if we also observe, in passing, all the workaholics on Wall Street, fearful that if they do not compete fourteen hours a day they might experience one more emotion besides greed; and if, finally, we recognize that despite, or possibly because of, the sexual revolution, marriage no longer "works"—which is another way of saying the people do not know how to love each other; if we put all this together, we get a perfect picture of a neurosis. Were an individual to display all of these attributes, the diagnosis would be obvious. Can one accurately describe a society as neurotic? What better name could one give to this confluence of symptoms?

It is important to determine the degree of pathology. We can observe that, since the 1930s we have as a nation pulled back from the worst manifestations of our illness. The crisis of the Great Depression was met vigorously with labor legislation, Social Security, and a determination to preserve the balance within society. The attempts of both McCarthyism and Watergate to seriously jeopardize the nature of our democracy were soundly rejected. When atmospheric nuclear testing threatened to ruin the planet, we were able to agree with the Russians to abolish that practice; we have even managed an ABM and a SALT I treaty, although both of these are threatened at this writing (early 1987). And when the war in Vietnam came close to tearing the nation apart, we managed to withdraw from that war, without, however, understanding what had happened and thereby making possible a repetition of such paranoid folly in the future. We have come to the brink of serious pathological behavior several times, but so far we have managed to walk away from that temptation. Neurosis seems the proper diagnosis; nothing more, but also nothing less.

A fundamental change in the system of values in the direction of moral regeneration would have the result, simply said, of making society healthy. It is tempting to resort to the rhetorical, mythical mode and write "healthy once again." But it is seriously to be doubted whether any past society can be accurately designated "healthy." There have been times of notable moral vigor—like the era of the founding of the Republic—but I think a truly healthy society has existed, up until now, only in our fantasies. Though I cannot find it in any of his published works, Freud is said to have pronounced that health can be measured by the capacities to love and to work. In order for society to institutionalize a radical change in values, there must be an essential

240

transformation in our capacity to work and to love. It may be profitable to look at what that might entail.

The view that any society takes of work is a crucial one in its total
system of norms. And that attitude has varied tremendously over time.
In the aristocratic pagan world of ancient Greece and Rome, to work
with one's hands or to labor in commerce was considered a degraded
life. Manual labor remains no great honor, but those striving in commerce have become our aristocracy. Similarly, in Max Weber's analysis
of the Protestant Reformation he demonstrates that one of the most
important results of that transformation was a radically new attitude
toward work, which established labor in the real world as a "calling."[6]
How important this Protestant work ethic is for industrialization has
been demonstrated with great irony only recently by the trials and
tribulations of Comrade Gorbachev, who cannot get his people to
work on time and who is in a deep quandary about how to inject more
of the work ethic into his society.

If we in the next fifty to one hundred years should witness a change
in the value of work no greater than the transformation wrought by
the Reformation, this would have an enormous significance for our
society. In the great failed experiment that was the 1960s much more
was going on than barefoot hippies depositing flowers in the gun bar-
rels of National Guardsmen. Hundreds of thousands of people became
active in political campaigns, some of them working twelve or fourteen
hours a day for little or no money. For a short while many Wall Street
law firms found they could not hire some of the best graduates of top
law schools unless they promised that the graduates could spend a half
or full day a week doing *pro bono* work—for the good of society. Of
course, that is all behind us now—for the moment. There remain, however, many thousands of people in our society—perhaps not hundreds
of thousands, it is true—who choose not to go for the big money and
insist that the work they do must have some deeper meaning in their
lives. This meaning comes from work suffused with the sense of
community.

The place of work in the moral universe has been from the start a
problem for the philosophy of liberalism and capitalism. Both a private
world of self-interest and a public world of virtue and citizenship were
recognized, but the world of work was somehow anomalous. Here one

pursued one's private selfish interest in a public context, but the public context was supposed to be the field of virtue. This moral contradiction was solved by the "invisible hand" of the marketplace that, somehow, turned "private vices into public virtues." The public virtue of work was achieved inadvertently, not by conscious purpose.

I propose that if we do witness in the years ahead a fundamental change in the value of work, it will take precisely the form of resolving that philosophical contradiction by making work an attribute of citizenship. Once a million or so people decide that working only for oneself leaves a hollowness in the middle of the soul, and that such work can give no real meaning to life; once a significant number of people join those thousands who already know that nothing satisfies more than work that preserves contact with community; once this new reformation in the meaning of work occurs in significant numbers, society will become unrecognizable compared with its current competitive and self-aggrandized state. Committed to the liberal tradition of the split between reason and feeling, Freud would talk of the capacities to love *and* work. If we go beyond liberalism, we can imagine a value system that combines work *with* Eros. In this dark hour any such hope may sound completely utopian. But history does teach us that changes in values even greater than this have been accomplished by people of no grander moral virtue than ourselves.

The great psychological value of work is that it provides the means for the sublimation of aggression, and without a new significant sublimation no fundamental transformation in values can occur. Competition is the characteristic form of aggression in our society. For most of us, it is within the work process that we seek our aggressive-competitive satisfactions. The psychologically and morally absurd individualism of our society maintains itself because it does provide a "civilized" amount of aggressive gratification. Working for the community is a less primitive, more sublimated way of obtaining that satisfaction, but it is not an activity devoid of aggression. This is so, first, because all work, of any kind, has an aggressive dimension, since it involves mastery in one form or another. And second, it is true because any communal work inevitably finds itself up against "the forces of evil" that have no intention of changing to make things better. Productively working for the community requires one to be a good fighter.

Change in the System of Values

Can we really expect that a significant number of people will give up the current competitive satisfactions of work, especially when they are economically rewarded so handsomely? That is *the* question, and it is hard to be optimistic in the face of it. And yet we have seen in this century as great, if not a greater, miracle of sublimation. Would anyone have dared to predict, in 1944, that Japan and Germany—the two greatest militaristic, "feudal" scourges of the century—would become stable, peaceful, nonauthoritarian societies? The great virtue of capitalism is that it provides a powerful way to sublimate the aristocratic-killing mode of aggressive satisfaction with the less primitive ones of competition and domination. The Japanese have discovered that it is easier, more pleasurable, and much less dangerous to conquer the world with the yen than with fighter planes. But that transition was made possible not only because it was reasonable and sensible, but also primarily because Japanese (and German) society was ready to take the step of a fundamental sublimation of aggression. In the sixties our society gave evidence that gross materialism and exhaustive competition were not necessarily coterminous with the human condition. There seemed, then, to be great hope for the young. We have been disappointed in that particular hope, but the young are born every day.

We have, last, to talk about love, eternal Eros. The realization of any of the humane hopes longingly expressed in this chapter ultimately depends on a fundamental redefinition of the relationship of women to men. This book has attempted to demonstrate that the greatest mind of this century was twisted in its thinking about morality, civilization, science, and reason because of an essential ambivalence about women. It is not too much to say that the basically inhuman relationship that still prevails between men and women continues to distort the whole nature of our morality and our politics. Aggression is the fundamental human problem, morality and love the fundamental cure. In all societies where women raise children, the most primitive forms of aggression are first experienced against mothers. There is no aggressive experience in an adult that does not resonate with an attack on women, no matter how much the superficial content of that aggressive act may disguise this fact. I cannot, at this point, rehearse the powerful argument that understands racism, the destruction of the environment, and the threatened elimination of the planet as reverberations of that overwhelming conflict with the mothers who raised us. Many others, most especially Dinnerstein, have performed that task much better than I could.

I do want, however, to point out that if we list the attributes that a new, more moral society might hopefully take up, all share one attribute: an emphasis on those qualities that, traditionally, frightened men have called "feminine." Such a society would be more nurturing and caring; it would substitute a sense of community for the pathologically competitive, isolated individualism of our current form of life; it would bear witness to the love we carry for our children by leaving them a world to live in; it would emphasize equality over tyranny in every human relationship. For men, this means abandoning a fragile masculine identity that has to be reinforced with a multitude of aggressive defense mechanisms that pronounce "I am not a woman"—because I preside over twenty thousand nuclear missiles. So long as men continue to define themselves in negative terms—not emotional, not weak, not womanish—just so long does the Age of Ambivalence dominate our lives.

Recognizing that there is an enormous distinction between where society must go and where it *will* go, it is incumbent on this argument to explore any indications that these two directions might possibly be the same. Despite the bombing of abortion clinics, the failure of the Equal Rights Amendment, the increasing hostility of some men, and certain temporary defeats, it seems clear that the feminist revolution goes forward. For one powerful reason: at the moment, at least, women give no indication of abandoning the project. If this continues to be true, it will powerfully distinguish this particular phase of that revolution from all previous eras. Over the past 350 years the feminist movement has advanced, then retreated or stopped, only to advance again many years later. Why this has been so is difficult to say. What does seem apparent today, however, is that the ultimate decision no longer rests with men. Women will be equal with men if enough of them wish to be. This situation has never, in all the history of the world, presented itself before. The moral implications are prodigious.

And by analogy with the Eisenhower years, when a significant forward thrust was compensated for by conservative defense mechanisms, it may be today that precisely because this revolution is continuing to advance, precisely because the majority of the people in society have accepted at least a good part of the sexual revolution, the counterreformation of the 1980s—the psychological defensive compensation for such progress—has had such force. "Backlash" is not an aptly descriptive term when we are lashing ourselves forward and backward simultaneously.

One further telling indication that this discourse is not entirely utopian: there is now more nurturing of infants and small children by fathers in our culture than possibly at any time since the transcending of "primitive" society. If one considers how our fathers were raised, and how we have raised our own children, and then how they, in turn, will nurture theirs, this development represents a veritable revolution in the degree to which fathers are involved with caring, especially for infants. Admittedly, in those 25 percent of families that are headed by a single parent (predominantly by a woman), this is not so. But this is another of those situations where things are simultaneously getting better and worse. In many of those families that have managed to preserve a stable marital situation, it is not incorrect to say that the quality of child nurturing is higher than it has ever been in historical times, giving weight most specifically to the psychological presence of the father from early on. One hears many tales these days of so-called Yuppie families, and even of those where the father has gone into the "real" world seeking big money, in which the men become passionate about fathering.

Admittedly, this is impressionistic reporting and hardly social "science," but one image remains in my mind as almost an archetypical symbol of a previously unimaginable change. It was the day of the 1987 Superbowl—the most macho of macho days, when American males revel in their manliness—and the Giants had just become the champions of the world. Some were dousing each other with liquids; others were dancing on the field; and one player brought his five-year-old son onto the battleground. He did not hold him high in rigid position, proclaiming triumph. First, he introduced him to other players, requiring him to shake hands all around, and when the boy became restless he picked him up, cradled him in his arms (the huge shoulder pads framing the scene), and nuzzled him. It was an image that would have been impossible twenty years ago. And, possibly, twenty years—

or less—from now, some player will even bring his daughter down onto the same field of triumph. One cannot know what weight to give to the multitude of contradictory and ambivalent impulses in our society. One thing seems certain, however: we are not only standing still or moving backward. There are powerful, morally progressive energies at work. The questions remain: How many, and with what force?

If women persevere in their refusal to give up the struggle, and if men continue to maintain, and even increase, their commitment to nurturing, it may yet be that Eros will win that fateful race with Thanatos. We are running, after all, for our own lives.

NOTES

Chapter 1. Freud's Dilemma and Freud's Solution

1. Ernst L. Freud, ed., *Letters of Sigmund Freud*, trans. Tania and James Stern (New York: Basic Books, 1960), pp. 308–9.

2. Sigmund Freud, 1923, *The Ego and the Id*, in *The Standard Edition of the Complete Psychological Works of Sigmund Freud*, ed. James Strachey et al. (London: Hogarth Press, 1953–74) [hereafter SE] 19:52.

3. Sigmund Freud, 1914, "On Narcissism: An Introduction," SE 14:94.

4. Sigmund Freud, 1933, *New Introductory Lectures on Psycho-Analysis*, SE 22:64–66.

5. Freud, 1923, *The Ego and the Id*, pp. 35, 36.

6. Ibid., italics added.

7. Ibid., p. 57.

8. Sigmund Freud, 1925, "Some Psychical Consequences of the Anatomical Distinction between the Sexes," SE 19:257.

9. Robert Jay Lifton, *The Nazi Doctors* (New York: Basic Books, 1986), p. 134.

10. Ibid., pp. 30, 15–16.

11. Ibid., pp. 204, 207.

12. Ibid., p. 115.

13. Ibid., p. 365.

14. Ibid., pp. 138, 150.

15. Sigmund Freud, 1930, *Civilization and Its Discontents*, SE 21:124.

Chapter 2. Huckleberry's Dilemma: The Conflict Between Conscience and the Superego

1. Mark Twain, *The Adventures of Huckleberry Finn* (New York: Viking Penguin, 1985), chap. 31.

2. Robert Coles, "Psychoanalysis and Moral Development," *American Journal of Psychoanalysis* 41, no. 2 (Summer 1981): 107.

3. Sigmund Freud, 1933, *New Introductory Lectures on Psycho-Analysis*, in *The Standard Edition of the Complete Psychological Works of Sigmund Freud*, ed. James Strachey et al. (London: Hogarth Press, 1953–74) [hereafter SE] 22:64–66.

4. Sigmund Freud, 1930, *Civilization and Its Discontents*, SE 21:145.

Chapter 3. Tyranny and Equality

1. Eli Sagan, *At the Dawn of Tyranny* (New York: Alfred A. Knopf, 1985), chap. 25.

2. Aristotle, *Politics*, ed. and trans. Ernest Barker (Oxford: Oxford University Press, 1958) III, #4.

3. Ibid., V, #1, 6–8.

4. Eli Sagan, *The Lust to Annihilate* (New York: Psychohistory Press, 1979), chap. 9.

5. Lawrence Stone, *The Family, Sex and Marriage in England 1500–1800* (New York: Harper & Row, 1977), pp. 81, 6, italics added.

6. Ibid., pp. 338, 339.

7. Ibid., p. 4.

8. Ibid., pp. 101–2.

9. Ibid., pp. 7–8.

10. Edmund Leites, *The Puritan Conscience and Modern Sexuality* (New Haven, CT: Yale University Press, 1986); Philip Greven, *The Protestant Temperament* (New York: Alfred A. Knopf, 1977); and Edmund S. Morgan, *The Puritan Family* (New York: Harper & Row, 1966).

11. Leites, *The Puritan Conscience and Modern Sexuality*.

12. Stone, *The Family, Sex and Marriage*, p. 6.

13. Greven, *The Protestant Temperament*, p. 35.

14. Stone, *The Family, Sex and Marriage*, p. 101.

15. Ibid., p. 424; and Daniel Beekman, *The Mechanical Baby* (Westport, CT: Lawrence Hill and Co., 1977), p. 34.

16. Beekman, *The Mechanical Baby*, p. 52.

17. Stone, *The Family, Sex and Marriage*, pp. 435, 20.

18. Ibid., pp. 405, 448.

19. Greven, *The Protestant Temperament*, pp. 159, 272.

20. Stone, *The Family, Sex and Marriage*, pp. 136, 137, 102.

21. William Shakespeare, *Hamlet*, act 3, sc. 4, line 69.

22. Stone, *The Family, Sex and Marriage*, pp. 8, 625, italics added.

23. Ibid., pp. 325, 237.

24. Morgan, *The Puritan Family*, pp. 45, 46.

25. Greven, *The Protestant Temperament*, p. 241.

26. Stone, *The Family, Sex and Marriage*, pp. 325, 277, 240.

27. Ibid., pp. 340, 512, 545.

28. Ibid., p. 342.

29. William Blake, "Milton" in Alfred Kazin, ed., *The Portable Blake* (New York: Penguin Books, 1974), p. 412.

Chapter 4. The Great Refusal

1. Lawrence Stone, *The Family, Sex and Marriage in England 1500–1800* (New York: Harper & Row, 1977), p. 240.

2. Sarah B. Pomeroy, *Goddesses, Whores, Wives and Slaves* (New York: Schocken Books, 1975), p. 78.

3. Stone, *The Family, Sex and Marriage*, p. 676.

4. Priscilla Robertson in Lloyd deMause, ed., *The History of Childhood* (New York: Psychohistory Press, 1974), p. 421.

5. Lloyd deMause in deMause, *The History of Childhood*, p. 49.

6. Robertson in deMause, *The History of Childhood*, pp. 413, 424, 425.

Notes

7. Quoted in Daniel Beekman, *The Mechanical Baby* (Westport, CT: Lawrence Hill and Co., 1977), p. 96.

8. Robertson in deMause, *The History of Childhood*, p. 416.

9. Edward P. Cheney, *The Dawn of a New Era, 1250–1453* (New York: Harper and Brothers, 1936), p. 132.

10. Edmund Leites, "The Family as History," *Partisan Review* 53, no. 1 (1986), passim; and Peter Gay, *Education of the Senses* (New York: Oxford University Press, 1984), passim.

11. Stone, *The Family, Sex and Marriage*, p. 666.

12. Gordon Rattray Taylor, *The Angel-Makers* (London: Heinemann, 1958), p. 36.

Chapter 5. The End of the Oedipus Complex and the Formation of the Superego

1. Sigmund Freud, 1933, *New Introductory Lectures on Psycho-Analysis*, in *The Standard Edition of the Complete Psychological Works of Sigmund Freud*, ed. James Strachey et al. (London: Hogarth Press, 1953–74) [hereafter SE] 22:129, italics added.

2. Sigmund Freud, 1926, *The Question of Lay Analysis*, SE 20:134, italics added.

3. Roy Schafer, "The Loving and Beloved Superego in Freud's Structural Theory," *Psychoanalytic Study of the Child* 15 (1960), passim.

4. Sigmund Freud, 1923, *The Ego and the Id*, SE 19:35.

5. Sigmund Freud, 1924, "The Dissolution of the Oedipus Complex," SE 19:173–74.

6. Ibid., p. 177.

7. Sigmund Freud, 1925, "Some Psychical Consequences of the Anatomical Distinction between the Sexes," SE 19:257.

8. Sigmund Freud, 1909, "Analysis of a Phobia in a Five-Year-Old Boy," SE 10:6–8.

9. Freud, 1924, "The Dissolution of the Oedipus Complex," pp. 174–77, italics added.

10. Ibid., pp. 177–79.

11. Freud, 1925, "Some Psychical Consequences of the Anatomical Distinction between the Sexes," pp. 257–58.

12. Sigmund Freud, 1912–13, *Totem and Taboo*, SE 13:142.

13. Freud, 1933, *New Introductory Lectures on Psycho-Analysis*, p. 63.

14. Hans Loewald, "The Waning of the Oedipus Complex," *Journal of the American Psychoanalytic Association*, 27 (1979):758–59, 762.

15. Freud, 1909, "Analysis of a Phobia in a Five-Year-Old Boy," p. 98, 99.

16. Ibid., pp. 131–32, italics added.

17. Anna Freud, *The Ego and the Mechanisms of Defense* (New York: International Universities Press, 1973), p. 72, italics added.

Notes

Chapter 6. The Harsh and Punishing Superego

1. Sigmund Freud, 1924, "The Economic Problem of Masochism," in *The Standard Edition of the Complete Psychological Works of Sigmund Freud*, ed. James Strachey et al. (London: Hogarth Press, 1953–74) [hereafter SE] 19:167.

2. Heinz Hartmann, 1956, "Reality Principle," in Heinz Hartmann, *Essays on Ego Psychology* (New York: International Universities Press, 1964), p. 256.

3. Roy Schafer, "Ideals, the Ego Ideal, and the Ideal Self," in *Motives and Thought*, ed. Robert R. Holt (New York: International Universities Press, 1967), pp. 140–41.

4. Talcott Parsons, *Social Structure and Personality* (New York: The Free Press, 1964), pp. 23–24.

5. Freud, 1926, *Inhibitions, Symptoms and Anxiety*, SE 20:115–16.

6. Sigmund Freud, 1924, "Neurosis and Psychosis," SE 19:149–50.

7. Roy Schafer, "The Loving and Beloved Superego in Freud's Structural Theory," *Psychoanalytic Study of the Child* 15 (1960):186–87.

8. Heinz Hartmann, *Psychoanalysis and Moral Values* (New York: International Universities Press, 1960), pp. 27, 38–39.

9. Schafer, "The Loving and Beloved Superego," pp. 186–87.

10. Sigmund Freud, 1940, *An Outline of Psycho-Analysis*, SE 23:175, italics in the original.

11. Sigmund Freud, 1923, *The Ego and the Id*, SE 19:57, 54.

12. Freud, 1924, "The Economic Problem of Masochism," p. 167.

13. Sigmund Freud, 1933, *New Introductory Lectures on Psycho-Analysis*, SE 22:62.

14. Sigmund Freud, 1912–13, *Totem and Taboo*, SE 13:67.

15. Sigmund Freud, 1928, "Dostoevsky and Parricide," SE 21:185.

16. Sigmund Freud, 1930, *Civilization and Its Discontents*, SE 21:130.

17. Freud, 1924, "The Economic Problem of Masochism," p. 167.

18. Freud, 1930, *Civilization and Its Discontents*, pp. 123–24.

19. Ibid., p. 129.

20. Herman Nunberg, *Principles of Psychoanalysis* (New York: International Universities Press, 1955), p. 172.

21. Edith Jacobson, *The Self and Object World* (New York: International Universities Press, 1964), p. 134.

22. 1 Kings 19:11–13.

23. Sigmund Freud, 1914, "On Narcissism: An Introduction," SE 14:96.

24. Jean Piaget, *The Moral Judgment of the Child*, trans. Marjorie Gabain (New York: The Free Press, 1965), pp. 192–93.

25. Melanie Klein, *Envy and Gratitude* (New York: Delacorte Press, 1975), pp. 251–52.

Chapter 7. Freud's Ambivalent Stance Toward Women and the Pre-Oedipal Mother

1. Sigmund Freud, 1933, *New Introductory Lectures on Psycho-Analysis*, in *The Standard Edition of the Complete Psychological Works of Sigmund Freud*, ed. James Strachey et al. (London: Hogarth Press, 1953–74 [hereafter SE] 22:151.

Notes

2. Ernst L. Freud, ed., *Letters of Sigmund Freud*, trans. Tania and James Stern (New York: Basic Books, 1960), p. 364.

3. Hilda Abraham and Ernst L. Freud, *The Letters of Sigmund Freud and Karl Abraham* (New York: Basic Books, 1965), pp. 185–86.

4. Sigmund Freud, 1927, "Humour," SE 21:159–66.

5. Sigmund Freud, 1930, *Civilization and Its Discontents*, SE 21:113n.

6. Ibid., pp. 109–10.

7. Ibid.

8. Abraham and Freud, *The Letters of Sigmund Freud and Karl Abraham*, p. 76.

9. Ibid.

10. Sigmund Freud, 1893–95, *Studies on Hysteria*, SE 2:103.

11. Sigmund Freud, 1905, *Three Essays on the Theory of Sexuality*, SE 7:220.

12. Herman Nunberg and Ernst Federn, *Minutes of the Vienna Psychoanalytic Society*, vol. 1, *1906–1908* (New York: International Universities Press, 1962), p. 35.

13. Sigmund Freud, 1908, " 'Civilized' Sexual Morality and Modern Nervous Illness," SE 9:185, 199.

14. Sigmund Freud, 1928, "Dostoevsky and Parricide," SE 21:193.

15. Sigmund Freud, 1931, "Female Sexuality," SE 21:227.

16. Sigmund Freud, 1925, "Some Psychical Consequences of the Anatomical Distinction between the Sexes," SE 19:257.

17. Freud, 1933, *New Introductory Lectures on Psycho-Analysis*, p. 134.

18. Ibid., pp. 116–17.

19. Freud, 1931, "Female Sexuality," p. 226.

20. Ibid., pp. 226–27.

21. Freud, 1930, *Civilization and Its Discontents*, p. 72.

22. Sigmund Freud, 1923, *The Ego and the Id*, SE 19:31, 32.

23. Freud, 1931, "Female Sexuality," p. 234, italics added.

24. Sigmund Freud, 1924, "The Dissolution of the Oedipus Complex," SE 19:174–75.

25. Ibid., pp. 175–76.

26. Freud, 1925, "Some Psychical Consequences of the Anatomical Distinction between the Sexes," p. 252.

27. Sigmund Freud, "On the Sexual Theories of Children," SE 9:217.

28. Sigmund Freud, 1923, "The Infantile Genital Organization: An Interpolation into the Theory of Sexuality," SE 19:145, italics in the original.

29. Freud, 1905, *Three Essays on the Theory of Sexuality*, pp. 199–200n, added in 1924.

30. Freud, 1925, "Some Psychical Consequences of the Anatomical Distinction between the Sexes," pp. 257–58.

Chapter 8. Ambivalence About Civilization

1. Sigmund Freud, 1908, " 'Civilized' Sexual Morality and Modern Nervous Illness," in *The Standard Edition of the Complete Psychological Works of Sigmund Freud*, ed. James Strachey et al. (London: Hogarth Press, 1953–74) [hereafter SE] 9:177–204.

2. Ibid., pp. 185, 186 (italics added), 187.

Notes

3. Sigmund Freud, 1912, "On the Universal Tendency to Debasement in the Sphere of Love," SE 11:178–90. Quotes on pp. 188 and 189.

4. Ibid., p. 189.

5. Sigmund Freud, 1916–17, *Introductory Lectures on Psycho-Analysis*, SE 16:354.

6. Sigmund Freud, 1926, *The Question of Lay Analysis*, SE 20:217.

7. Sigmund Freud, 1910, "The Psycho-Analytic View of a Psychogenic Disturbance of Vision," SE 11:215.

8. Sigmund Freud, 1924, "A Short Account of Psycho-Analysis," SE 19:207.

9. Sigmund Freud, 1930, *Civilization and Its Discontents*, SE 21:122.

10. Sigmund Freud, 1933, *New Introductory Lectures on Psycho-Analysis*, SE 22:110.

11. Freud, 1912, "On the Universal Tendency to Debasement in the Sphere of Love," p. 190.

12. Ibid., pp. 187, 190.

13. Sigmund Freud, 1915, "Thoughts for the Times on War and Death," SE 14:284–85.

14. Freud, 1930, *Civilization and Its Discontents*, p. 134.

15. Freud, 1915, "Thoughts for the Times on War and Death," p. 285.

16. Freud, 1930, *Civilization and Its Discontents*, p. 141.

17. Ibid., p. 122.

18. Freud, 1933, *New Introductory Lectures on Psycho-Analysis*, p. 110.

19. Margaret Mahler et al., *The Psychological Birth of the Human Infant* (New York: Basic Books, 1975), passim.

20. Herman Nunberg and Ernst Federn, *Minutes of the Vienna Psychoanalytic Society*, vol. 2 (New York: International Universities Press, 1967), p. 174, italics added.

21. Freud, 1933, *New Introductory Lectures on Psycho-Analysis*, p. 110.

22. Quoted in Lloyd deMause, ed., *The History of Childhood* (New York: Psychohistory Press, 1974), p. 2.

Chapter 9. The Split Between the Soul and the Body, Between Reason and Feelings

1. Mary Midgeley, *Beast and Man* (New York: New American Library, 1980), p. 44.

2. 1 Corinthians 7:1–9.

3. Sigmund Freud, 1910, "A Special Type of Choice of Object Made by Men," in *The Standard Edition of the Complete Psychological Works of Sigmund Freud*, ed. James Strachey et al. (London: Hogarth Press, 1953–74) [hereafter SE] 11:165.

4. Romans 8:5–12.

5. Sigmund Freud, 1927, *The Future of an Illusion*, SE 21:48, 53, italics added.

6. 1 Corinthians 7:32–33.

7. Galatians 5:19–21.

8. Karen Horney, "The Dread of Women," *International Journal of Psycho-Analysis* 13 (1932):353.

9. Dorothy Dinnerstein, *The Mermaid and the Minotaur* (New York: Harper & Row, 1977), pp. 66–67.

Notes

10. Sigmund Freud, 1928, "Dostoevsky and Parricide," SE 21:193.

11. René Descartes, *Discourse on Method* (Baltimore: Penguin Books, 1968), p. 54.

12. Quoted in Sheldon Wolin, *Politics and Vision* (Boston: Little, Brown, 1960), p. 318.

13. Sigmund Freud, 1940, *An Outline of Psycho-Analysis*, SE 23:148.

14. Jean-Jacques Rousseau, *Second Discourse*, trans. Robert D. Masters and Judith R. Masters (New York: St. Martin's Press, 1964), pp. 131, 95–96, 133.

15. Jean-Jacques Rousseau, *Emile*, trans. Alan Bloom (New York: Basic Books, 1979), p. 235.

16. Sigmund Freud, 1933, *New Introductory Lectures on Psycho-Analysis*, SE 22:160.

17. Ibid., pp. 158, 159.

18. Ibid., p. 181.

19. Ibid., pp. 162, 171, italics added.

20. Sigmund Freud, 1930, *Civilization and Its Discontents*, SE 21:112.

21. Heinz Hartmann, *Psychoanalysis and Moral Values* (New York: International Universities Press, 1960), pp. 24, 60.

22. Ibid., p. 26.

23. Ibid., p. 102, italics added.

Chapter 10. Love, Identification, and the Origins of Conscience

1. William McGuire, ed., *The Freud/Jung Letters*, trans. Ralph Manheim and R. F. C. Hull (Princeton, NJ: Princeton University Press, 1974), pp. 12–13.

2. Herman Nunberg and Ernst Federn, *Minutes of the Vienna Psychoanalytic Society*, vol. 1, *1906–1908* (New York: International Universities Press, 1962), p. 60.

3. Sigmund Freud, 1916, "Some Character-Types Met with in Psycho-Analytic Work," in *The Standard Edition of the Complete Psychological Works of Sigmund Freud*, ed. James Strachey et al. (London: Hogarth Press, 1953–74) [hereafter SE] 14:312.

4. Ida MacAlpine, "The Development of the Transference," *Psychoanalytic Quarterly* 19 (1950):501–39.

5. Phyllis Greenacre, "The Role of Transference," *Journal of the American Psychoanalytic Association* 2 (1954):671–84.

6. René A. Spitz, "Transference: The Analytical Setting and Its Prototype," *International Journal of Psycho-Analysis* 37 (1956):380–85.

7. Ibid., p. 382.

8. Heinz Hartmann, *Psychoanalysis and Moral Values* (New York: International Universities Press, 1960), passim.

9. Sigmund Freud, 1933, *New Introductory Lectures on Psycho-Analysis*, SE 22:62.

10. Sigmund Freud, 1920, *Group Psychology and the Analysis of the Ego*, SE 18:90–92.

11. Sigmund Freud, 1930, *Civilization and Its Discontents*, SE 21:55, 122.

12. Sigmund Freud, 1933, *Why War?* SE 22:212.

13. Ruth Mack Brunswick, "The Preoedipal Phase of the Libido Development," *Psychoanalytic Quarterly* 9 (1940):307–8.

14. René Spitz, "On the Genesis of Superego Components," *Psychoanalytic Study of the Child* 13 (1958):391.

Notes

15. Jean-Jacques Rousseau, *Emile*, trans. Alan Bloom (New York: Basic Books, 1979), p. 213.

16. Spitz, "On the Genesis of Superego Components," p. 394.

17. Rosalind Gould, *Child Studies Through Fantasy* (New York: Quadrangle Books, 1972), passim.

18. John B. McDevitt, "The Role of Internalization in the Development of Object Relations during the Separation-Individuation Phase," *Journal of the American Psychoanalytic Association* 27 (1979):339–40, 331.

19. Gould, *Child Studies Through Fantasy*, p. 231.

20. Hartmann, *Psychoanalysis and Moral Values*, pp. 55, 60.

21. Mary Midgeley, *Beast and Man* (New York: New American Library, 1980), p. 333.

22. Ernest Jones, *The Life and Work of Sigmund Freud*, vol. 1 (New York: Basic Books, 1953), p. 389.

23. Anna Freud, *The Ego and the Mechanisms of Defense* (New York: International Universities Press, 1983), passim.

24. Spitz, "On the Genesis of Superego Components," p. 384.

25. Gould, *Child Studies Through Fantasy*, pp. 214–15.

26. Ibid., p. 232.

27. Ibid., p. 142.

28. Spitz, "On the Genesis of Superego Components," p. 384.

29. Sigmund Freud, 1923, *The Ego and the Id*, SE 19:35.

30. Rousseau, *Emile*, pp. 222, 235.

31. Sigmund Freud, 1905, *Three Essays on the Theory of Sexuality*, SE 7:192–93.

32. Manuel Furer, "Some Developmental Aspects of the Superego," *International Journal of Psycho-Analysis* 48 (1967):277.

33. Margaret Mahler et al., *The Psychological Birth of the Human Infant* (New York: Basic Books, 1975), pp. 97–98.

34. Sigmund Freud, 1931, "Female Sexuality," SE 21:passim.

35. McDevitt, "The Role of Internalization in the Development of Object Relations," p. 340.

36. Talcott Parsons, *Social Structure and Personality* (New York: The Free Press, 1964), p. 29.

Chapter 11. The Capacity and the Need for Idealization

1. Quoted in Arnold D. Richards, "The Subordinate Self in Psychoanalytic Theory and in Self Psychologies," *Journal of the American Psychoanalytic Association* 30 (1982):944.

2. Sigmund Freud, 1923, *The Ego and the Id*, in *The Standard Edition of the Complete Psychological Works of Sigmund Freud*, ed. James Strachey et al. (London: Hogarth Press, 1953–74) [hereafter SE] 19:58.

3. Sigmund Freud, 1914, "On Narcissism: An Introduction," SE 14:94.

4. Sigmund Freud, 1933, *New Introductory Lectures on Psycho-Analysis*, SE 22:64–65.

5. Heinz Hartmann and Rudolf Loewenstein, "Notes on the Superego," in Heinz

Notes

Hartmann, Ernst Kris, and Rudolf M. Loewenstein, *Papers on Psychoanalytic Psychology, Psychological Issues* 4 (ND) (Monograph 14), p. 163.

6. Edith Jacobson, *The Self and Object World* (New York: International Universities Press, 1964), p. 94.

7. Freud, 1933, *New Introductory Lectures on Psycho-Analysis*, p. 65.

8. René Spitz, "On the Genesis of Superego Components," *Psychoanalytic Study of the Child* 13 (1958):387.

9. Melanie Klein, *Envy and Gratitude* (New York: Delacorte Press, 1975), pp. 251–52.

10. Heinz Hartmann, *Essays on Ego Psychology* (New York: International Universities Press, 1964), p. 231.

11. Ernst L. Freud, ed., *Letters of Sigmund Freud*, trans. Tania and James Stern (New York: Basic Books, 1960), p. 309.

12. Hanna Segal, *Introduction to the Work of Melanie Klein* (New York: Basic Books, 1974), passim.

13. Jacobson, *The Self and Object World*, p. 66.

14. Freud, 1923, *The Ego and the Id*, p. 37.

15. Sigmund Freud, 1933, *Why War?* SE 22:212.

Chapter 12. Moral Contradictions in Adult Life

1. Sigmund Freud, 1920, *Group Psychology and the Analysis of the Ego*, in *The Standard Edition of the Complete Psychological Works of Sigmund Freud*, ed. James Strachey et al. (London: Hogarth Press, 1953–74) [hereafter SE] 18:92.

2. Hannah Arendt, *The Origins of Totalitarianism* (New York: Harcourt Brace Jovanovich, 1973), p. 377.

3. Heinz Hartmann, *Psychoanalysis and Moral Values* (New York: International Universities Press, 1960), p. 27.

4. Sigmund Freud, 1927, "Humour," SE 21:166.

5. Sigmund Freud, 1933, *New Introductory Lectures on Psycho-Analysis*, SE 22:65.

6. Sigmund Freud, 1923, *The Ego and the Id*, SE 19:52.

7. Nathan G. Hale, Jr., ed., *James Jackson Putnam and Psychoanalysis* (Cambridge, MA: Harvard University Press, 1971), p. 188.

8. Talcott Parsons, *Social Structure and Personality* (New York: The Free Press, 1964), pp. 18, 17.

9. Eli Sagan, *Cannibalism: Human Aggression and Cultural Form* (New York: Harper & Row, 1974), passim.

10. Freud, 1933, *New Introductory Lectures on Psycho-Analysis*, p. 64, italics added.

11. Parsons, *Social Structure and Personality*, p. 29 and chap. 2.

12. John Frosch, *The Psychotic Process* (New York: International Universities Press, 1983), passim.

13. Jean-Jacques Rousseau, *Emile*, trans. Alan Bloom (New York: Basic Books, 1979), p. 253.

14. Herman Nunberg and Ernst Federn, *Minutes of the Vienna Psychoanalytic Society*, vol. 1, *1906–1908* (New York: International Universities Press, 1962), p. 35.

15. René Spitz, "On the Genesis of Superego Components," *Psychoanalytic Study of the Child* 8 (1958):387.

16. Dorothy Dinnerstein, *The Mermaid and the Minotaur* (New York: Harper & Row, 1977), passim.

17. Margaret Mahler et al., *The Psychological Birth of the Human Infant* (New York: Basic Books, 1975), passim.

18. Sigmund Freud, 1930, *Civilization and Its Discontents*, SE 21:122.

Chapter 13. Some Reflections on a Fundamental Change in the System of Values

1. Livy, *Annales*, vol. 1, trans. B. O. Foster (Cambridge, MA: Harvard University Press, 1976), book 1, preface, p. 9.

2. Peter Brown, review of *Pagans and Christians*, by Robin Lane Fox, *New York Review of Books*, 12 March 1987.

3. Quoted in E. R. Dodds, *The Greeks and the Irrational* (Berkeley: University of California Press, 1951), p. 254.

4. Dorothy Dinnerstein, *The Mermaid and the Minotaur* (New York: Harper & Row, 1977), passim.

5. "Single Parents Head 25% of Families in the United States," *New York Times*, 6 November 1986, p. C13.

6. Max Weber, *The Protestant Ethic and the Spirit of Capitalism*, trans. Talcott Parsons (New York: Charles Scribner's Sons, 1958), passim.

BIBLIOGRAPHY

Freud: Published Works and Letters

All quotations from Freud come from *The Standard Edition of the Complete Psychological Writings of Sigmund Freud*, 24 volumes, edited by James Strachey et al. (London: Hogarth Press, 1953–74). The abbreviation "SE" is used to indicate this work, followed by the volume number and page numbers on which the work appears.

Letters of Freud, edited by others, are listed after Freud's published works.

1893–1895, *Studies on Hysteria*, SE 2.

1905, *Three Essays on the Theory of Sexuality*, SE 7:125–243.

1908, " 'Civilized' Sexual Morality and Modern Nervous Illness," SE 9:179–204.

1908, "On the Sexual Theories of Children," SE 9:207–26.

1909, "Analysis of a Phobia in a Five-Year-Old Boy," SE 10:3–147.

1910, "The Psycho-analytic View of a Psychogenic Disturbance of Vision," SE 11:210–18.

1910, "A Special Type of Choice of Object Made by Men," SE 10:163–175.

1912, "On the Universal Tendency to Debasement in the Sphere of Love," SE 11:178–90.

1912–1913, *Totem and Taboo*, SE 13:1–161.

1914, "On Narcissism: An Introduction," SE 14:69–102.

1915, "Thoughts for the Times on War and Death," SE 14:273–302.

1916, "Some Character-Types Met with in Psychoanalytic Work," SE 14:309–333.

1915–1916, *Introductory Lectures on Psycho-Analysis*, Part 1 and Part 2, SE 15.

1916–1917, *Introductory Lectures on Psycho-Analysis*, Part 3, SE 16.

1920, *Group Psychology and the Analysis of the Ego*, SE 18:67–143.

1923, *The Ego and the Id*, SE 19:3–59.

1923, "The Infantile Genital Organization: An Interpolation into the Theory of Sexuality," SE 19:141–145.

1924, "The Loss of Reality in Neurosis and Psychosis," SE 19:183–187.

1924, "The Dissolution of the Oedipus Complex," SE 19:172–79.

1924, "The Economic Problem of Masochism," SE 19:157–70.

1924, "A Short Account of Psycho-Analysis," SE 19:190–209.

1925, "Some Psychical Consequences of the Anatomical Distinction between the Sexes," SE 19:243–58.

1926, *The Question of Lay Analysis*, SE 20:179–250.

1926, *Inhibitions, Symptoms and Anxiety*, SE 20:77–172.

1927, *The Future of an Illusion*, SE 21:3–56.

1927, "Humour," SE 21:159–166.

1928, "Dostoevsky and Parricide," SE 21:175–194.

1930, *Civilization and Its Discontents*, SE 21:59–145.

1931, "Female Sexuality," SE 21:223–43.

Bibliography

1933, *New Introductory Lectures on Psycho-Analysis*, SE 22:3–182.
1933, *Why War?* SE 22:197–215.
1940, *An Outline of Psycho-Analysis*, SE 23:141–207.

Abraham, Hilda, and Freud, Ernst L. *The Letters of Sigmund Freud and Karl Abraham*. New York: Basic Books, 1965.
Freud, Ernst L., ed. *Letters of Sigmund Freud*, trans. Tania and James Stern. New York: Basic Books, 1960.
McGuire, William, ed. *The Freud/Jung Letters*, trans. Ralph Manheim and R. F. C. Hull. Princeton, NJ: Princeton University Press, 1974.

Other Works

Arendt, Hannah. *The Origins of Totalitarianism*. New York: Harcourt Brace Jovanovich, 1973.
Aristotle. *Politics*, ed. and trans. Ernest Barker. Oxford: Oxford University Press, 1958.
Beekman, Daniel. *The Mechanical Baby*. Westport, CT: Lawrence Hill and Co., 1977.
Bellah, Robert N., et al. *Habits of the Heart*. Berkeley: University of California Press, 1985.
Brown, Peter. Review of *Pagans and Christians*, by Robin Lane Fox. *New York Review of Books*, 12 March 1987.
Brunswick, Ruth Mack. "The Preoedipal Phase of the Libido Development," *Psychoanalytic Quarterly* 9 (1940):293–319.
Cheney, Edward P. *The Dawn of a New Era, 1250–1453*. New York: Harper and Brothers, 1936.
Coles, Robert. "Psychoanalysis and Moral Development," *American Journal of Psychoanalysis* 41, no. 2 (Summer 1981):101–113.
deMause, Lloyd, ed. *The History of Childhood*. New York: Psychohistory Press, 1974.
Descartes, René. *Discourse on Method*. Baltimore: Penguin Books, 1968.
Dinnerstein, Dorothy. *The Mermaid and the Minotaur*. New York: Harper & Row, 1977.
Dodds, E. R. *The Greeks and the Irrational*. Berkeley: University of California Press, 1951.
Freud, Anna. *The Ego and the Mechanisms of Defense*. New York: International Universities Press, 1973.
Frosch, John. *The Psychotic Process*. New York: International Universities Press, 1983.
Furer, Manuel. "Some Developmental Aspects of the Superego," *International Journal of Psycho-Analysis* 48 (1967):277–80.
Gay, Peter. *Education of the Senses*. New York: Oxford University Press, 1984.
Gould, Rosalind. *Child Studies Through Fantasy*. New York: Quadrangle Books, 1972.
Greenacre, Phyllis, "The Role of Transference," *Journal of the American Psychoanalytic Association* 2 (1954):671–84.
Greven, Philip. *The Protestant Temperament*. New York: Alfred Knopf, 1977.
Hale, Nathan G., Jr., ed. *James Jackson Putnam and Psychoanalysis*. Cambridge, MA: Harvard University Press, 1971.

Bibliography

Hartmann, Heinz. *Psychoanalysis and Moral Values*. New York: International Universities Press, 1960.

———. *Essays on Ego Psychology*. New York: International Universities Press, 1964.

———, and Loewenstein, Rudolf. "Notes on the Superego," in Heinz Hartmann, Ernst Kris, and Rudolf M. Loewenstein, *Papers on Psychoanalytic Psychology*, *Psychological Issues* 4 (ND) (Monograph 14).

Horney, Karen. "The Dread of Women," *International Journal of Psychoanalysis* 13 (1932):348–60.

Jacobson, Edith. *The Self and Object World*. New York: International Universities, 1964.

Jones, Ernest. *The Life and Work of Sigmund Freud*, vol. 1. New York: Basic Books, 1953.

Klein, Melanie. *Envy and Gratitude*. New York: Delacorte, 1975.

Lasch, Christopher. *The Culture of Narcissism*. New York: W. W. Norton, 1979.

Leites, Edmund. *The Puritan Conscience and Modern Sexuality*. New Haven, CT: Yale University Press, 1986.

———. "The Family as History," *Partisan Review* 53, no. 1 (1986):111–25.

Lifton, Robert Jay. *The Nazi Doctors*. New York: Basic Books, 1986.

Livy, *Annales*, trans. B. O. Foster, vol. 1. Cambridge, MA: Harvard University Press, 1976.

Loewald, Hans. "The Waning of the Oedipus Complex," *Journal of the American Psychoanalytic Association* 27 (1979):751–75.

MacAlpine, Ida. "The Development of the Transference," *Psychoanalytic Quarterly* 19 (1950):501–39.

McDevitt, John B. "The Role of Internalization in the Development of Object Relations during the Separation-Individuation Phase," *Journal of the American Psychoanalytic Association* 27 (1979):327–44.

Mahler, Margaret, et al. *The Psychological Birth of the Human Infant*. New York: Basic Books, 1975.

Midgeley, Mary. *Beast and Man*. New York: New American Library, 1980.

Morgan, Edmund S. *The Puritan Family*. New York: Harper & Row, 1966.

Nunberg, Herman. *Principles of Psychoanalysis*. New York: International Universities Press, 1955.

———, and Federn, Ernst. *Minutes of the Vienna Psychoanalytic Society*, vol. 1, *1906–1908*. New York: International Universities Press, 1962.

———. *Minutes of the Vienna Psychoanalytic Society*, vol. 2. New York: International Universities Press, 1967.

Parsons, Talcott. *Social Structure and Personality*. New York: The Free Press, 1964.

Piaget, Jean. *The Moral Judgment of the Child*, trans. Marjorie Gabain. New York: The Free Press, 1965.

Pomeroy, Sarah B. *Goddesses, Whores, Wives and Slaves*. New York: Schocken Books, 1975.

Richards, Arnold D. "The Subordinate Self in Psychoanalytic Theory and in Self Psychologies," *Journal of the American Psychoanalytic Association* 30 (1982):939–57.

Rousseau, Jean-Jacques. *Emile*, trans. Alan Bloom. New York: Basic Books, 1979.

———. *Second Discourse*, trans. Roger D. Masters and Judith R. Masters. New York: St. Martin's Press, 1964.

Bibliography

Sagan, Eli. *Cannibalism: Human Aggression and Cultural Form.* New York: Harper & Row, 1974.

————. *The Lust to Annihilate.* New York: Psychohistory Press, 1979.

————. *At the Dawn of Tyranny.* New York: Alfred A. Knopf, 1985.

Schafer, Roy. "The Loving and Beloved Superego in Freud's Structural Theory," *Psychoanalytic Study of the Child* 15 (1960):163–88.

————. "Ideals, the Ego Ideal, and the Ideal Self," in *Motives and Thought*, ed. Robert R. Holt, pp. 131–74. New York: International Universities Press, 1967.

Segal, Hanna. *Introduction to the Work of Melanie Klein.* New York: Basic Books, 1974.

Spitz, René A. "Transference: The Analytical Setting and Its Prototype," *International Journal of Psychoanalysis* 37 (1956):380–85.

————. "On the Genesis of Superego Components," *Psychoanalytic Study of the Child* 13 (1958):375–404.

Stone, Lawrence. *The Family, Sex and Marriage in England 1500–1800.* New York: Harper & Row, 1977.

Taylor, Gordon Rattray. *The Angel-Makers.* London: Heinemann, 1958.

Twain, Mark. *The Adventures of Huckleberry Finn.* New York: Viking Penguin, 1985.

Weber, Max. *The Protestant Ethic and the Spirit of Capitalism*, trans. Talcott Parsons. New York: Charles Scribner's Sons, 1958.

Wolin, Sheldon. *Politics and Vision.* Boston: Little, Brown, 1960.

INDEX

Abbott, Jacob, 55

ABM treaty, 240

Abortion, 56, 220

Abraham, Karl, 106

Abstraction, capacity for, 204–7

Acting out, 100; aggressive, 164; and negative idealizations, 213

Adams, Abigail, 47–48

Adams, John, 47

Adler, Alfred, 105

Adolescence: capacity for generalization and abstraction in, 204, 205, 213; conflict between superego and conscience in, 173; idealized values in, 187; repression of sexuality in, 140; revolt in, 201; reworking of Oedipus complex in, 78, 81–82; superego attributes in, 87

Affective individualism, 38

Aggression: biological basis of, 222; toward childhood sexuality, 141; against children, 49; conflicts between love and, 28, 164; control of, 200; as defense against anxiety, 52, 236; guilt and, 99; Hartmann on, 154; inhibition of, 98–99; mother as original object of, 211; of Nazi superego, 13; in nurturing, 189; projection onto parents of, 97–98; relationship of civilization to, 120, 121, 124–35; relgion and, 139–40; "spoiling" and, 96; sublimation of, 180, 188, 242, 243; turned on the self, 96–97

Aggressor, identification with, 69, 124, 173–78, 188, 191, 193, 212

Ambivalence: about civilization, 119–35; conscience and, 164; and current moral problems, 65; about equality for women, 33, 238; toward first nurturer-destroyer, 211; Freud and, 8–9, 61–64; about morality, 172; nineteenth-century, 55–56, 59; of nurturing, 28; perpetuation of, 234–35; of present age, 227–28; about racism, 22; relativism and, 31; social norms and, 203; and split between reason and feeling, 137;

and structural model, 5; within superego, 200; in systems of values, 220

American Revolution, 48, 53

Anal stage, 73, 80, 111, 114, 117, 132–33

Anatomical distinctions between the sexes, 73, 75

Anger, sexuality and, 130–31

Anthony, Susan B., 58

Anti-Semitism, 201

Anxiety: toward childhood sexuality, 140; defenses against, 52, 53; about homosexual impulses, 142; male, about female sexuality, 142, 143; moral progress prevented by, 234–39; and preoedipal mother, 113; about reengulfment by symbiotic mother, 143; sexual, of men, 45–47, 49; see also Castration anxiety; Separation anxiety

Aquinas, St. Thomas, 231

Argentina, 199

Aristotle, 28–30, 32, 33, 64

Arlow, Jacob, 184

Arms control, 195, 233

Arranged marriage, 44

Astell, Mary, 48

Atheism, 223

Athenian democracy, 37, 51–52

Augustine, Saint, 135

Augustus Caesar, 230

Auschwitz, 11, 12, 31, 33, 168

Authoritarianism, 57, 58, 60, 191, 234, 236, 239; superego and, 72, 101–2

Autonomy, achievement of, 208–10, 214

Ball, John, 58

Bellah, Robert N., 225n, 233n, 239

Bergen-Belsen, 31

Berlin, University of, 10

Bible, 49, 93, 101

Black Death, 231

Blacks, prejudice against, see Racism

Bodelschwingh, Fritz von, 11–12

261

Index

Death instinct, 126, 127; *see also* Thanatos

Debs, Eugene, 206

Defense(s): apotheosis of science as, 155–56; against castration anxiety, 76; contempt for women as, 116; domination as, 60; giving up of, 52, 60; against homosexual impulses, 142; identification with aggressor as, 174, 176; reification of reason as, 139; religious, 140; social, 235–36

Democracy, 34, 50, 214, 215, 225, 227; Athenian, 37, 51–52; child-rearing practices and, 41; imperialism and, 52; in nineteenth century, 49, 56–57

Democratic Party, 232

Depression, 96

Descartes, René, 144–45

Dickens, Charles, 54

Dickinson, Emily, 123

Dinnerstein, Dorothy, 143–44, 238, 244

Disadvantaged, neglect of, 223, 224

"Dissolution of the Oedipus Complex, The" (Freud), 72

Dodds, E. R., 137

Dostoevski, Feodor, 61

Dostoevsky and Parricide (Freud), 95

"Dread of Woman, The" (Horney), 143

Drives: destructive, 130, 146, 164, 176, 200, 222; differential treatment of, 134; relationship of civilization to, 120, 125; and soul-body split, 137; sublimation of, 134, 135

Durkheim, Emile, 192, 203, 221

Dutch republic, 34

Economic equality, 58

Edgeworth, Maria, 54

Education: seventeenth- and eighteenth-century attitudes toward, 39, 42; universal public, 57

Ego, 5, 70n, 80, 199; aggression directed toward, 97; domination of superego over, 72; estrangement of superego and, 71; external reality and, 89; formation of, 6; and good object, 103; and

identification with aggressor, 174; and identification with good object, 188; introjection of id's libidinal impulses into, 86; loss of autonomy of, 143; lower classes and, 107; as metaphorical structure, 184; positive relationship of superego and, 91, 92; superego demands on, 8; and symptom formation, 90

Ego and the Id, The (Freud), 4, 5, 72, 92

Ego ideal, 5, 6, 8, 20, 183, 185; conflict between superego and, 200; maintenance of, 5; narcissism and, 185–86; origin of, 112

Ego instincts, 126

Eisenhower, Dwight D., 220, 236, 244

Ela, Daniel, 47

England, 199; child-rearing practices in, 40–43; constitutional monarchy in, 53; imperialism of, 56; Peterloo massacre in, 53, 57; women's suffrage in, 59

English revolution, 36–37

Englishwoman's Domestic Magazine, 56

Enlightenment, the, 53

Equality, 32–33, 37, 53, 225; ambivalence about, 190; economic, 58; Freud's attitudes toward, 104, 107, 108, 118; ideal of, 214; and Levellers, 36; and political candidates, 232; and Puritanism, 40; and sexuality, 45–49, 51; in system of values, 223; for women, *see* Feminism

Equal Rights Amendment, 244

Eros, 14, 15, 44, 211, 222, 243, 246; and adult moral contradictions, 200; and ambivalence, 28, 65; and child-rearing practices, 42, 191; and civilization, 63, 120, 126–31, 167, 182, 215; and group concern, 196–97; and intelligence, 139; and morality, 21; and mother-infant dyad, 168–69; Plato on, 138, 166; power of, 214; repression of, 147, 193; and scientific *Weltanschauung,* 153; and Thanatos, 165; and work, 242

Euripides, 30

Euthanasia, Nazi program of, 10, 11

Evangelicals, child-rearing practices of, 40, 54

Index

Himmler, Heinrich, 197, 199
Hippocratic oath, 11
Hiroshima, 33, 168
Hitler, Adolf, 10–12, 212
Hobbes, Thomas, 38, 145, 147
Hochschild, Arlie, 156n
Holland, Henry Lord, 41–42
Homer, 227
Homosexuality, 140, 142, 148
Horney, Karen, 143
House of Representatives, U.S., 195
Human sacrifice, 214
Hus, Jan, 228, 231
Hysteria, 162

Id, 5, 45, 70n, 199; formation of, 6; instinctual demands of, 90; lower classes
and, 107; as metaphorical structure,
184; origins of superego in, 86, 88, 89
Idealization, 65, 183–94, 200, 204, 205,
212–13, 233; of Freud, 215n; superego
capacity for, 92
Identification, 80, 107–8, 200, 204, 206,
212; with aggressor, 69, 124, 173–78,
188, 191, 193, 212; and conscience,
160, 169–82; with evil, 192; Freud on,
167–68; idealization and, 188; with
nurturer, 14, 171–73, 191; pre-oedipal,
112; splitting and, 190; with victim
and comforter, 178–81; in warfare,
192–93
Imperialism, 28, 56; democracy and, 52;
equation of moral universalism with,
31
Incest taboos, 121, 123, 124; and anxiety
toward childhood sexuality, 140
Incorporation, oral, 79–80
Independent judgment, 208
Individualism: affective, 38; radical, 225,
239
Infanticide, 214
Infantile sexuality, 54, 57
Inquisition, 12
Instincts: defusion of, 96; fusion of, 140;
Mill on, 145; relationship of civiliza-

tion to, 120, 121, 125–27, 131–35; and
symptom formation, 141; triumph of
reason over, 138, 139
Intrasystemic conflict, 200
Introductory Lectures on Psycho-Analysis
(Freud), 124, 165
Isakower, Otto, 19, 100

Jacobson, Edith, 100, 186, 190–91
James, William, 208
Japan, 243
Jews: derogatory generalizations about,
110; intellectual, 104; Nazi genocide
of, 10–13; Orthodox, 94; prejudice
against, 124
Johnson, Lyndon, 52, 232
Judgment, independent, 208
Jung, Carl, 161, 222

Kennedy, John, 232
Kennedy, Robert, 232
Kernberg, Otto, 222
King, Martin Luther, 168
Kingship, 34
Klein, Fritz, 11
Klein, Melanie, 102–3, 174, 187–89

Lady's Monthly Museum, The, 49
Lasch, Christopher, 225n, 239
Latency period, 72, 75
Leites, Edmund, 40n
Levellers, 36
Leviathan (Hobbes), 147
Liberalism, 53, 145, 227; and child-
rearing attitudes, 40; feminist, 47, 51; of
Freud, 104–8; of Locke, 38; work and,
241, 242
Liberties of the Massachusetts Colony, The,
47

265

Index

Index

Regression: in response to anxiety, 235; social, 148

Relativism, cultural, 30–32

Religion: during Eisenhower era, 236; fundamentalist, 53; idealization in, 186; imperative of good conduct in, 152; science versus, 151, 223; *see also* Catholic Church; Jews; Protestantism

Renaissance, 227, 230

Repetition compulsion, 78, 163, 165

Repression, 189; of aggression, 96, 97; and civilization, 120–28, 131–35; of excremental interests, 123; of masturbation, 55; of memory of pre-oedipal mother, 9, 14, 62–64, 105, 111–13, 118; nineteenth-century, 48, 49; of Oedipus complex, 72, 73; overly aggressive, 141; and punishing superego, 87; and Puritanism, 39; and racism, 124; and reason, 147; religious, 139–40; of sexuality, 45–46; social, 141–42; and soul-body split, 137; sublimation distinguished from, 134; and symptom formation, 89–90

Rolland, Romain, 105

Rome, ancient, 128, 224, 230, 231, 241

Rousseau, Jean Jacques, 33, 41, 145–47, 160, 170, 178, 205, 207

Sadism, 14, 174; control of impulses of, 123; and eroticism, 121, 125, 130, 131; of Nazis, 11–13, 192

SALT I, 240

Schafer, Roy, 88, 90–92

Schliemann, Heinrich, 111

School integration, 19, 204

Science: apotheosis of, as symptomatic behavior, 149–56; as basis of morality, 152–53; Freud on, 63, 137–39; and system of values, 223

Selective identification, 190–91, 201

Self-esteem, 208

Self-observation, 5, 20

Senate, U.S., 195

Separation and individuation, 131, 132, 145, 202n; and selective identification, 190

Separation anxiety, 213, 214; defense against, 237

Sexism, 8, 9, 13, 32, 33, 53, 154, 223–25; and anxiety, 237–38; commitment to ending, 233; as defense, 52; encouraged by superego, 63; of Freud, 110–11; and identification with aggressor, 174; late Victorian, 147–48; and male sexual anxiety, 46; and repression of memory of pre-oedipal mother, 105; in seventeenth century, 36; and social norms, 201

Sexuality, 51; adolescent, 208–9; and civilization, 120–31, 133; cultural degradation of, 87; and equality, 45–49, 51; Freud and liberation of, 64; infantile, 54, 57; and love, 44, 165–66; male fear of, 45–47, 49; nineteenth-century, 58; and Puritanism, 39, 40; and religion, 138–40; and shifts in values, 225, 226; social repression of, 141–42; sublimation of, 188; *see also* Libido

Shakespeare, William, 234

Shame, hidden, 4

Slavery, 9, 13, 23, 33, 148, 213; abolition of, 49, 57, 214, 225, 226; in ancient Greece, 28–30, 32, 64, 213, 222; Huckleberry Finn and, 16–19, 22; institutionalization of, 28; legitimized by superego, 63; in seventeenth century, 35, 36; as universally immoral, 27

Social conscience, 161

Socialism, 104, 105

Social norms, 201, 203, 223

Socrates, 146, 202

Sophocles, 129

Soul, split between body and, 136–56

Soviet Union, swaddling in, 50

Spitz, René, 55, 162, 169, 170, 175, 177, 188

Splitting, 46, 102, 144, 189–90, 211; Freud's capacity for, 108; and idealization, 212; and moral contradictions, 199; on moral issues, 172, 196

Index

Spock, Benjamin, 55
"Spoiling" of children, 95–96, 98
SS, 197
Stalinism, 33, 53, 223
Stanton, Elizabeth Cady, 58
Sterilization, Nazi programs of, 10
Stone, Lawrence, 38, 41, 46, 60
Structural model of psyche, 5, 199
Studies on Hysteria (Breuer and Freud), 108
Sublimation, 121, 133–35; of aggression, 131, 180, 242, 243; capacity for, 188; civilization's demand for, 120; differentiation of repression and, 55; of narcissism, 185–86; women's capacity for, 109
Suburbs, move to, 236–37
Suffrage, 57, 59
Superego, 4–9, 123, 222; and adult moral contradictions, 199–200, 202–3; and aggression, 135; and authoritarian conception of morality, 57, 62–63; basic functions of, 5; biopsychological inevitability of, 86, 88; capacity of conscience to judge, 21; challenging commands of, 19; and civilization, 120, 181–82; conflict between conscience and, 172–73; conflicting values within, 22–23; emergence of, 6–7; and end of Oedipus complex, 69–85; harsh and punishing, 86–103, 118, 214; of Huckleberry Finn, 17, 18, 20; and identification with aggressor, 177; impersonal, 205; and independent judgment, 209, 210; internalization of, 100–101; and lower classes, 107; masculine attributes of, 62; as metaphorical structure, 183–85; and moral capacity of psyche, 159; moral values incorporated by, 186–87, 198; and Nazi genocide, 10–14; parental disturbances in, 90–91; pathology of, 13–15, 71; and penis envy, 117; and reason, 147; reinforcement of sexism by, 111; and religious repression, 140; repression as main function of, 145, 146, 189; and selective identifica-

tion, 191; social and cultural determinants of, 9, 87; and social norms, 201; and split between reason and feeling, 138; and Twain's views of society, 22; values internalized in, 19–20; in women, 109, 118
Swaddling, 35, 38, 41, 42, 50, 202n
Switzerland, 34
Symbiotic mother: fear of reengulfment by, 113, 143, 145; separation from, 181
Symposium, The (Plato), 137–38
Symptomatic behavior, 147–48; apotheosis of science as, 149–56
Symptom formation, 89–90; and instincts, 141

Taboo: concept of, 94; incest, 121, 123, 124
Taylor, Gordon, 60
Temperamental factors, 172, 174
Thanatos, 165, 168, 246
Thompson, Kurt, 193n
Three Essays on Sexuality (Freud), 108
Titian, 206
Tocqueville, Alexis de, 29
Totem and Taboo (Freud), 78–79, 94
Trade unionism, 58
Transference, 92, 161–63
Trespass-punishment configuration, 94
Truth, scientific, 149–51
Tyranny, 32–33, 37, 53; as defense against anxiety, 53; masculine challenge to, 51; repression in service of, 140; in seventeenth century, 36; in system of values, 223
Twain, Mark, 18, 22

Unconscious, 45; permanence of connections in, 122
Underclass, 224, 225
Utilitarianism, 105, 137, 145, 192

269

Index

Value systems, 65, 159, 192; and emotional affect, 193; fundamental change in, 219–46; and moral autonomy, 210; parental and social, 201–3; radical change in, 104–5; superego incorporation of, 191

Vanbrugh, John, 51

Venetian republic, 34

Victim, identification with, 178–81

Victorianism, 39

Vienna Psychoanalytic Society, 108, 132, 162, 208

Vietnam war, 56, 106, 195, 203n, 204, 223, 240

Wadsworth, Benjamin, 44

Walpole, Horace, 49

Warfare, 33; ancient Greek commitment to, 30; identifications and idealizations in, 192–93; as symptomatic behavior, 148

Watergate, 240

Weber, Max, 192, 221, 241

Welfare state, 220, 224, 226

Weltanschauung, scientific, 149–54

Wesley, John, 40

Wet-nursing, 35, 38, 41, 42, 202n

White man's burden, 31

Why War? (Freud), 167

Willard, Samuel, 47

Wollstonecraft, Mary, 48–49

Women: ambivalence about, 9; in ancient Athens, 51–52; anger toward, 131; debasement of sexuality and, 122; during English revolution, 36; equality for, *see* Feminism; Freud's ambivalence about, 61–62, 104–18; in nineteenth century, 54, 57–60; prejudice against, *see* Sexism; in seventeenth and eighteenth centuries, 35, 37–40, 43–44, 53; sexuality of, 45–47; sexual repression of, 142–43; superego development of, 8, 76, 77; tyrannization of, 27, 28, 30

Work, capacity for love and, 240–46

Working-class political parties, 58

World War I, 106, 165

Wycliffe, John, 228, 229, 231

Yuppies, 220, 235, 236, 245